Business Darwinism: Evolve or Dissolve

Adaptive Strategies for the Information Age

Business Darwinism: Evolve or Dissolve

Adaptive Strategies for the Information Age

ERIC A. MARKS

John Wiley & Sons, Inc.

This book is dedicated to my father, Lyle Thomas Marks. His strength, wisdom, and integrity have inspired my life's journey.

This text is printed on acid-free paper. ♾

Published simultaneously in Canada.

The author gratefully acknowledges Harvard Business School Press for their permission to use portions of their works in this book:+

Gary Hamel, *Leading the Revolution* (Boston, MA: Harvard Business School Press, 2000), pp. 70–113.

Peter Weill and Marianne Broadbent, *Leveraging the New Infrastructure* (Boston, MA: Harvard Business School Press, 1998).

ISBN 0-471-43441-8

Printed in the United States of America

10 9 8 7 6 5 4 3 2 1

CONTENTS

Foreword x

Introduction xv

Chapter 1 Business Darwinism and Digital Evolution 1

Adaptive Advantage: Culture 3
Human versus Corporate Evolution 4
Information: A Key Adaptive Mechanism 5
Principle of Information Darwinism 8
Breaking Down Information Darwinism: Part One 10
How Do Winning Firms Survive Information Darwinism? 13
Information Mastery: Value Discipline of the Next Wave 15
Breaking Down Information Darwinism: Part Two 17
How Do Winning Firms Survive Information Darwinism? 19
Business 2.0 E-Biz 100 21
Examples of Companies That "Get It" 23
Evolution of Organizational Models to Support Information Functions 28
Corporate Brain-to-Body Ratio 28
Unleashing Information Value 29
Notes 31

Chapter 2 Welcome to Today (Yesterday Revisited) 32

Laboratory of Change 32
Change as Life—Life as Change 34
Technology-Driven Change 34
Brief Technology Tour 35
Industrial Revolution 37
Second Industrial Revolution 37
Enter the Transistor 39
Enter the Internet: Why the Internet Is Different 40
Incumbents and Hybrids Move to the Middle 41
Internet Impact 42
Welcome to the Network Age 43
End of the First Wave: Recent Technotrends 44
Beginning of the Next Wave 45
Business Implications 45
Competitive Technologies (for the Next Wave) 46

Digital Dilemma: Preparing for the Next Wave 47
Looking Ahead to the Nth Wave 48
Notes 48

Chapter 3 Evolutionary Metaphors for Business 50
Evolution as a Guide to the Future 52
Environment, Natural Selection, and Survival of the Fittest 52
Evolution and Adaptation 53
Natural Selection 53
Competition 54
Business Environment 56
Punctuated Equilibrium and Change 56
Punctuated Equilibrium and the Business Environment 57
Corporations Are Living Organisms 59
Nature of the Firm: How Companies Survive, Compete, Replicate, and Adapt 61
How Did Corporations Evolve? 62
How Corporations Survive 66
Business Darwinism: What Is Fitness for Corporations? 67
How Corporations Compete 67
Replication: How Do Corporations Reproduce? 69
Corporate DNA 72
Corporate DNA versus Corporate Culture 74
What Is the Difference between Corporate Culture and Corporate DNA? 75
How Corporations Adapt (or Competing Against Change) 75
Change: The Competitive Constant 76
Adaptation for Short and Long Time Frames 76
Proactive Adaptation: Future-Focused Change 77
Notes 78

Chapter 4 Evolution of Information Technology Organizations and Strategies 81
Rise of Information Technology 82
Origins of Financial Applications 83
Client-Server Architecture and the Rise of the Departmental Application 85
Manufacturing Meets the Wintel Duopoly 86
Enter the Enterprise Application 87
Organizational Structures and Outcomes 89
Organizing IT: Principles First 91

Why Alignment Is *Not* the Problem 95
Role of IT Has Changed, But Management Did Not Realize It 96
IT Organizational Strategies and Principles 96
Notes 98

Chapter 5 Information Management in Business Evolution 99
New Role of IT 100
Architecture, Architecture, Architecture 101
Mapping IT Architecture to Business Fitness 105
Infrastructure 105
Transactional Systems 110
Informational Technology 111
Strategic Technology 113
Developing an Evolutionary IT Portfolio 114
Patterns of Evolutionary IT Architecture Management 115
Implications for Information Mastery 120
Notes 122

Chapter 6 Information-Based Business Modeling 123
Corporate Strategies and Business Initiatives 123
Core Strategy 128
Strategic Resources 129
Configuration: Linking Core Strategy to Strategic Resources 130
Information's Role in Configuring the Corporation 130
Customer Interfaces 132
Customer Benefits: Linking Core Strategy to Customer Interface 135
Information Role in Benefit Creation and Delivery 135
Value Network 136
Company Boundaries: Linking Strategic Resources to the Value Network 138
Information Role in Defining Company Boundaries 138
Wealth Potential of the Business Model 139
Strategic Flexibility 141
Portfolio Breadth 142
Operating Agility 143
Lower Breakevens 144
Information-Based Force Multipliers 144

	Creating the Information Mastery Agenda in an Evolving Corporation	145
	Conclusion	155
	Notes	155
Chapter 7	**Business Evolutionary Strategies**	**156**
	Macro-Model of Business Evolution: Orchestrating Change	158
	Capacity for Change: Corporate Mutation Rates	163
	Flexing Corporate Muscle: Business Architecture and IT Architecture	169
	Flexing the Business Architecture	169
	Flexing the IT Architecture	171
	Double Flexing: Business and IT Architecture Interplay	174
	Fitness Levers: Metrics and Feedback	175
	Examples of Business Evolution in Action	181
	Hewlett-Packard's Journey	181
	Working the Model	183
	Conclusion	189
	Notes	190
Chapter 8	**Business Evolution Theory and Practice**	**191**
	Business Evolution Strategies: Survive and Compete	195
	Protect the Core Business Survival System	195
	What Is Core?	196
	Make Core Process as Efficient as Possible: Conservation of Energy	197
	Secure Market Share and Protect "Franchise Customers"	198
	Insurance Example: Survive and Compete	199
	Competitive Strategies	207
	Survive and Compete Conclusion	212
	Business Evolution Strategies: Replicate and Adapt	213
	Business Replication: Crossing the Generation Gap	214
	Intel: Crossing the Semiconductor Technology Generation Gap	218
	The Nokia Story: Business at the Edge of Chaos	219
	Business Adaptation in Corporate Evolution: Anticipating the Unknown	223
	Conclusion	229
	Notes	230

Chapter 9 Information Darwinism in the Future **232**
Waiting for the Future 234
Next Golden Age of IT 237
How to Avoid Being Digitally Deselected 238
Create Your Own Information Mastery Agenda 240
Steps to Information Mastery 244
Treat the IT Future as an Opportunity, Not a Threat 244
Invest in IT to Enhance Evolutionary Fitness 246
Develop Boardroom IT Awareness and Promote IT Professionals to Operations Roles 250
Ensure Corporate Agility and Evolutionary Capabilities 252
Digital Hunter-Gatherers and Corporate Velociraptors 255
Real-Time Evolution 257
The Darwinian Road Ahead 260
Notes 261

Index **263**

FOREWORD

The basic premise of the book you are about to read is that business must rethink how it looks at, invests in, and uses information technology in order to deal with and survive constant change. Smart companies may also be able to prosper if they adopt new attitudes about information technology (IT).

Author Eric Marks first began developing his ideas about information technology and its relationship to business, particularly in manufacturing companies, in articles written for *Managing Automation,* the magazine I edit. When he first approached me about his ideas, an immediate intellectual friendship ensued; we were both frustrated with the progress businesses were making with information technology, continually disturbed with worn-out arguments about IT's seeming lack of positive impact on productivity, and generally puzzled with why businesses were mired in applying IT strategically. In two articles which appeared in the summer of 1998, Marks began to lay out the groundwork for "Business Darwinism," advancing his ideas about a new conceptual model or framework that embraced manufacturing operations, IT, and the business overall.

In *Business Darwinism,* Marks sets forth not only the information technology elements of this framework, but also the crucially important business model that must accompany it. Most important, though, he identifies a new value discipline he calls Information Mastery, which is at the heart of a new way of thinking about the business with information, and information technology, at the core.

I believe this book is important because it can help move a very big rock up a very slippery slope. The rock, of course, is conventional wisdom—and I use that phrase, particularly the second word in it, advisedly—about the relationship between IT and business. It is a mind-set that breeds inertia, but one that must progress if we are to unlock the true potential of IT. The slippery slope, perhaps a bit more obscure, is the different dynamics of IT and business cycles and the managerial and organizational dimensions to the business—all of which must be brought into harmony if the new concepts that Marks advances are to succeed.

It would be unfair to underestimate the challenge posed by all of these factors. Certainly, *Business Darwinism* does not shy away from presenting this challenge nor does it shrink from saying what the consequences will be to businesses that fail to meet it. The glass, though, is half full, not half empty, and the rewards that will attend those with the courage, vision, persistence, and execution skills to rise to a higher level of relationship with IT will be rich indeed.

Such a challenge is not only timely and needed in today's business world, but will be, Marks suggests, an ongoing effort that will test the intellectual flexibility as well as organizational stamina of businesses in every industry segment everywhere.

This will be a daunting task for most corporations and a far greater one than they have ever had to grapple with before when it comes to dealing with IT. For the electronic information technology systems whose "brains" are the software creations of human beings, and which are unlike physical labor-saving inventions that defined earlier eras and business, social, and political paradigm shifts, are truly one of the most unique inventions in all human experience.

The software-controlled electronic information system is fundamentally different from physical labor-saving devices such as the cotton gin, the locomotive, or the telephone. Rather than extend the ability of hand motion, leg motion, or the ability to hear and speak across distances, IT systems extend the capabilities of the mind—to think, to organize and disseminate information, to create.

Because these systems are of the mind rather than of the body, they take a lot more effort and time to understand. This is one of the central problems in managing IT today. The fact of the matter is that people simply don't have all that much experience yet with IT systems to truly understand their impact on people, organizations, methods of management, and the fabric of culture that weaves through all. The development of the ENIAC was only about 50 years ago, a short time in the history of human invention and one far more brief than attended the invention and adoption of cars, telephones, and even television. Perhaps more important, the development of the groundbreaking IBM 360, the first electronic computing system to be widely used in businesses, arrived on the scene only about 35 years ago. How can we begin to understand the effects of what has become increasingly complex software systems on equally complex organizational entities such as multinational businesses when the body of experience we must rely on for judgments about those effects is in itself immature?

There are several other factors that compound the experience problem. The first is what I have often referred to in my writings about IT, which have been stimulated by Marks's first two articles in *Managing Automation* and now by *Business Darwinism,* as the Absorption Problem. The mere fact that a corporation buys an IT system and installs it says very little about the extent to which the capabilities of that system are used and by how many people within that business. Getting to know the "mind" of even a relatively simple PC-based software system such as Microsoft Office has proven to be beyond the capabilities of most people who use that system. Imagine what business faces in fully understanding and fully exploiting a so-called enterprise system such as SAP's R/3 software, a system exponentially more complex and rich in functionality than the systems we use as individuals.

Factor in to this equation the notion of frequent and periodic updates to these systems that their inventors delight in continually introducing and providing to users. Unlike adding chapters to a book, which could be read without having to reread the entire book, these changes often permeate a system, restarting the Absorption Problem.

The Absorption Problem is also deeply affected by such associated issues as training and education. Most corporations still don't have ongoing, companywide IT training programs that are woven into the fabric of their cultures. The lack of training, of course, inhibits wider usage of the technology by more people as well as more functionality lying not used or underutilized in those systems. The net effect is to limit the development of the all-important body of experience with the systems.

Our education system, too, still regards IT as a compartmentalized discipline rather than a tool whose full use could more profoundly improve the educational experience. Schools treat IT much like business still views the IS department, along the lines of what Marks calls Industrial Age thinking. Changing the ways that our educational system views IT, particularly at the grammar and secondary school levels, is perhaps the single most important goal all must embrace in the evolution of IT now taking place. Generational change may indeed be the key in our coming to a fuller understanding of IT.

But for now, an equally important factor in the IT challenge facing business is what I have called, in articles in *Managing Automation,* the Alignment Problem. There are two major branches to the Alignment Problem. The first branch has to do with the tension between technology cycles and business cycles. Contrary to some conventional notions, technology does not change and progress at the same speed and pace as business cycles. Even though the venture capital spigot has been severely tightened this year due to the economic downturn, technological innovation continues in many sectors even as the business slowdown worsens and companies hold back on investing in IT.

While the tension is most pronounced during a downturn, even in good times businesses face the continual challenge of marrying and synchronizing IT to business cycles and processes that are often unpredictable and changing. The closer a business can get to aligning the two, the more benefit can be derived from the IT investment, but the alignment is a continual challenge that requires much ongoing effort. Without flexible software architectures that can accommodate change and without adaptable business policies to go with them, a business can end up on the rocky shoals of a failed IT investment. Like the developing body of experience we have with the impact of IT systems on the corporate entity itself, we are also just beginning to understand how to deal with the alignment problem between technology and business cycles.

The other branch of the Alignment Problem is a multidimensional issue having to do with organizational and management factors. Simply thinking about and trying to understand the impact of IT on a company's business processes will not lead to a full understanding of IT's effect on the corporate entity nor will it allow for maximum utilization and exploitation of the technology.

Any time information technology is injected into the corporate entity, the technology has an effect on the entity's organizational structure and the way that structure is managed. The impact on organizational structure has to do with how work is organized, how people are deployed to accomplish that work, the process by which the work is carried out, how decision making is structured, and how the hierarchy of authority, responsibility, and compensation is organized. Obviously, the more pervasive the technology, the more intense the impact on these characteristics. Equally important, the impact of the technology injection on management has to do with the setting of goals and objectives associated with the technology, policies, and procedures for employing the technology, and overseeing the processes by which the technology is used.

It's important to understand, too, that the technology factor itself has a set of effects associated with it that are distinct from the organizational and management factors. In today's world, it would be rare indeed to find the corporation that did not have some existing technology base or what the IT industry calls legacy systems installed and running, and in many cases running well. Consequently, the injection of new technology, whether it is a customer relationship management system, a web-based ordering system, or a broad-scale enterprise resource management system, will in itself have an impact on the existing technology infrastructure that must be understood if the new investment is to be successfully leveraged.

The key here, though, is that the three factors—technology, organization, and management—are present and inseparable in the calculus of a progressive IT and business framework. Certainly, each factor may take on different and varying weights depending on the particular circumstances of a corporate entity, but in the final analysis all three must be in equilibrium for the technology to succeed, and by succeed I mean to be used to its full potential and advantage.

Discussions of identifying and sustaining competitive advantage with IT often miss the point because of a lack of understanding of this three-factor calculation, which I have called the Theory of Trilateral Alignment. Competitive advantage can be found in how well IT is used. And successful use can only be attained when the whole of the corporate entity, its structure and methods of management, is geared to and aligned with the technology.

Marks is dead-on correct in arguing that business must make the intellectual shift in regarding IT in a new, more intimate way. Having a philosophy of IT that is rooted in Industrial Age concepts is a surefire prescription for underutilization, and even failure, with IT. The language we use to communicate about IT reveals the scope and depth of the problem. Today, IT is widely referred to as a "tool," something mass produced, used to accomplish a task and then stored, much like a wrench, a saw, or a screwdriver is used and then placed in a toolbox.

Surely such conceptualizations reflect the limitations of today's language and vocabulary, but they also reveal a mind-set or attitude that is not holistic with regard to IT and the business. It is rather an Industrial Age notion of compartmentalized and sequential tasks directed to predefined objectives. But this approach, of course, misunderstands the essence of IT, the extension of the mind. Most businesses need to make the shift to the broader and more natural vision, and most as well need to learn, understand, and adopt disciplines associated with executing Trilateral Alignment. Likewise, most consultancies and research firms in the IT industry need to embrace this new philosophy if they are going to be able to truly help their clients.

The real value that can come from what Marks calls Information Mastery lies in what one great writer called the "undiscovered country." Reducing cost and improving efficiency and productivity will get businesses to first or even second base, but home runs will be scored only when information is exploited in new ways to extend the business or even create new businesses. It is the opening of new realms and dimensions to the business that leverage the power of IT. Like the power of thought itself, can there be any limit to it?

The gating factor—that opens it, limits it, or closes it off—lies in only one area. It lies in the makeup of the mind, or, to put it in hierarchical business terms, within the brain of the business, the person who is managerially in charge. Simply put, leadership will either make or break a business's involvement with IT. If the leadership has a mind-set to focus on efficiency and productivity, then the leadership will most probably achieve those limited and limiting objectives. But in doing so it will have ignored the essence of IT and will not reap the rewards its potential has to offer.

Only enlightened leadership can make the leap to the new philosophy. Only enlightened leadership can approach the business based on a vision of IT as not only woven into the fabric of the business but a business driver itself, as important as new geographic markets and new customers. Only enlightened leadership can create, develop, and sustain a culture in which this new IT philosophy will flourish.

The history of technology strongly suggests that if it can happen, it will happen. Mankind will eventually figure out a way. The philosophy of IT I have discussed here, and which Eric Marks explores in much greater depth in the pages to come, will take root over time. As much as we would like to take credit for these ideas, they are in large part self-evident, as knowable and as inexorable as other forces in nature.

This book, therefore, is a valuable guide to understanding that nature and devising ways to harness its forces. In the end, that may be all we can do. And that may just be enough.

David R. Brousell
Editor-in-Chief
Managing Automation Magazine
New York, October 2001

INTRODUCTION

During the writing of this book, several insights and changes of direction occurred that were unplanned and unanticipated. I began this project intending to author an e-business and information technology (IT) strategy book; however, as I completed the research and the initial chapters, I realized that what I was writing did not provide businesses with the tools needed to adapt themselves to business change. The initial premise of the book was that information plays a strategic and critical role in today's corporations, and therefore the firms that are best able to drive business value with information assets and processes will survive, whereas those that do not will be deselected. Although I had established a clear need for unleashing IT from the management paradigms of the Industrial Age through a new value discipline called Information Mastery, I soon realized that I had written myself into a corner. Corporations need to do more than fix the way the information value is created and managed to help them adapt to their business environment. They need a broader framework for business change based on the evolutionary and biological analogies developed earlier in the book.

At the same time, the business landscape was undergoing rapid change with the economic slump of 2001 following so closely on the heels of the Internet boom and dot-com bust. The sanguine growth predictions of Internet business models were soon proved fraudulent by the business version of natural selection. Firm after firm folded because of fundamental flaws in their business models. That means that these business models were not well adapted to their business landscape. They were unfit in Business Darwinism fitness terms. They were incapable of demonstrating positive results in the four fitness levers we settled on as keys to fitness: (1) revenue, (2) profit, (3) cash flow, and (4) market share. We witnessed business evolution with the sudden emergence of new species of companies based on exciting new e-business models, doing business on the web in ways never imagined before. The sudden and rapid speciation of corporations captured the hearts and minds of executives around the world who were enamored of business models that were capable of creating so many 20-something millionaires in such a short time based on their successful initial public offerings (IPOs). This is why I introduced Stephen Jay Gould's concept of Punctuated Equilibrium to describe this sudden flourishing of new species of businesses and rapid change.

I realized that Darwinian fitness was an appropriate way to characterize corporations, and the fitness levers we settled on seemed to make the most sense for short-term survival of a corporation. Companies that do not perform according to the fitness metrics of revenue, profit, cash flow, and market share will not survive, and they surely will not be able to replicate or transition themselves across a generation of change. These fitness metrics are good enough for Dell Computer, so they should be good enough for other corporations. The dot-com demise of 2000 and 2001 demonstrated the criticality of business fitness in business evolution. We now know that the business version of natural selection is as absolute as nature's version of natural selection.

At this point, I spent two days scratching my head and pondering what framework or methodology would be useful to help businesses adapt their business models to changes in the business landscape, competitor threats, customer preferences, fundamental technology that affects entire industries, and corporate leadership. I realized that my IT premise was correct and completely valid, but it needed to be augmented by a framework that added corporate structure, organizational design, company and industry value chains, business processes, and all other related *business architecture* components to the *IT architecture* elements of increasingly information-based business models. A *business evolution model* was needed to encompass corporate strategy, information-based business modeling, and four evolutionary activities that any corporation must perform to remain viable—survive, compete, replicate, and adapt. In performing these four activities, a firm must be able to flex its respective business architecture and IT architecture in order to implement the necessary changes to drive better fitness against the fitness metrics mentioned previously. This ongoing process continually assesses the fitness of a firm's business model to the business landscape and adjusts it through business and technology initiatives that support surviving, competing, replicating, and adapting. Business Darwinism, then, provides an overarching framework for corporations to evolve themselves proactively, as well as reactively, to business change.

A brief review of the book's chapters provides readers with the flow and structure of this book:

- Chapter 1 lays the groundwork for a new paradigm of information management. The Principle of Information Darwinism is developed, suggesting that corporations and business leaders must invest in information technology more aggressively to ensure business survival. The executives and companies that do will not only survive, they will thrive. Those that do not will be deselected. A new value discipline of Information Mastery is presented as a critical core capability of any modern organization. Information Mastery is a way of conducting business based on superior use of information in a broader and more strategic sense. The role, organization, processes, and metrics of information are different under the value discipline of Information Mastery. Information is the evolutionary and adaptive machinery of a firm.
- Chapter 2 provides a review of major technology trends over the course of history, beginning with the printing press and ending with the Internet. This abbreviated technology review shows how technology has had a dramatic impact on human history and how innovation complexes can coalesce and

drive a sustained, disruptive wave of massive business and societal change. The Internet is one of these events, much as the printing press was in its time. They are similar in their impact on human civilization in that they broke an information bottleneck and unleashed access to information to the masses. Information, we maintain, is clearly power.

- Chapter 3 develops the evolutionary framework for businesses, equating them to living organisms. We suggest that corporations must conduct four fundamental evolutionary activities—survive, compete, replicate, and, over generations of business change, adapt. We posit four business fitness metrics—revenue, profit, cash flow, and market share—as the most critical measures for corporations to be "fit" and able to transition their business models across a generation of business change. The trajectory of human evolution is equated with the increased use of information to drive corporate evolution. If culture replaced physical evolution in humans, then information is the cultural equivalent for firms. All activities that manage information and knowledge of a firm are those that will augment and, in some cases, replace competing on physical assets alone.
- Chapter 4 traces the development of information technology and information delivery as a formal corporate discipline. From the early computer applications in GE's Louisville facility to the rise of the personal computer (PC), client-server computing, and the Internet, we show how these changes in information technology have strained the organizations that were devised to "manage" the changes. This historical review suggests that today's corporations are still managing information delivery with an Industrial Age management paradigm. Chapter 4 concludes with the idea that the IT results from the last 10 years or so are logical outcomes of managing information delivery from an Industrial Age perspective.
- Chapter 5 explores the notion of IT architecture. We review several leading IT strategists' views and approaches to IT management, IT architecture management, and portfolio management, and then settle on the approach of Weill and Broadbent, which breaks IT into four categories of spending—infrastructure, transactional, informational, and strategic technologies. We then introduce a business evolution framework and integrate these IT categories into it to show how the IT architecture can be "flexed" in response to the needs of the business to incorporate change and facilitate business evolution.
- Chapter 6 presents a discussion of corporate strategy and business modeling. Gary Hamel's compelling business modeling methodology is reviewed and adapted to the discussion of information management. The result is a concept called *information-based business modeling,* which builds information management concepts into the fabric of corporate strategy and the resulting business model. Information-based business modeling eliminates the classic alignment problem that has plagued

corporations managing their businesses with an Industrial Age information management model.

- Chapter 7 extends the discussions of IT architecture and information-based business modeling into a larger context: a model of business evolution. We devise a macro-model of business change based on corporate strategy, an information-based business model, and the ability to successfully implement business initiatives by flexing the business architecture and the IT architecture. We show how the evolutionary activities of a firm—survive, compete, replicate, and adapt—have different objectives and requirements for implementation, but they all involve flexing the business and IT architecture for success.
- Chapter 8 embellishes the business evolution framework with examples. The business evolution model is "worked" to demonstrate how the four evolutionary processes of a corporation—survive, compete, replicate, and adapt—are accomplished by a firm. We describe how survive and compete are core business model activities, with their respective goals for success. We describe how corporate replication *repositions* a firm for its next future, essentially transitioning the firm across a generation of business change, using the business evolution model. Finally, we show how adaptive activities of a firm *preposition* it for multiple futures by adding the corporate variability and agility to respond to multiple unknown outcomes.
- Chapter 9 closes the book with some forward-looking ideas on what the future of IT and business holds. We forecast what the next Golden Age of IT might involve, and we offer ways that corporations can create their own Information Mastery value disciplines customized for their firm in their competitive situation. Finally, several suggestions are made about how corporations can build adaptive processes and capabilities into their fundamental structure and culture. This is the ultimate core competency—the adaptive agility of a corporation in response to environmental change.

Business evolution is not unlike evolution in nature, and the parallels we have developed to help businesses use information to facilitate better fitness resemble those of humans as a species. The business evolution model and information-based business modeling approach have been developed to help companies adapt in their immediate environments, to help reposition them for their next futures, and to help preposition themselves for the unknown, or multiple futures.

This book is about evolution and change. I hope that the story of how I wrote this book serves as a metaphor for what corporations must do to compete and remain viable as business entities. Change is constant in nature and in business. Corporations that can build adaptive capabilities into their culture, their structure and organization, and their information and business processes will truly be the winners based on Business Darwinism. Happy evolution!

1

BUSINESS DARWINISM AND DIGITAL EVOLUTION

Darwin is probably a better guide to business competition than economists are.

—Bruce Henderson,
Boston Consulting Group

When I was young, perhaps 12 or 13 years old, I was fortunate to live on a dairy farm in upstate New York in the Chenango River Valley region. This dairy farm was not unlike many in the area. It ran along the banks of the Chenango River for perhaps three-quarters of a mile as the river flows, with fertile flats replenished by nutrients from upstream, winter and spring floods that covered the land then eventually receded, followed by the growing season for alfalfa, corn, and other feed crops. But our family farm was different from most in one important way: two archaeological sites were located there. Nothing would intrigue me more than walking those fields after the first rainfall following the spring plowing. The rain would wash away the top layer of soil, revealing the secrets of people who occupied that land thousands of years ago. I would find potsherds, flint chips from the manufacture of stone tools, and even the tools themselves, some of them in perfectly preserved condition and others worn and broken. My prehistoric finds included scrapers, knives, mortar and pestle, and pottery, all from the Woodland Era of North American prehistory. This village site was large and was likely occupied year-round.

There was also another archaeological site on our farm, closer to the river than the first, but also different. This site was a small hunting camp, with fire-cracked rock marking a fire pit for cooking and heating, and older-style pottery and stone tools from the Archaic Period, which was roughly 7,000 years B.C. More than nine thousand years ago this particular group of Archaic Indians camped at this location, repeatedly for several years perhaps, building their campfires and dining from the game they managed to kill on that hunting trip, and telling stories about life and perhaps musing about the future. Who knows? But it surely was fascinating to me to walk along this field, between the rows of corn, picking up the remnants from a time long past, and wondering who they were and what they did here.

It would occur to me that the nameless, faceless inhabitants of this land two thousand years ago did not leave an epitaph. There was no signpost, no gravestone, no historical marker to tell a curious 13-year-old farmer's son what happened here and why the previous inhabitants were no longer here. As I write these paragraphs about business strategy and business change, I am wondering what the epitaph will be for the many new companies that sprang from the venture capitalists' fold only to fall victim to the recent pattern of dot-com failure. What would a corporation's gravestone read if someone were to write an epitaph?

> Here lies the remains of the dot-com known as Nolonger.com, and it was a good firm. It was based on the New Economy formula of "get market share now, worry about profits later." It was based on measures of success where the stock valuation was more important than revenue, cash flow, and profitability. But they did give us free food, provided Ping-Pong tables for after-lunch games, bagels every Monday for breakfast, and generally created a great working atmosphere. If only it had lasted . . .

As I am writing this book, firm after firm is folding. Venture capitalists have turned off the free-flowing faucet of easy funding for many of the firms they spawned as part of the First Wave of e-business. These firms, which were taking advantage of a stock market that valued their New Economy business model, unfortunately did not have viable, market-focused strategies that allowed for sustainable growth in market share, revenues, and profits. The firms that did make it to the initial public offering (IPO) stage and posted enviable stock valuations are now seeing their stock get pounded by the markets and disparaged by the analysts. They are realizing that with no venture capital money, and a revenue stream that barely resembles a trickle, their future is bleak.

They are not alone. This is the state of many firms, both New Economy and Old. The relative condition of New Economy firms versus Old Economy firms may not be entirely comparable, although on the measures of market share, revenue, cash flow, and profitability they are. These metrics determine fundamentally whether a firm has a viable business model and a product or service that the market considers valuable. The First Wave of the New Economy was an experiment. Some made it, but most did not. Some are still trying to make it. Regarding the relative viability of any start-up firm over the last 10 years, many struggled only to eventually shutter their windows. Of course, the venture capitalists like this situation. They prefer a 10 percent success rate in their startups, which helps ensure that the ideas they fund are unique and different. But this ratio is probably similar to the success rate of start-up businesses historically, regardless of whether they are venture capital funded or not. Like nature and the life-and-death struggles in the wild every day, some companies survive and others do not.

This book is about all corporations. This book draws on evolutionary metaphors to attempt to provide a framework for handling change, which is sorely needed today with the pace of change increasing, the amount of change becoming overwhelming, and the nature of the changes turning unpredictable. Evolutionary processes are at work in the business world, much as they are at work in the natural world. Survival of the fittest applies to the world's corporations as much as it applies to the variety of living organisms in existence today, as well as those long extinct. Darwinian principles can be employed to build an adaptive framework for corporations. This adaptive framework will lead to a set of principles that will ultimately help today's corporations better compete against other firms, but more important, compete against the unknown; compete against change; and compete for a business landscape that is as yet unknown and unknowable.

This book also makes some points that will seem to be tautologies. For example, I will suggest that technology-driven change is forcing companies to adopt more technology as the solution to problems that arose largely as a result of technology changes. Technology changes things, which requires more technology to solve the problems that technology largely enabled. So technology is part of the solution to technology-driven change. For companies, then, the two primary competitors they face in making a living are change, which is accelerating, and their competitors, which are also changing. Technology as an adaptive mechanism provides a pathway to solving both problems, but only in a corporation whose leadership understands the role of technology in enabling corporate strategy.

ADAPTIVE ADVANTAGE: CULTURE

Corporations, by virtue of consisting of human beings, share the evolutionary trajectory of human beings. Humans have distinguished themselves from all other living species in the development of intelligence, or culture, as a primary adaptive mechanism. Culture replaced physical adaptation as the primary evolutionary capability by virtue of the speed, efficiency, and flexibility it provides. Companies evolve and adapt to their surroundings as living organisms do. Above all, the ability to evolve and adapt to the environment—both the immediate conditions and maintaining the ability to adapt to future change—is the ultimate evolutionary advantage. For corporations, the adaptive mechanisms involve information processing. Corporate replication is the successful copying of corporate culture and corporate DNA, by either growing the existing firm in new directions or using other variation-enhancing strategies such as increased research and development (R&D), mergers and acquisitions, and divisional spinoffs. The information management assets, processes, and capabilities of a firm support all corporate replication activities. In fact, without those elements of the corporate DNA of a firm, its replication processes, as well as its core survival, competing, and adaptive processes would be endangered.

HUMAN VERSUS CORPORATE EVOLUTION

Humans have not changed much physically over the last million years. Two million years ago, *Homo erectus* domesticated fire, used language to communicate, and crafted weapons; 500,000 years ago, *Homo sapiens* emerged. They were distinguished by their ability to create technology as demonstrated by increased innovation and progressive sophistication of their tool-making. Ninety thousand years ago, *Homo sapiens sapiens,* our immediate ancestors, emerged. Again, physically, we have not changed significantly over these timeframes; however, we have continued to adapt, acclimate, and thrive in our environment; interact with other cultures; and adapt to new climates and geographies. This is because as a species we have learned, through cultural adaptation as opposed to physical adaptation, to survive in varying geographies and climates and to respond to unforeseen changes in the conditions around us.

Now, to be accurate, cultural evolution does not replace genetic evolution. It does, however, augment survivability and adaptive responses to environmental changes in a more efficient manner, and it does represent a body of accumulated knowledge of the species. In that manner, then, culture is similar to the DNA contents of an individual or the genome of a species. As Matt Ridley[1] observes, our genes represent our 4-billion-year biography as a biological lineage, the cumulative documentation of all the changes to the human gene sequence as captured by the species. Human culture works within the generational timeframe, whereas genetic evolution, being a function of reproduction, works across many generations and, ultimately, over millions of years. The ability to augment the rate of change of the species with behavioral adaptations is a tremendous evolutionary advantage. This explains why human beings are an ecological success as a species, perhaps the most successful ever. Humans are the most abundant animal on Earth, with some 6 billion of us populating virtually every possible habitat, and representing some 300 million tons of biomass.[2] As a species, we would not be as successful without the information-processing capabilities that culture represents.

Culture in humans can be compared to information technology for corporations. These are "software-like" adaptive mechanisms that allow for flexible responses to unforeseen changes. They allow responses in timeframes that are much faster (e.g., web speed) than geologic and evolutionary time fences, which are measured in hundreds of thousands, even millions of years. As much as DNA is a digital code for the development of an individual of a species, information technology (IT) is the digital strategy that will allow corporations to craft their ability to survive in the New Economy. The ability of firms to harvest information and drive their business based on information will separate the winners from the losers in the New Economy. Strategic use of IT will be a key adaptive mechanism for all firms in the coming years, but especially so for global corporations in all industries.

INFORMATION: A KEY ADAPTIVE MECHANISM

Information is the primary adaptive mechanism for global corporations to survive and compete in the Information Economy. The ability of global manufacturers to harness information *firmwide* in *every* operation—to harvest knowledge and turn it into competitive advantage—will be the primary source of competitive advantage for firms intent on winning in the new millennium. Information technology must be a central theme of any modern business strategy today. Firms that do not subscribe to this view will not be around in the long term. The strategic value of information—as well as the corporate assets that store, manipulate, analyze, print, and present information about the business, the customers, and the products and services provided to the customers—is increasing.

Corporations are undergoing a fitful transition from their Industrial Age mode of operation to an Information Age of operation. Some are doing so faster than their competitors, and they will survive. Recognizing the need for the change has not been easy, nor will the transition be smooth. The changes required to be an Information Age corporation are many and varied because of the differences between managing physical assets, such as factories, machines, and inventory, and managing bits and bytes, or information. Information is a different economic medium than physical goods, as Evans and Wurster point out in their fascinating book, *Blown to Bits*. They note that the objects of strategy, things such as business structures, supply chains, customer and supplier relationships, and even entire industries, are held together by a kind of "glue." That glue, according to Evans and Wurster, is information.[3] Information is different. It is bits and bytes, ones and zeros, as opposed to atoms and molecules, the world of physical products, machines and equipment, buildings and manufacturing plants. Exhibit 1.1 shows how information is a business driver in today's information-based economy.

Information "makes a vastly disproportionate contribution to competitive advantage," according to Evans and Wurster.[4] Information, as well as the assets and processes for managing it, provides the fabric for the boundaries, stability, organizational structure, and ultimately the competitive advantage of corporations and industries. In fact, for many companies not typically classified as members of the "information industries," their mastery of information distinguishes their performance from that of their competitors. "Every business is an information business," according to Evans and Wurster.[5] Whether the business is manufacturing or a typical services industry, it is indelibly shaped by its ability to manage information in various ways. Slywotsky and Morrison define a digital business as the following:

> One in which strategic options have been transformed—and significantly broadened—by the use of digital technologies. Under this definition, it's not enough to have a great Web site or a wired workforce or neat software that helps run a factory. A digital business uses digital technologies to devise entirely new value propositions for customers and for the company's own talent; to invent new methods of creating and capturing profits; and, ultimately, to pursue the true goal of strategic differentiation: uniqueness.[6]

Information strategies expand the range of business options a company can employ in executing its business strategy, as well as being critical for the *execution*

- Information is of strategic value to a firm.
- Information technology has a new role in the corporation of the New Economy. The role is strategic, not tactical, and the responsibilities are enormous.
- Information assets have surpassed physical assets in strategic value to the firm.
- The secret is to find ways to unleash the informational value embedded in the corporation. This means identifying, inventorying, assessing the value, and packaging information content into sources of value for new customers, new suppliers, new markets, new products, and new industries.
- Products are increasingly being bundled with information, which adds additional value to products.
- Information services are being "productized," continuing to demonstrate the increased value of various forms of information.
- Information Technology is no longer a support organization. It is now a strategic organization.
- Information is an economic driver. It has added productivity, jobs, and growth to the world economy at a phenomenal rate.

Exhibit 1.1 Information as a Business Driver

of the strategy and tactics. Clearly, then, managing information today is more critical to a company's survival than maintaining the same IT objectives of the past.

The mastery of information-based business models is different because information is a different type of competitive play. As noted by Evans and Wurster, the economics of physical entities versus information is different.[7] When a physical thing is sold, the seller no longer can claim ownership, but when an idea, a book, or a song is sold, the seller still technically "owns" it through copyright protection, and therefore the piece of information can be sold repeatedly. Information can be copied at nearly zero cost forever, as opposed to physical things, which require manufacturing facilities, machinery and equipment, specially trained personnel, and the materials and components to manufacture the physical goods.[8] Information has limitless boundaries and can be transmitted quickly and easily across networks. Physical things can be large and bulky, and require packaging for transportation. Some things in the physical world have diminishing returns, such as farmland, which does not double in productivity despite doubling the labor or fertilizer applied to it. Other physical entities, such as factories and "economy-of-scale" production settings, are subject to increasing returns by virtue of having lower unit costs per quantity made (e.g., big factories have lower unit costs than smaller factories). Information, however, has perfectly increasing returns. Money spent to learn something once allows one to reuse that knowledge at zero additional cost indefinitely. Slywotsky and Morrison amplify this notion:

> Managing atoms is manipulation of physical assets: stockpiling inventory, shipping products, buying equipment, installing machinery, building factories. Managing bits is manipulation of information: gathering, analyzing, modeling, sorting, sharing, and replicating data.[9]

The economics of information requires imperfect markets, or asymmetries of information. The value of information resides in limiting access to information such that rents can be charged for access. If access is not limited or restricted, the information is worthless. If access is restricted, then the information is a monopoly.[10] As many authors have observed, managing atoms compared to managing bits is a different game. There are fundamental differences between them. The technology review in Chapter 2 shows how the printing press released the value of information from the book container in the 1400s. Similarly, the Internet and related information technologies are continuing this trend but on a far grander scale. The bond between the medium and the message, the product and the information about the product, the physical value chain and the information flowing bidirectionally through that value chain, has been shattered. The boundless nature of information-based businesses relies on the ability to transform value equations from those of physical infrastructure and physical products to those of information infrastructure, product and process data, and metadata.

PRINCIPLE OF INFORMATION DARWINISM

In the transition to an Information Age economy from an Industrial Age economy, the strategic management of information becomes an all-important differentiator. The strategies and skills required to manage an information-based business model are different from those required to manage an Industrial Age business model. The metrics are different, the inputs and outputs are different, and the valuation of assets is different. In fact, the valuation of "value" is different with information-based business models and processes. During this transitional period and for the foreseeable future, one principle will dominate the business landscape—the Principle of Information Darwinism. This principle states:

> Firms that invest in information technology (IT) as a strategic resource for the future will survive. Those that do not will perish. Executives who invest in IT as one of their primary strategic levers will thrive. Those who do not will be deselected.

The Principle of Information Darwinism is the business equivalent of natural selection. The "filter" that will sort the survivors from the failures is the degree to which these firms have positioned themselves around the fundamental capabilities of harnessing information and driving value from it. The firms that have the information management capabilities required of the Information Age will succeed over those that do not. The business environment of the Information Age will select those firms that can harness and exploit information to survive, to compete, and to adapt to business change. Before breaking down the Principle of Information Darwinism into its components, a few concepts must be clarified.

First, the Principle of Information Darwinism does not espouse reckless spending on IT just for fun. Rather, it promotes a more strategic view of information as an asset, as a value driver of the New Economy, as something increasingly valued by customers—both internal and external to the firm. This requires a new and broader definition of the role and objectives of information management. It requires new metrics of success based on contribution to the success of the business, not in terms of how well the budget was managed. In our treatment of IT, we do not limit our discussion to how IT has been used and applied to business problems in the past. Information Darwinism seeks to define IT and assets as a much deeper and more fundamental element of competing in today's high-charged business environment. So when IT is discussed, we are referring to the typical IT management capabilities of a firm, but we are also significantly broadening our treatment of information management to include information and knowledge assets of all types, including the accumulated paper in file cabinets, the blueprints hanging in vaults in engineering departments of manufacturing firms, and any documentation of a firm's history, its customers, and its values, culture, and norms. This information also includes the mobile knowledge repositories in the minds of knowledge workers. We consider all of these elements of a firm as information assets, and firms must learn how to harness and derive value from them all.

Second, the Principle of Information Darwinism does not consider IT strategy to be a separate activity from business strategy. In fact, increasingly, if information management is not woven into the essence of today's business strategy, as well as into the goals, objectives, and activities that operationalize strategy, then that firm will be severely handicapped. This concept is similar to the recent realization that e-business is, after all, business. The two are inseparable and rightfully so. We seek to unify business strategy and IT strategies as increasingly the same fundamental exercise. This idea is similar to what Slywotsky and Morrison advocate by the term "Digital Business Design" in their book *How Digital Is Your Business?*[11] Businesses of the Next Wave will embed information capabilities into all core business processes to deliver superior value to all customers. There will be an IT organization, and there will be a chief information officer (CIO), but the CIO will be a business leader of the next generation of world-class firms. The CIO will provide thought leadership on how to run a business using information as a core value driver, not using IT systems to support core business processes. Information will be so integrally bundled with products and services of the firm, as well as with the processes that produce and deliver products and services, that thinking of IT separate from them will be impossible. Information and products will be the yin and yang of a firm. No products and services will exist without information, and no information will exist without products and services. Information in this scenario will be valued much differently than it was as a function of the IT organization.

Finally, the Principle of Information Darwinism expands and modifies the role of information management from the Industrial Age view of IT as something to be controlled and managed as a support organization to a view of IT as a critical component of all business operations, with a role in driving revenue growth, customer acquisition and retention, cost savings and operating efficiencies, innovation processes, and all other business functions. The CIO's function will be an operations role, not a support role. The users of IT will be more sophisticated as the Internet and technology become more pervasive in everyday human lives. Therefore, as the users become more information enabled and information capable, leading firms will be in a position to create the next generation of knowledge workers—employees with more basic computing skills and more knowledge of how they can use information in their everyday tasks to reach out to customers and deliver new value streams and ultimately new revenue streams. But this will be possible only by achieving the first two goals mentioned earlier—(1) defining information differently as a strategic element of all firm operations, and (2) melding IT strategy and corporate strategy into one united information-driven view of how the leaders of the Next Wave will win. They will win by using information in superior ways to survive, compete, replicate, and adapt to change. That is the essence of Information Darwinism.

BREAKING DOWN INFORMATION DARWINISM: PART ONE

Firms that invest in IT as a strategic resource for the future will survive. Those that do not will perish.

The first component of the Principle of Information Darwinism addresses how firms view IT, as a strategic weapon or as a budgetary necessity. It concerns how corporations invest in IT, at minimal levels required to perform fundamental business transactions to survive, or as an option, a financial investment that will provide superior returns over time. The firms that view IT as an expense and their IT department as an overhead expenditure will not survive the Next Wave of change. These firms will be outflanked by nimble new competitors and destroyed head-on by their direct competitors. In short, they will be deselected by the business version of natural selection. Consider the IT spending spree generated by the millennium hype, or Y2K. Billions of dollars were spent on software, hardware, consulting services, and remediation tools to prepare for the Year 2000 transition. Companies had multiple options for dealing with this situation. One option was to remediate systems while maintaining the existing architecture, even though in many cases the IT infrastructures and application portfolios were outdated, proprietary mainframe architectures. The firms that invested the bare minimum in their IT assets to achieve Y2K compliance missed an opportunity to upgrade their systems' capabilities and prepare for the newly digital and Internet-based competitive landscape.

Some firms, however, invested aggressively in their IT infrastructures, updated their application portfolios with modern, n-tier web-based tools, and now are positioned for the Next Wave. These firms are now poised to compete in a new way, in a digitally enabled fashion that adumbrates what Slywotzky and Morrison call "digital business design." These firms have not fully transitioned to the Information Age model of operation yet; in fact, no corporation has. Incremental improvements in Industrial Age corporate structures and strategies foreshadow aspects of how informationalized corporations might operate in the Internet Age, but these are merely extensions of older business designs. We have yet to witness the new species of firms that will emerge from the Internet shakeout of 2000–2001, but they will be based on sound business fitness metrics combined with a cutting-edge view and implementation of IT to drive their business models.

Exhibit 1.2 highlights the traits of the firms that will lead the Next Wave. These characteristics will separate these corporations from their competitors because they understand the strategic value of information and of the assets that capture, manage, and create customer value from information. They have threaded the core competencies of superior IT management throughout every business process, linking them all to delivery of superior customer value. These value processes will have increasing information content and will be delivered by information assets to attain category supremacy in the markets in which these firms choose to compete.

Dell Computer is an example of a firm that is based on an information-intensive mode of competition. Dell's make-to-order manufacturing model is envied by IBM, Hewlett-Packard, and many other PC manufacturers that covet one of its key internal benefits—its negative working capital business model. Simply put, Dell orders components for its products only after the customers have paid for them in advance. In other words, Dell receives the order information from its customers, as well as payment in advance, and then purchases the

- Leading firms of the Next Wave understand the strategic value of information.
- Leading firms have processes in place to continuously evaluate their information competitiveness and how to improve it.
- Leading firms of the Next Wave constantly look for new sources of information value, both within and outside the boundaries of the organization.
- Leading firms of the Next Wave build processes that are information-based and communication-centric.
- Leading firms have recognized the shift from asset-intensive competitive advantage to information-intensive competitive advantage and have organized themselves accordingly.
- Leading firms seek out the information value in their information assets—products, processes, personnel, customer interactions, knowledge bases.
- Leaders of the Next Wave will drive cycles of innovation using information-based tools, processes, assets, and teams.

Exhibit 1.2 Traits of the Next Wave Winners

inventory to make the product and ship it. This approach is the reverse of most manufacturing companies, which forecast demand for products, purchase inventory in advance using their own working capital, and manufacture and ship the product to distributors, wholesalers, and eventually retailers, who sell them to end customers. Eventually, these companies get paid by this distribution channel for their products. Dell, in other words, has replaced the need for inventory with information. Dell takes in demand information from the marketplace, as well as revenue from its customers, before it commits to purchasing inventory from its suppliers. Dell's manufacturing velocity is tremendous, with a six-hour cycle time from the receipt of a customer order to shipping the final product. To support its direct sales model and to achieve the negative working capital model of finance super-efficiency, in 1993 Dell invested heavily to overhaul its information systems in manufacturing and logistics and implemented manufacturing automation to continue to drive costs down and improve manufacturing throughput. Dell is the industry benchmark for make-to-order manufacturing, where information replaces inventory. Dell's ability to obtain customer order information, process it and aggregate it into purchasing information for its suppliers, translate it into manufacturing information to drive make-to-order assembly of computers of multiple configurations, and then perform logistics and shipping with unmatched speed, makes it an information-intensive manufacturing firm. Dell's mode of operation is as much based on information management skills as manufacturing asset management skills.

This is an example of a new breed of firm, where its business and operating models are predicated on information assets driving physical manufacturing assets rather than the reverse. These companies will survive and thrive in the face of heightened competition because of their information-harvesting capabilities. The others, as the Principle of Information Darwinism suggests, will either modify their business models if possible or be deselected. Many firms represent the new breed of firm, the information-based competitors with the capabilities required for the Information Age, but many other firms are struggling with an Industrial Age method of competing. Recent examples include AT&T, Lucent, Kodak, and Xerox, which have failed to adapt to today's times for a variety of reasons. They have failed to adapt to the requirements of the Information Age economy. These firms, and many others like them, have not embraced the power of information as a weapon for reaching new customers and markets, as a tool for driving costs down, as a way of competing against both the competition and the unknown—rapid, technology-driven change. They have not seized the opportunities afforded them by the rapid changes caused by globalism, by the Internet explosion, and by the increasing pace of change. They simply do not have the proper tools to compete in this environment.

HOW DO WINNING FIRMS SURVIVE INFORMATION DARWINISM?

The Dell example should provide some clues regarding the activities that world-class corporations pursue to drive their business models to higher performance levels, or greater fitness, than their competitors. Information Darwinism suggests that firms must invest in IT at greater levels and in smarter ways than their competitors in order to dominate their markets and beat their competition. But Information Darwinism requires more than investing hard-fought company dollars blindly into an information budget and hoping for a return of some kind; it requires the processes and capabilities of a firm to be information-based processes, and those processes rely on the firmwide processes of creating, harnessing, managing, and distributing information to provide value to the corporation and its customers. In short, the *processes* of a firm must be information-based, but company processes must support a larger firmwide goal and operating credo that is based on the corporate strategy and the business model. The coherence of these goals determines the ability of a firm to concentrate its efforts on accomplishing them.

Consider Treacy and Wiersema's landmark book[12] on how a company's (actually, the business unit's) focus on a particular system of value delivery has requirements for the processes, behaviors, and ultimately the information systems that help drive that value delivery model. Treacy and Wiersema identified three central concepts for operating a business unit[13]:

1. A value proposition, or the value provided to customers by the firm's processes and products
2. An operating model for delivering the value proposition to the customers
3. A value discipline, or the ways that companies may combine their operating models and value propositions to be market leaders in their chosen competitive arena

In their book, Treacy and Wiersema also identified three fundamental value disciplines:

1. Operational excellence
2. Product leadership
3. Customer intimacy

Each of these disciplines had certain characteristics and operating models that accompanied them. Essentially, the total system of value delivery that underlies each of these disciplines is driven by a set of processes and capabilities of the firm. The firm must cultivate the particular bundle of processes and capabilities in order to fully and repeatedly deliver the total value demanded of competing on a particular value discipline. Each value discipline also has a bundle of information processes that accompanies it.

Consider the value discipline of operational excellence. Operational excellence demands that a firm deliver quality, price, and ease of purchase in a superior fashion compared to its competitors. Operational excellence companies execute their business models well and as a result can offer the lowest prices and better service as a result. In order to deliver on the operational excellence value proposition, the operating model must have tightly synchronized business processes driven by information-intensive capabilities. The operating model of operational excellence demands a set of core processes, both business processes and information processes, that will allow efficiency, low cost structure, and superior execution of the business model that results in quality, service, overall price value, and ease of purchase for customers. The processes of operational excellence deliver the value proposition to customers in a repeatable, efficient fashion.

Similarly, the value proposition delivered by the product leadership value discipline is based on executing a set of processes, both business and information processes, that allow the repeatable delivery of products that meet and exceed the expectations of customers. The value discipline of product excellence requires creative processes of research and development (R&D) and invention, followed by commercialization skills and product development capabilities. Once basic research is focused on new product development objectives with commercial viability, information processes begin to drive the downstream activity. Computer-aided design (CAD), computer-aided manufacturing (CAM), product data management and collaborative design tools, and simulation and other tools facilitate product development, manufacturing, and distribution to customers. The combination of business processes and information processes to drive product execution allows a firm to excel at the product leadership value discipline in the fashion described by Treacy and Wiersema.

The same phenomenon applies to customer intimacy, a value discipline based on development and nurturing of customer relationships and the customized delivery of product and service solutions for those customers. The customer intimacy value discipline is based on a value proposition of relationships and trust with the vendor firm. The customers may not pay the best price on a given procurement or service transaction, but over the lifetime of the relationship both parties will win and sustain one another. Again, this value discipline is driven by a core set of business and information processes that make it possible to generate above-average performance relative to a firm's competitors. Information technologies that support the customer intimacy value discipline might include customer relationship management (CRM) tools, sales force automation and contact management software, account management processes and tools, and related processes and technologies that foster knowing customers well and providing what they desire from the relationship.

While Treacy and Wiersema do emphasize the critical contribution of IT to the execution of some of the processes that underlie value disciplines, that view is not sufficient anymore. Operationally excellent companies are particularly reliant on technology, so much so that "one usually has to look inside the companies' computer systems to understand their core business processes."[14] These systems do not merely monitor and track process performance, they contain the process and execute it. This is clearly the case in financial services and insurance industries, where core business processes *are* computers systems that employees use every day to execute the basic processes of the corporation. Clearly, then, operational excellence heavily relies on IT and other automation tools for consistent and efficient process execution.

But the role of IT extends deeper today than it ever has before and is more of a driving force for the other value disciplines of product leadership and customer intimacy as well. Furthermore, it is important to note that this perspective includes both the basic business processes that drive execution of a particular value discipline and the processes that create, harvest, manage, and distribute information value across the firm's value chain in support of corporate activities. To that end, a new value discipline separate from the embedded concepts of IT management that we are accustomed to is introduced—Information Mastery.

INFORMATION MASTERY: VALUE DISCIPLINE OF THE NEXT WAVE

The value discipline of the Next Wave is based on the ability of a corporation to harness and deliver superior information value. The strategic contribution that information makes in this new value discipline is the new imperative of the Information Age. Like the value disciplines devised by Treacy and Wiersema, Information Mastery has a value proposition and an operating model.

The value proposition of Information Mastery is different from the IT management practices of the past. Information technology management as a company discipline is typically managed as a budgetary expense, where relative performance is assessed on compliance to that budget. The value proposition of Information Mastery is substantially different. Information Mastery demands a different definition of information's contribution to company success. Information Mastery requires a new way of funding itself, where it is not treated as an overhead allocation. Rather, it is considered a core production asset of the firm, regardless of the industry. The value of information is based on new metrics and new methods for evaluating the information contribution to corporate strategy execution. The following are attributes of Information Mastery:

- *Information-based business processes.* Business process are not designed or redesigned without explicit consideration of how information is used by and created through those processes. Information has value in and of itself in the business processes of a corporation.
- *Information management processes.* Information processes are defined and built in conjunction with business processes, with an explicit role and well-defined metrics. Information-based business models not only enable the business to achieve superior results, but information itself is also released from its Industrial Age tethers and constraints, which allows information value to be realized in new ways, with new processes and new valuation techniques.
- *Business execution.* Execution of the business with information-intensive processes will place a new demand on the organization to develop the core capabilities, the skills, and new ways of managing information assets more effectively.
- *Unleashing information value.* Creating more value with information means more than managing information systems. It means defining a larger role for intellectual property management, licensing information assets, identifying and inventorying information assets, and placing appropriate value on them.
- *New information assets.* Information Mastery demands new valuation processes and techniques for information content, assets, processes, and tools than before. For leading firms, the information assets will become more valuable in the ongoing business enterprise, and information processes will enhance the value of other noninformation assets as well.
- *New information metrics.* Information Mastery requires new metrics for assessing the contribution of information to the success of the business. Traditional, Industrial Age metrics will not suffice in today's business environment.

Information Mastery as a value discipline in and of itself clearly raises the bar for the information management functions of any corporation. At first, many executives will view this as heresy. After all, they have gotten by just fine with spending 2 to 5 percent of revenues on information technology. Why should they change that view? The answer is simple. Following our biological and evolutionary examples, the pattern should be obvious. The ability of companies to adapt to change and replicate business models across generations of technology change and leadership transitions is a strategic advantage. Information management processes and capabilities clearly resemble the evolutionary trajectory of intelligence and the development of culture, language, and technology. These developments are all part of the human experience. Corporations must not view themselves as separate from the evolution of human organizations and culture. They are a direct result of human development and are therefore subject to many of the same fundamental processes. Knowing this, and knowing what to do about it, will become a differentiator for corporate leaders. The information function today will help firms adapt to the business environment tomorrow.

BREAKING DOWN INFORMATION DARWINISM: PART TWO

Executives who invest in IT as one of their primary strategic levers will thrive. Those who do not will be deselected.

The second component of the Principle of Information Darwinism involves the leadership of corporations and how they view, invest, and guide the IT initiatives of their firms. Those executives who recognize the value of IT in today's business environment and leverage it as a strategic weapon will be the survivors. Their firms will win more market share, retain more customer loyalty, and demonstrate superior financial performance as a result of choosing IT as one of their main competitive weapons. This generation of enlightened executives will outpace their peers in all measures of personal and business success because they will have elected to drive IT investments as competitive differentiators against firms in the same industry. They may also threaten adjacent or related industries as forces of convergence blur traditional industry boundaries. In the Information Age, competitive advantage, barriers to entry, and industry and company boundaries are all transient entities. Their existence is increasingly fleeting. The next generation of business executives will herald a new breed of leaders. They have all been exposed to IT, they have all grown up with PCs and the Internet, and they know how fleeting competitive advantage can be—it can appear and disappear in the wink of an eye given today's rates of change. These seemingly transient episodes of competitive advantage result from several possible factors. Either the business model was not a good one, where sustained revenues, profits, and cash flows were not possible, or it was a good model but the execution was flawed. Another possibility is that rapid change in the industry structure, customer choices, or other factors invalidated the business model, forcing companies to exit the industry. The new breed of executive will be more accustomed to these changes. More IT-savvy executives will be promoted to C-level slots in the coming years than ever before. Chief information officers will begin to move into more operational roles in leading-edge firms because of the way Y2K planning and execution was managed.

Most IT professionals demonstrated that they had far deeper knowledge of company operations than was thought to be the case by their operational peers. This recognition will lead to the wholesale transition of leadership positions to those who are IT literate and not only understand IT, but can also engage their technology organizations as partners in running the business, in satisfying customers, and in creating and delivering new products to the marketplace.

Exhibit 1.3 highlights the traits of executives who will survive the Next Wave. These characteristics separate them from their peers because they

Next Wave leaders understand the strategic value of information.

- CEOs of the Next Wave will unleash their IT organizations from the management practices of the past; CEOs will establish a formal partnership and clear dialogue with their CIO partners and establish a concurrent business and technology strategy process.
- CEOs of the Next Wave will increase IT budgets, but with this increase will come a new responsibility: demonstrating IT value above and beyond the normal expectations, which will require new metrics based on corporate fitness—revenue, profit, cash flow, market share.
- Next Wave CEOs will establish an IT research and development function that drives information innovation for both internal efficiencies and potential licensing revenue from software developed in-house; IT will become a future source of revenue as world-class technologies—once their advantage has been realized internally by the firm—are licensed to other firms and potentially spun off as new corporations; IT will serve as an incubator in this role, creating yet again more potential revenue streams from investing in technology.
- Next Wave leaders value their IT assets and staff, and seek their guidance and support for all aspects of corporate strategy and execution.
- The CEOs of Next Wave firms will be technologically savvy. They will seek out the information needed to turn IT into the driving force of business strategy execution.
- CEOs of Next Wave companies will not use IT as an excuse for overspending on their budgets or for not meeting planned orders or shipments.
- Leaders of the Next Wave have shifted their organizations to compete less on physical assets and more on information assets. This does not mean, though, that they must shed physical assets and outsource manufacturing. It merely means wrapping the physical processes with information tools to drive more efficient utilization of physical assets, as well as providing more information content bundled with products and extracting information value from all business processes.

Exhibit 1.3 Traits of the Next Wave

understand the strategic value of information, of the assets they capture, and they manage and create customer value from information.

Many more executives will be deselected as their firms falter in the Information Age. They will not have anticipated how to confront and anticipate the changes in the New Economy. They will not know that their training in the Industrial Age management techniques taught in most business schools has ill equipped them to manage an information-intensive competitive landscape. They must learn or be deselected.

HOW DO WINNING FIRMS SURVIVE INFORMATION DARWINISM?

Review the value disciplines or, for that matter, any strategies of leading corporations. A common recurring theme appears: the firm's corporate culture and values have a larger affect on its ultimate success than many of the superficial business initiatives do. Winning firms avoid deselection by Information Darwinism because of their ability to change their information management structures from the financially driven orientation of the past to the information-value driven model of the future. This change begins at the top of a corporation with the view of IT and how it can be used to drive the formulation and execution of business strategy. Executives of the Next Wave will be trained in the concepts of strategic information management. These leaders will aggressively recruit technology-savvy members of their staff to develop and implement information-based processes based on new ideas for harnessing and delivering greater value from IT processes, assets, and core capabilities.

As with the value disciplines described earlier, Information Mastery contains elements in its operating model that are essential for its ascendance as a legitimate value discipline. Information Mastery as a value discipline requires the following attributes of the leaders of the Next Wave and how they view and empower the information management functions of their respective corporations:

- *Role of IT.* The role of IT as a value discipline requires more scope and responsibility for business operations and business results. Information technology must be defined as a key business value driver, and it must be explicitly linked as a critical path process for achievement of corporate success. Executives who embrace Information Mastery as a value discipline will reap the rewards from this new stance toward IT management in the Next Wave. Information Mastery will allow IT to increasingly be a business function rather than a separate supporting function. Information technology will have profitability, market share, and customer satisfaction goals, but it will be clearly tied to external results, external customers, and corporate profitability. The role of IT in the value discipline of Information Mastery will be much broader, with a deeper impact on corporate success than was ever contemplated or allowed under the Industrial Age IT management practices of the past.

- *Organization and structure of IT.* Organizing the information functions under Information Mastery will not be an afterthought of corporate strategy and business model definition. It will be a carefully premeditated act that explicitly recognizes the value contribution of information in driving execution of business profitability and customer satisfaction. Information technology organizations will not be constrained by Industrial Age thinking and management principles. Unfettered by the cost-control paradigm that resulted from the reporting relationship to the financial organization of a firm, IT will become a value-driven business unit that creates information value in its own right in conjunction with driving the execution of core business process.
- *IT and business leadership blur.* The critical attribute of Information Mastery is the technology literacy of the leaders of the Next Wave. IT leaders will be more business savvy than ever before, and business leaders will be more technology savvy. Their leadership roles and responsibilities will blur across business boundaries that are fluid and intertwined. Common business objectives will gel business and IT leaders together despite fluid business boundaries, which will make the teaming of IT and business leaders a natural function of how IT is organized and structured. Adaptive mechanisms will be built into business and IT functions to support rapid rollout of new ideas for business and technology. Their roles and goals will be interdependent, and their success will be mutually reinforcing, resulting in a coadaptive relationship for success.
- *Structure of IT.* Information Mastery requires that the IT organization be structured to adapt and respond to business and technological change. This approach is different from IT structures of the past, which were meant to maintain control over technology and organizational change. These approaches evolved out of the IT management of the past. Information Mastery will demand dynamic IT structures that can rapidly change with technology and help the business functions of the firm adapt quicker than those of its competitors. This requires fluid and dynamic structures that do not resist change but, rather, are built on change and are expected to change. As technology and business change accelerates, companies will be hard pressed to respond without the appropriate organization and structure based on a culture of change. This is no time to

plan for stasis—the business environment will continue to be a vibrant and inherently unstable setting for the foreseeable future. Plan on it with IT structures.

- *Expectations of IT.* Information Mastery raises the expectations of IT beyond those of the typical paradigm of IT management. Information Mastery enables IT to generate new value for the organization beyond the narrow expectations of the Industrial Age. Those expectations were for IT managers to keep systems running, not exceed the paltry budget they were allocated, and with the 30 percent of the budget remaining to engage in creative IT research on behalf of the business and spend it wisely. This approach is wrong. Information technology expectations of Information Mastery might include conducting research to invent new value streams for the corporation and identify new ways to drive more value with less investment. Information technology R&D functions will be a mission-critical function of leading firms, where pure IT research is conducted as a part of the ongoing role and function of IT. Research will be directed at business processes that help serve customers, lower costs, increase market share, and innovate new products and services. Patents and intellectual property goals will be established for IT organizations, with a goal of licensing new ideas and innovations on behalf of the firm. Patents may result in spinoffs from the parent company based on new technology innovations and patents from R&D. These are examples, but they are intended to demonstrate how releasing IT from the "lack of expectations" of the Industrial Age of information management can result in dramatic innovation and business value creation.
- *Culture of IT.* Information Mastery requires a new culture of IT that is centered on business results based on information value. Information technologists will no longer be considered the nerds in the backroom. Information technology gurus will be the next generation of leaders for the Next Wave, and therefore the culture and training of IT professionals must be as much in the business of the firm as in the business of generating superior value based on Information Mastery. The culture of IT will be based on knowledge of both business and information management and will be recognized as a critical driver of corporate initiatives and success.

BUSINESS 2.0 E-BIZ 100

In an April 1999 *Business 2.0* article, the top 100 e-business companies were ranked by web revenue. In this list, manufacturing companies were well represented. In fact, more than 50 percent of e-commerce involves logistics activities such as managing warehouses, distribution centers, and transportation of physical goods. UPS and Federal Express, for example, are considered e-business leaders and have positioned themselves for the e-business age. Their strategies are clearly oriented toward shipping smaller parcels associated with the wave of business-to-consumer (B2C) commerce of the First Wave of the Internet boom.

Continuing to break down this list, 66 of the top 100 e-business companies were pure Internet firms. Twenty-one of the top 100 e-business firms are retailers. Thirteen were financial services firms, and fourteen were media publishing firms. Even manufacturing is well represented on the e-business 100, including Dell, Cisco, Nortel, IBM, and other related high tech-firms. Fourteen high-tech manufacturing firms were listed on the April 1999 e-business 100 list. *Business 2.0* has not updated its list, but many of the Internet pure plays have probably been deselected as a result of unsound business models and poor execution.

A recent *Business Week* article detailed a new list of IT companies that are performing well in the post–dot-com era.[15] Two types of companies are winning according to the "*Business Week* Info Tech 100": those that have achieved the efficiencies and business improvements long promised by the technology revolution, and those that sell products and services that help businesses achieve business improvements and improve their bottom line. The Internet hubris spurred a tremendous wave of technology investments by most companies; however, the dot-com demise combined with the current economic slowdown has companies looking for ways to put those technology investments to work, and the Internet is part of the equation. It turns out, at least for now, that companies are using the Internet to drive cost savings and inventory reductions by using the web to take slack out of supply chains, for example, or to drive procurement processes, or to implement customer-facing systems such as CRM. Focusing on outsourcing, customer self-service, business process enablement, and supply chain management have helped corporations drive significant cost savings.

This is reminiscent of General Electric's (GE's) efforts to scale its Internet plans back to in-house improvements, which will generate some $1.6 billion in savings.[16] GE is increasing its computer budget by some 12 percent in 2001, to approximately $3 billion. Although this plan is less far-reaching than its original Internet plans, GE plans to digitize as many business processes as possible with web applications enabled by e-mail capabilities. This internal focus was initiated because many of its customers and suppliers were not able to support what GE was trying to accomplish. Their IT systems and capabilities were not able to meet the needs of GE's Internet strategy. GE's internal e-business plans are clearly valid and valuable applications of technology to drive new business value for a company, even though they are scaled-back business initiatives from their original intent.

The *Business Week* Info Tech 100 list, similar to the e-business 100 list, has manufacturing companies well represented. The important lesson from both of the lists is that the Internet and, more broadly, information technology still have tremendous promise for companies seeking new ways to drive business value based on information capabilities. This theme will be a constant throughout this book.

EXAMPLES OF COMPANIES THAT "GET IT"

The important point is that there really *are* companies that "get it." They really understand what the Internet opportunity means for their operations, for managing their supply chains, and for their marketing, sales, and customer care processes. But what is the difference between the companies that do understand e-business and the companies that do not?

- *Business first.* These companies understand business first, and e-business and technology initiatives are the execution mechanisms for their business strategy. But they drive business models that are based on traditional business fitness levers of revenue, cash flow, and profits. Increasingly, information-based assets will drive a higher percentage of revenue and profit as firms learn how to embed information into all their sources of revenue.
- *Agility and speed.* Leading companies understand that agility and speed are competitive differentiators, and they have designed their corporations to compete on these dimensions. Agility and speed are woven into their cultures, their strategies, their processes, and their technology capabilities. Speed allows rapid cycles of learning, which as learning curve studies have demonstrated, promotes faster adaptation, lower costs, and other crucial benefits.[17]
- *New definition of information value.* These firms have broadened the definition of information management from one of traditional Industrial Age thinking to a new, Information Age definition. The new view of information changes how information assets are valued and bundled into all processes and activities of the firm. It values information innovation on par with product development. For firms that compete on nondigital products, or products that do not process or contain information, the use of information is embedded into those products by virtue of the processes and market intelligence used to design, manufacture, distribute, and sell them.

- *Customer and market proximity.* They are close to their customers and markets and have instituted strategies, processes, and technologies to ensure market proximity and customer intimacy. Information processes are deployed to ensure transactional efficiency and ease of doing business for all customer and supplier interfaces. Market knowledge and customer needs are continuously sought as inputs into organizational learning engines that sift and analyze this information in support of process and product innovations.
- *Do not build monuments; build the future.* They do not build monuments to reflect on their past achievements; they build cultures and processes to guarantee their future survival. Monuments in this case refer to assets as trophies, such as large headquarters buildings or huge factories that do not provide competitive advantage (although they make for great tours for visitors). Building for the future means investing in value-creating activities, which are increasingly information-based.
- *Constantly seek and deliver new value to customers.* Increasingly, value drivers will be information-based, whether in the products a firm sells, in the processes that make the products, or in the servicing of both the processes and products by internal customer-support processes. Information-based business models will generate new value in new ways based on a superior ability to manage information and harvest knowledge.

In the First Wave of e-business, IT investing was spurred on by the need to explore selling over the web. Corporations are just beginning to "walk upright" with their incipient responses to the Internet opportunity (or challenge) facing them. Evolutionarily speaking, we have seen the environment change, conferring sudden advantage on certain companies (e.g., dot-coms and other new entrants), and now we are seeing the old guard respond as best they can. Their adaptive calculus may allow them to respond in time, or it may not.

Competing on information is a different game from competing on physical assets. An example from the cell phone industry illustrates competing on information intensity as opposed to physical asset intensity. In this case, a manufacturing firm augmented limited manufacturing capacity with outstanding information management capacity, which ultimately allowed them, through superior revenue and market share growth, to become the largest manufacturer in their industry.

This is precisely what happened with Nokia in their competition with Motorola and Ericsson in the cellular phone industry.[18] On January 26, 2001, Ericsson announced that it was outsourcing manufacturing to contract manufacturer Flextronics International Ltd. Ericsson's exit from manufacturing its cellular phones involved the transfer of six factories and some 4,200 employees to Flextronics. Ericsson's announcement preceded Motorola's announcement to outsource most of its cellular phone manufacturing capacity just weeks earlier. These announcements signal attempts by Ericsson and Motorola to trim production costs and bolster the already slim margins—as low as 3 percent for Motorola—on their phones. But Nokia is keeping production of phones in-house, believing that it constitutes a competitive advantage over its rivals by allowing it to control costs and perhaps even drive them lower. Lower costs will allow Nokia to drive prices down and take more market share from its manufacturing-outsourced competitors. Nokia currently produces more phones than both Motorola and Ericsson combined, the number two and three players in cell phone revenue, respectively.

But how has Nokia managed to usurp the dominant position in this industry from its erstwhile competitors? What changes in Nokia's operating model allowed it to achieve the dominant market position in cell phones? What strategic decisions did it make to help achieve its enviable business success? The answer is replacing or augmenting manufacturing asset intensity with information asset intensity. Nokia was originally a paper manufacturer, and eventually became a manufacturing conglomerate with a diverse portfolio of businesses such as multiple paper products, rubber boots, and even televisions and computers along the way. Nokia decided to exit those lines of business and elected to shed those manufacturing assets in favor of becoming a cell phone pure-play. Nokia was on the verge of bankruptcy in the early 1990s, lacking the global manufacturing muscle of competitors Motorola and Ericsson. Nokia restructured for a global economy at that time, instituting streamlined product design and flexible process design for manufacturing, allowing it to be nimble and agile in its production capabilities. This redesign allowed Nokia to respond quickly to the radically increased demand for cellular phones by creating sleek new designs to address regional global tastes, as well as being a first-mover in the digital cell phone market. In lieu of building expensive worldwide manufacturing capacity, which was impossible for Nokia at that time, it reorganized to compete on information capabilities. The information that allowed Nokia to optimize its limited manufacturing capacity at the time was customer preference and choice information, combined with product design information, all used to build manufacturing and distribution processes, which leveraged that information as well. Nokia needed the ability to gather, harness, and manage information globally more than it needed to manufacture globally at that time. This turned out to be the strategic lever that, ultimately, has allowed Nokia to compete both on manufacturing capabilities as well as information capabilities, but the information decision created its current manufacturing dominance, not the reverse.

Nokia is able to produce 24 new phone designs per year, a pace that neither Motorola nor Ericsson can match. Nokia built the proper processes, as well as the information management capabilities, that not only enabled those processes, but also sustained and energized them to achieve the performance it is realizing today. Product design processes involve tremendous information management resources such as computer-aided design (CAD) for the phone itself, the computer boards inside, the microprocessor and memory chips that reside on the boards, and even the software that is embedded on the chips. The rich suite of design and development tools for all components of the typical cellular phone are complex, and they require large investments in information management tools, such as product data management (PDM) software and enterprise document management (EDM) software, to coordinate a concurrent design through the development cycles of a cell phone.

These are all elements of competing on the basis of information intensity, not by physical asset intensity. The information content of a single manufacturing facility of 100,000 square feet that can produce 100 product types with the same processes, equipment, and personnel is higher than a 100,000-square-foot factory that can only produce 50 product types. In other words, the manufacturing automation, the processes and process documentation, and the work instructions that are displayed to operators to inform them how to assemble a particular variant of a product are all information assets required to perform those processes. A flexible manufacturing facility will have more investments in flexible tooling, which is based on programmable automation, downloadable machine instructions, CAD/CAM tools, and other information-based manufacturing tools. Once again, these information assets allow more capability per square foot of facility than would otherwise be possible.

Industrial automation has been an interesting field to watch over the last half decade as sensors, devices, motors and drives, and programmable logic controllers (PLCs) have become more information-capable and more information-enabled than ever before. More and more, these industrial automation systems are transitioning from the proprietary architectures and standards of the 1980s and early 1990s to architectures based on the standards and general-purpose technologies of IT organizations. Industrial automation products are now based on PCs, using web browsers for visualization and information search and retrieval, Microsoft Windows for the operating system, Ethernet transmission control protocol/Internet protocol (TCP/IP) for the networking, and Java, VisualBasic, C, and C++ languages as the programming tools. The plant floor has become a dynamic environment based on its ability to process and manage process and product information, quality control and process control, and reporting of production status, capacity, and quality. This has not always been the case.

These investments in information management tools on the plant floor can allow a firm to compete on an information basis with manufacturing assets as opposed to competing on a physical asset basis with manufacturing assets, which require large investments in capital, facilities, equipment, and personnel. Information allows a firm to do more with less, as Nokia has proven. Informationalizing manufacturing facilities eliminates the bottleneck of information flowing between the order-taking processes and the delivery processes, and all processes in between. This is what Dell has done, among others. Dell, Cisco, and others manufacture, but they do it in such a way that the plant floor environment is an integral element of their information management capabilities. That achievement is the result of information-enabled manufacturing assets, processes, and skills.

As discussed earlier, Treacy and Wiersema have three winning formulas for business success:

1. Customer intimacy
2. Product leadership
3. Operational excellence

Their observation is that winning firms have selected one of these major competitive dimensions as their primary competitive lever and have implemented the processes and technology solutions to emphasize and drive that particular competitive discipline. The firm then has to maintain a minimum level of competence in the other two disciplines to achieve market leadership. Consider Intel, which competes on product and process innovation for microchip design and manufacturing, as an example of product leadership. Intel must have outstanding product development and innovation, creating processes and capabilities in order to be the product leader it is recognized as being. But it must also maintain acceptable performance levels in customer intimacy and operational excellence in order to succeed overall by competing on its primary discipline—product leadership. I believe, however, that Treacy and Wiersema miss an important point in their outstanding book. Today a firm can achieve excellent results along all of these dimensions with sound investments in the processes and technologies to support them. They do not have to make a choice of one over another, but they must know what confers competitive advantage for them versus their competitors and what helps them serve their customers better than their competitors. Then they must design the strategies, processes, and information systems that drive those competitive levers, or disciplines, to winning levels. Information management capabilities underlie every one of Treacy and Wiersema's "disciplines" just as they underlie any winning competitive strategy for a leading firm.

EVOLUTION OF ORGANIZATIONAL MODELS TO SUPPORT INFORMATION FUNCTIONS

Firms must successfully transition from an Industrial Age strategy, structure, and core capabilities to an Information Age strategy, structure, and core capabilities. Chapter 2 shows how today's firms are bound by their Industrial Age legacies. They have not successfully been able to unleash the informational value that is embedded in their business model, their products, or their services. That value is constrained by their strategy, structure, core capabilities, corporate culture, and value system, all of which are carryovers from their Industrial Age roots. In order to devise an organizational design that allows a firm to understand its information assets and how it can add tremendous incremental value, we must discuss brain-to-body ratios.

CORPORATE BRAIN-TO-BODY RATIO

Most corporations have invested in information systems to manage their businesses. The level of investment in IT varies by industry, strategy, and a host of other factors. By and large, though, IT investments are managed as stable proportions of the overall budget spending. Manufacturing firms on average spend roughly 2 percent of their gross revenues on IT. Financial services firms and telecommunications firms spend more, approximately 5 to 6 percent of gross revenues on IT. With extraordinary events such as the Year 2000, the spending was increased to address the problem across all industries, but in general IT spending has not increased as a percentage of budgets. If we equate IT capabilities of corporations with the brains of living organisms, then there is an interesting inconsistency. The evolution of mammals, primates, and human beings witnessed first the development of brains, followed by the dramatic increase in size over evolutionary time. The evolution of the human brain is one of the most remarkable and rapid evolutionary phenomena known. In just 3 million years, which is a very short time in evolutionary terms, the human skull increased from 500 cubic centimeters to roughly 1,400 cubic centimeters. This near tripling in brain volume from the *Australopithecine*s to today's modern *Homo sapiens sapiens* not only represents a rapid pace of evolution, but also tends to correlate with the ways in which life-forms make a living in nature. In the human case, the largest explosion in brain size occurred during the time between *Homo erectus* and *Homo sapiens,* some 500,000 to 100,000 years ago. Overall, human brains began increasing in size relative to apes around 2 million years ago, apparently concurrently with the making of tools. *Homo erectus* was an innovative species. They were inventors of several innovations, including fire, clothing, weapons, and early language. *Homo sapiens* continued this trend with continued innovations in language and art, as well as developing even more sophisticated weapons and technology.

Whether researchers use cranial capacity as a measure of intelligence, or brain-to-body ratios, or even the more widely (though still not an exact measure of intelligence) encephalization quotient (EQ), the trend has been clear: mammals, then primates, followed by early hominid forms leading to *Homo sapiens sapiens,* have all demonstrated increasingly larger brain size, and the rate of increase in humans has been dramatic. If we compare IT spending of corporations since the early days of IT, we can make a case that IT spending tends to be capped at previous budget levels because of the attitudes of executives toward IT as an expense as opposed to a strategic resource. Companies must increase their brain-to-body ratios, by investing in IT, in order to match the evolutionary trajectory of humans. Why should corporations trust this analogy? Increased investments in IT correlate with better returns for all firms, and we have clearly demonstrated the increased dependence on information for managing businesses—and that means all businesses.

Today's corporations must increase their brain-to-body ratios as well. Instead of limiting their IT investments to historical spending benchmarks, forward-looking companies will look for new and creative ways to leverage technology to create competitive advantage. This increase in digital content, or intelligence, must be targeted at customer value and business process enablement. Information technology must be applied toward success metrics that create competitive advantage for the firm.

UNLEASHING INFORMATION VALUE

In order to unleash the information value that is embedded in a business, in the information assets that comprise the firm, a corporation has to turn itself upside down, or look within itself, to examine its makeup and structure with a new lens and from a completely new perspective. The required perspective is one of exploration, curiosity, and wonder at how much informational value is contained within the firm's entire enterprise, within the minds of its employees or "knowledge workers," within the reams of documents and files that still exist in the Industrial Age containers of the past such as file cabinets, blueprints, microfiche, and photocopies. How much information is contained in the embedded devices that are used to control critical manufacturing processes, information that may have clues about how the process might be improved, how the products manufactured by those processes might be improved, and more? This is the accumulated competitive advantage of a firm in its historical context; however, most corporations have no idea what assets they posses, what their value is internally or externally, and most important, how to capture, harness, or release the embedded value of these assets.

In order to unleash information value as described previously, the following activities might be considered as initial steps to inventorying and ascribing value to the information assets within a corporation:

1. Define the information value opportunity that exists in how the firm serves its external and internal customers.
2. Define how the current business strategy is information-based: how information is integral to the products, the business and production processes, and the firm's internal customers.
3. Understand the information-value gap that may exist between the strategy and needs of future business opportunities.
4. Inventory the information assets in the firm—this means any processor or container of information that exists in the firm.
5. Inventory the value of that information, from at least two perspectives: (1) How can these information assets and this body of knowledge support our current business model? How can it help us survive and compete and maintain our current business today? and (2) What is the value of that information in supporting new value and revenue streams? How might this information be used to create a completely new value proposition for new customers, new industries, and new markets? How might competitors or partners use this information? How can our firm be the locus of the new value chain in this new market?
6. Perform a valuation exercise. What is it worth to us? What might it be worth to others? How can we place the proper value on our information assets? How can we make money with this information? How do we value the contents of our information assets?
7. Determine how the firm organizes to unleash the informational value contained in these resources. What strategies and tactics are needed? What structures, processes, and competencies are necessary to make this body of information a viable value stream for the firm to potential customers? What new core competencies are needed to drive this as a viable business model?

The normal view of IT is not sufficient. The traditional view of IT, even in today's sophisticated high-technology firms, is a constrained, cost center view of information management. In fact, the word "management" suggests that they are only managing information, not doing internal mining of information, inventorying information, creating knowledge wealth for the firm, and creating strategic and competitive advantage for the firm. Clearly there must be a better way.

NOTES

1. Matt Ridley, *Genome* (New York: HarperCollins Publishers, 1999), p. 35.
2. Ibid., p. 25.
3. Philip Evans and Thomas S. Wurster, *Blown to Bits* (Boston, MA: Harvard Business School Press, 2000), p. xi.
4. Ibid., p. 12.
5. Ibid., p. 9.
6. Adrian J. Slywotzky and David J. Morrison, *How Digital Is Your Business?* (New York: Crown, 2000), p. 3.
7. Evans and Wurster, *Blown to Bits,* p. 15.
8. Ibid., p. 15.
9. Slywotzky and Morrison, *How Digital Is Your Business?* p. 29.
10. Evans and Wurster, *Blown to Bits,* p. 15.
11. Slywotzky and Morrison, *How Digital Is Your Business?*
12. Michael Treacy and Fred Wiersema, *Discipline of Market Leaders* (Reading, MA: Addison-Wesley, 1995).
13. Ibid., p. xiv.
14. Ibid., p. 55.
15. "*Business Week* Info Tech 100 Annual Report," *Business Week* (June 18, 2001), p. 91.
16. Matt Murray and Jathon Sapsford, "GE Reshuffles Its Dot-Com Strategy to Focus on Internal 'Digitizing,'" *The Wall Street Journal* (May 4, 2001), p. B1.
17. George Stalk, Jr. and Thomas M. Hout, *Competing Against Time* (New York: The Free Press, 1990).
18. Stephen Baker, "Outsourcing Alone Won't Save Nokia's Rivals," *Business Week* (February 12, 2001), p. 38.

2

WELCOME TO TODAY (YESTERDAY REVISITED)

I was lucky that at an early age I hitched my wagon to the electron.

—David Sarnoff,
Former President of RCA, 1967

We have explored the impact of technology on human society and how the pace of change has been driven by technology. We have also demonstrated how the Internet is our most recent example of technology-driven change. In this chapter, we show how the forces of evolution that affect living organisms also affect businesses. The analogy of the evolution of living organisms is extended to the evolution of corporations to show that, fundamentally, they are following a similar trajectory, similar processes, and similar mechanisms for survival, competition, reproduction, and adaptation.

LABORATORY OF CHANGE

Evolutionary and biological metaphors are rife in business literature today. For example, a recent *Fortune*[1] article talked about Dell's corporate culture being part of its DNA. Charles Fine uses evolutionary analogies in his book *Clockspeed.*[2] Evan Schwartz published a book entitled *Digital Darwinism.*[3]) The use of evolutionary analogy is appropriate in today's world. A living laboratory of change is occurring with the Internet macrocosm of today. The rapid growth and maturation, albeit still nascent, of the Internet and the World Wide Web is ongoing. New companies are rising up to threaten the established multinational conglomerates, sometimes successfully and other times not. Recently, the demise of many dot-coms has executives wondering whether the Internet and its associated wave of innovation and change will actually affect them after all. The same executives were endangered by the widespread and rapid adoption of the Internet. They all watched as the stock valuations of these incipient corporations based on incredibly new, sexy business models soared to heights rivaling such venerable high-technology stars as Cisco, Sun Microsystems, Microsoft, and so on. They all scrambled to devise Internet strategies of their own to capitalize on this new wave of profitability and technology sizzle. Brick-and-mortar firms created new divisions—e-business divisions—that were supposed to create new revenue streams, new channels to market, and new access to untapped markets and customers. Many firms soon realized, however, that this new experiment in e-business required more fortitude than they had anticipated. Success was not guaranteed just because they were established companies. The incumbent advantage was not an advantage at all in the end. Success is also not assured simply because a company declares itself a dot-com either. The upstart status is not necessarily an advantage just because these companies have no physical infrastructure or predisposition to operate in an Old Economy way. In fact, one realization should be clear to all firms: success is not a foregone conclusion just because they can erect a nice web site and post company literature on it. There is more to it than that.

What we were and are witnessing is evolution. This example of evolution involves corporations, with natural selection acting on them to pick the survivors based on today's business conditions. Corporations can be likened to populations of organisms. A corporation is a collection of individuals, organized into functional groupings or departments, with the collective goal of "making a living" as a firm. "Making a living" can be defined as the fundamental purpose of the corporation, specifically companies that are for-profit institutions. Therefore, a firm that is making a living better than another firm is more profitable, has more market share, and has the most talented employees contributing to its success.

Corporations that are successful at providing value to customers enjoy high profits, high market share, and strong customer loyalty, but this success will be sought by others. The industry that a company serves is similar to an ecological niche in biology. Like living organisms, corporations occupy an ecological niche by extracting profits from its customers. The company is adapted to making a living in this way; however, other firms can elect to make a living the same way and may decide to compete for the same profits. The number of competitors is limited by the amount of profit or energy that can be extracted. The size of a market, much like an ecosystem, has a finite amount of resources that can be exploited by its occupants in order to survive.

Firms that are better at extracting profit from their ecological niche will thrive at the expense of their competitors. They will be rewarded with faster growth, more market share, higher profits, more employee loyalty, and loyal customers. The less efficient competitors will gradually lose market share, profit, and customers. They may go out of business eventually and, in Darwinian terms, become extinct. They will have been deselected based on the differential ability of firms to survive in their economic niche. However, a more fundamental problem faces today's corporations: change.

CHANGE AS LIFE—LIFE AS CHANGE

Today's business conditions can be described as chaotic. The business world is fraught with the risks of the unknown, with change as a normal feature of the business landscape. The pace of change has accelerated, driven by the increased rates of technological innovation, changes we have developed by ourselves. That is the main difference of the world of today versus the world of our ancestors: we have created many of the challenges that confront us today.[4] We also have the ability to create solutions to our problems, by evolving to adapt to the changes. But change, the constant force that we perceive as normal, is inevitable. Companies have always dealt with change. Changing customers, changing needs and demands of customers, new competitors, and new regions. Globalism. Economic fluctuations. These forces all act on firms in different ways depending on how corporations are able to respond. Some corporations have dealt with change better than others, although for varied reasons.

By and large, these same forces have confronted living organisms since the beginning of time. These same forces have been affecting humankind, and humankind's creations as well. Among humankind's creations are today's corporations. Lo and behold, corporations are subject to the same evolutionary forces and natural laws that the world's living creatures are subject to. Entropy. Laws of thermodynamics. Evolution. These same laws act on living species every day. But is this time of rapid technological change unique to today? The answer is no.

TECHNOLOGY-DRIVEN CHANGE

A review of some major technological advances throughout recent history shows that rapid societal changes have always followed major innovations. The rapid changes first occur as part of an "innovation complex," or a series of rapid technological advances that follow and build on a major breakthrough invention or idea. That watershed breakthrough suddenly enables other innovations and inventions that are similar enough to take advantage of the breakthrough. Once this takes place, the innovation complex picks up speed with the increasing adoption of these associated technologies by society.

Jared Diamond summarizes the accelerating pace of innovation:

> Technology's history exemplifies what is termed an autocatalytic process: that is, one that speeds up at a rate that increases with time, because the process catalyzes itself. The explosion of technology since the Industrial Revolution impresses us today, but the medieval explosion was equally impressive compared with that of the Bronze Age, which in turn dwarfed that of the Upper Paleolithic.[5]

Technology is cumulative. It self-propagates. This is because technological advances rely on mastery of simpler problems, which in turn allow the next series of innovations. In addition, new technologies provide the foundation for other advancements by recombination of ideas. The printing press innovation complex aptly demonstrates this phenomenon. The invention of movable type in 1452 by Gutenberg is widely considered to be the primary innovation that culminated in the development of the printing press; however, movable type was one of six technological advances that ultimately manifested themselves in the printing system represented by the printing press.[6] Without concurrent advances in paper, movable type, metallurgy, presses, inks, and scripts, the printing press would not have been the invention that it ultimately became. We can trace similar instances of the innovation complex phenomenon and show how massive sociocultural changes followed major advancements in technology. We begin with the printing press and finish with the Internet.

This technology review demonstrates that technology is indeed accelerating and that the human appetite for technology is increasing as well. Our ability to accept and use technology to support our lifestyles makes increased innovation inevitable. The real revelation is that technology is our adaptive framework as a species. This historical review demonstrates that there are parallels in history to the Internet explosion occurring today. The forces that are making the Internet a part of our everyday lives are the same forces that made the printing press so important.

BRIEF TECHNOLOGY TOUR

In the fifteenth century, the printing press was changing the world. The printing press was shifting the value of books from the book itself to the message within the book. At the time, books were lovingly crafted on vellum by monks in monasteries as an act of devotion to God. As a result, books were very expensive and not available to the public. The advent of the printing press, and related innovations of ink, paper, and others, shifted the value equation. The book no longer was the value driver; the message became the value driver instead.

Consider George Gilder's book,[7] in which he argues that unlimited bandwidth will fundamentally change how the world will work. The invention of the printing press, or more accurately movable type, in 1452 was an exercise in bandwidth. The printing press removed a major bottleneck blocking access to information. The bottleneck was book production. The printing press unleashed the value of information from its physical container, the book. It shifted the value from the medium to the message. The power of information would be one of the major forces in the development of scientific endeavor, creation of new technologies, and exploration and conquest of other nations. Jared Diamond captures the importance of written materials at the time:

> Writing empowered European societies by facilitating political administration and economic exchanges, motivating and guiding exploration and conquest, and making available a range of information and human experience extending into remote places and times.[8]

The printing press allowed mass distribution of information to the content-hungry citizens of the time, breaking the information bottleneck and raising the level of education of the masses to new heights. Information was no longer restricted to the aristocracy; it was suddenly available to everyone. The same is true of the Internet. Although many believe that access to personal computers (PCs) and the Internet is not possible for all socioeconomic groups, this techno-sociostratification will not be a problem for long. The cost of technology will continue to decline, and the ubiquity of the Internet in our everyday lives will break all barriers to the Internet.

Evans and Wurster[9] describe the Internet as being the main mechanism for breaking the richness versus reach trade-off that has plagued businesses in the pre-Internet era. Before the Internet, business strategies had two options: focus on "rich" information in the form of customized products for specific customers or focus on "reach," or reaching a larger, more diverse market with a less specific "message." This richness–reach trade-off no longer has to be the case. In the old days, product information was tightly linked to the product itself. In order to learn about products available on the market, one would have to physically travel to where products are actually sold to see them, to compare them, to learn about them, and to compare the prices to similar products. The information content of products was tightly bound to the physical distribution of the product, as well as to the packaging on the product. Nutritional information and marketing content are co-resident on the labels of canned goods, for example, along with a price stamped on the top.

Evans and Wurster's discussion of the economics of things versus the economics of information makes perfect sense in explaining the impact of the printing press on society in the fifteenth century. The printing press released the value of information from the physical bounds and constraints of books. The printing press was just such an innovation as the Internet. It broke the bottleneck of information distribution by feeding the nature of humankind—our curiosity about the world in which we live, our need for information about our world. The innovation complex of the printing press was a major historical technological breakthrough, but its impact on society and culture worldwide was even more impressive. The significance of printed publications on society continues to be a central part of the human experience, and we owe it to the work of Gutenberg and the other inventors of his time.

INDUSTRIAL REVOLUTION

Similarly, the Industrial Revolution caused massive upheaval of the established order when it blossomed in the early to mid-1700s. The Industrial Revolution had a dramatic impact on society at the time, bringing innovations and change that would ultimately lead to the concept of the factory system and other asset-intensive modes of production. The innovations of the Industrial Revolution initially revolved around the textile industry, which at the time was a major driver of the world economy. The flying shuttle, when it was invented in 1733 by John Kay, allowed weavers to cut cotton twice as fast as before, which shifted the production bottleneck to other areas of production, namely weaving and spinning. The spinning jenny and the hydraulic spinning machine followed. Together with the related innovations leading to the cotton loom, these devices caused the creation of the modern factory system because the cotton loom was far too large and too expensive to reside in family dwellings. By building a factory for his machine in 1769, Richard Arkwright became the founder of the modern factory system, which paved the way for the economic and social changes that characterized the Industrial Revolution. But the series of innovations around the cotton loom and the cotton production industry caused massive societal change that rapidly impacted all facets of the soon-to-be industrialized world. The modern factory system was one result. Poor working conditions were another. This era marked the beginning of the accelerating technology cycle that is occurring now.

SECOND INDUSTRIAL REVOLUTION

The Second Industrial Revolution was even more far-reaching. It was catalyzed by the invention of electricity. Noteworthy innovations that characterize this age of innovation include the telegraph, the telephone, and the light bulb. Two major trends that emerged were communications and transportation. These trends would be built on the previous foundations of technology and would rapidly shape the world in dramatic, unpredictable ways. How could people wrapped up in the midst of such sweeping change anticipate how it would affect them? That task would probably be impossible. The invention of electricity and the steam engine would bring massive changes to the world and set the stage for advancements in virtually all fields of scientific and industrial endeavor. Many of today's modern industrial firms are the products of this era, including General Electric, General Motors, Sears Roebuck & Company, and a host of others. Frederick Taylor made his mark on the world of manufacturing by introducing what he termed "scientific management," a form of industrial engineering involving organization of work. His work with Ford and Bethlehem Steel established the field of scientific management at a time when the Second Industrial Revolution was just picking up steam after the Civil War. Many national industries grew out of local trades, including textiles, steel, glass, and shoes, and many small factories of the time grew to become large manufacturing complexes.[10]

A quick scan of the 2000 *Fortune* 500 list shows how many of the firms that sprouted from the Industrial Age have transitioned their businesses into the Information Age of today. The electric light bulb, invented by Thomas Edison in 1879, led to the formation of many of today's industrial giants. On October 21, 1879, when the candescent light bulb passed the 40-hour test in Menlo Park, New Jersey, it heralded a new generation of corporation—the industrial giants of today. General Electric was formed in 1892 in a merger of Edison General Electric Company and The Thomson-Houston Company, a direct descendant of the invention of the light bulb. General Motors (actually, Olds Motor Vehicle Company) was formed in 1897, followed in 1908 by the creation of General Motors Corporation. IBM even had its roots in the late 1800s, beginning with the formation of the Bundy Manufacturing Company in 1888, changing to the Computing Scale Company of America in 1891, becoming Computing-Tabulating-Recording Company (C-T-R) in 1911, and eventually changing its name to International Business Machines, or IBM, in 1924 under the reign of Thomas Watson.

The Industrial Revolution set the stage for more technological innovation, commercialization, and eventual adoption by human society. Entire industries emerged from the dynamic years of the Industrial Revolution, which in turn created yet more technology. The human appetite for technology and innovation was just beginning to be fed with invention after invention, built on the ideas of previous innovators. The technological developments that evolved from the two major innovations of the Second Industrial Revolution—electricity and the steam engine—paved the way for the next wave of technology-driven change. The amount of innovation and technology continued to increase along with the pace of adoption, a theme that has continued throughout history.

ENTER THE TRANSISTOR

Continuing to trace technological watershed moments, fast forward to the creation of the transistor in 1948 by inventors at Bell Laboratories. The transistor was a digital device that consumed low power and had smaller space requirements than the vacuum tube technology that it displaced, which made its adoption into electromechanical devices a *fait accompli.* The transistor was followed by the integrated circuit in 1958. Jack Kilby, a Massachusetts Institute of Technology reject turned researcher at Texas Instruments, solved the tyranny-of-numbers problem when he penned his ideas in his lab notebook:

> The following circuit elements could be made on a single slice: resistors, capacitor, distributed capacitor, transistor.[11]

Kilby had described the basic principles of the integrated circuit, or microchip, and went on to build and test this new device on September 12, 1958, for the Texas Instruments brass. Six months later, Robert Noyce developed a similar solution to the same problem, with a design that was easier to manufacture. Both are now considered to be co-inventors of the microchip, although Kilby was awarded the Nobel Prize for his accomplishments on December 10, 2000. (Noyce died in 1990 and Nobel prizes are not awarded posthumously.)

The invention of the integrated circuit led to the first computer chip in 1969, computer kits in 1975, and the now-famous first personal computer in 1981, the well-chronicled story of how IBM created and then gave away one of the most important inventions in human history. Here again the pace of digital change accelerated as more and more powerful chips were being stuffed into smaller devices. This same innovative wave of digital technology witnessed the increased calculating power of the computers of this time. The early computers, such as the noteworthy ENIAC, were capable of 1,000 additions per second. These were the vacuum tube–based machines before the invention of the transistor. The next generation of computing machines was capable of 10,000 additions per second, which represented a factor of 10 increase. By 1965, calculations of 1,000,000 per second were reached. These increases in computing technology were truly impressive and launched the current Computer Age. The rapid enhancements of computing power, though, in a sense are not the most impressive innovation of the modern Computer Age. They enabled an increasingly technologically savvy society to develop and adopt ever more far-reaching innovations. The combination of societal readiness for innovation and technology sows the seeds of massive change as much as the technology itself.

ENTER THE INTERNET: WHY THE INTERNET IS DIFFERENT

The Internet has been the most quickly adopted technology in all of human history.[12] As of August 2000, 61 percent of U.S. homes, or some 64 million households, had PCs in them, which makes the PC rival the television in importance.[13] The primary reason for home PC adoption is not the need for computing at home, but the desire for Internet access, which is considered important for U.S. homes. The time spent online by users will continue to rise as more functionality, products, and content are moved to the web, and as it becomes even more threaded into our everyday lives.

The Internet has been adopted more quickly than the telephone, radio, and television, faster than the automobile, and faster than electricity itself. Electric lights required approximately 50 years to reach 95 percent penetration in the United States. Radio took roughly 35 years to reach 95 percent penetration. The telephone needed 80 years to achieve a 90 percent diffusion rate, while television took 30 years to achieve 90 percent penetration.[14]

The Internet has surpassed the adoption rate of the PC, which is arguably the precursor to its success. It is standing on the shoulders of the success of the PC; the Internet came at a time when it was able to piggyback off the adoption of the PC into U.S. households. As PCs became commonplace "appliances," the use of them as access devices to the World Wide Web was a simple and natural extension. What were people really doing on their computers at home before the web? Writing software? Not most users. The Internet became the "killer app" that used the home PC and gave those who owned them something else to do with them—surf the Net. Research. Learn. Organize into communities. Connect with one another. Share information and ideas. All of these activities are part of the human experience and have been so since the development of language and culture. As Davis and Meyer state, we have entered the second half of the information economy, in which we are using computers less for computing and, instead, more for connecting.[15] Connecting people, organizations, countries, and continents—this is the real power of the Internet. Binding together people with a web of ideas and thought and intellectual pursuit. The Internet created new business models, spawned new industries, and disrupted the world as we now know it. From small family-owned businesses to large multinationals, the Internet is making business both more difficult and easier in another sense. A review of the e-business First Wave will show these trends and set the stage for the next steps of our journey forward.

INCUMBENTS AND HYBRIDS MOVE TO THE MIDDLE

At the time of publication of this book, the evolutionary forces of business are at work. The incumbent brick-and-mortar firms watched as the stock valuations of e-business firms skyrocketed to astronomical heights, dwarfing the stock valuations of venerable retailers such as Wal-Mart, Kmart, and others, and rivaling the valuations of high-tech leaders such as Nortel, Cisco, Intel, and many others. The brick-and-mortar firms rapidly commissioned Internet divisions to erect their web sites, developed fulfillment capabilities that would support a virtual business model, and even began offering stock options to their staffs as ways to demonstrate their commitment to the New Economy business model and culture. But the carnage of 2000–2001 will be long remembered by many e-business start-ups, which were denied additional venture capital funding because of a loss of faith in their business models and viability of their operating economics.

Every day another Internet retailer goes out of business and its assets are shopped around to other survivors of the demise of that particular species of web corporation. Again, these are evolutionary forces at work. The brick-and-mortar firms are examining the landscape and, in many cases, are buying the assets of these failed e-businesses as a way to add the skills and technologies of the Internet to their own firms. This is a way to augment the corporate DNA of a firm, to enhance the core competencies to compete over the Internet without necessarily having to "bet the farm" on a particular course of action. These "hedging strategies" are fine, as long as firms understand that the Internet is here to stay and that the First Wave of e-business was simply that. It was an evolutionary wave of trial and error, of learning and growing, of finding new ways to conduct business, to find information, to build virtual communities of users, and to provide a social context to the Internet in grand ways beyond what its creators perhaps envisioned.

One thing is clear from the First Wave: the move to the middle is in progress. This is evidenced by the addition of web capabilities by the brick-and-mortar firms as well as by the addition of physical infrastructure by Internet firms such as Amazon. The real lesson of the First Wave may be that there is huge value in a blended business model that combines the best of a highly optimized physical infrastructure with the best of a leading-edge Internet business model. For incumbent firms with investments in physical assets, it may be advisable for them to get the best performance possible from these physical assets by augmenting them with information technologies and Internet technologies and knowledge management and supply chain management techniques. These are all viable, Internet-enabling strategies for firms striving for a better way.

Virtual firms without large investments in physical infrastructure, however, have other opportunities available. They have more strategic degrees of freedom available because they are unencumbered by manufacturing plants, distribution centers, and other monuments of the post–Industrial Age. But as Amazon has aptly realized, there is merit to adding physical assets in support of an excellently conceived and operationally viable Internet business model. It comes down to customer-based metrics of service, delivery, and overall quality of the transaction. Whether a business is virtual or brick-and-mortar, these things support a viable business model that is based on revenue, cash flow, and profits.

The hybridization of Internet business models by all firms seeking competitive advantage will continue to morph and change as new capabilities are devised to answer the needs of this burgeoning landscape of opportunity. For virtual firms getting "real" or "physical" with their business model, and for brick-and-mortar firms getting "virtual" by selling off their factories and distribution centers, there is plenty of room in the middle for variations of the two. The range of variations will differ by the amount of legacy physical infrastructure to be carried forward into the Internet business model and by the minimal amount of physical presence required by virtual firms to handle returns and to display product samples. New hybrids based on small kiosks in malls and other retail centers, combined with highly virtual business models, are being experimented with by visionary new start-ups and existing retailers. All that can be said for sure is that more experimentation and more variety of business models will ensure that ultimately, there will be winning Internet business models for all firms based on their industry, their product/service bundles, and how the future unfolds.

INTERNET IMPACT

Why has the web become so popular in so short a time? As established previously, the Internet is the fastest-adopted technology in the history of humankind. But what about the web makes it so integral and so natural for us? What makes it the most significant idea the world has known so far? The Internet is characterized by some unique attributes that make it a natural extension of human needs. These human needs include the notion of social organization and structure, communication, and sharing of ideas, for storytelling and social interaction and for fulfillment of basic desires such as obtaining life's necessities. These attributes have implications for how the Internet can also affect both the B2B and the B2C business models today. Only because these attributes are so basic to our human needs can the web be the business tool it is becoming today. Four critical attributes explain the adoption of the web:

1. Organization and community for the participants
2. Choice and control of content
3. Connectivity and sharing of ideas
4. Culture of Now and Anywhere (time and distance compression)

Each of these aspects of the Internet has implications for how the web has developed so far, as well as how it will develop in the future. In all cases, the diffusion of the Internet will have to support these fundamental human needs to remain the tool of choice for the Internet Age.

WELCOME TO THE NETWORK AGE

The Internet is an amazing technological phenomenon. A massive wave of change is coming. As participants, we cannot expect to be in a position of omniscience, of knowing what the technological phenomenon is that we are experiencing and where it is heading. We will not have the luxury of hindsight for some time to come, because according to some futurists (e.g., Newt Gingrich), we are only partially through the innovation and change in communications and computing that we have already experienced. The Computer Age is still unfolding, and it has plenty of fuel remaining in its innovation engine. According to Roger McNamee of Integral Capital Partners, we are shifting from the PC-centric, database-centric, client/server-centric technology businesses of the 1990s to network-centric, communications-centric, Internet-based technology businesses.[16] This means that we are in the midst of the transition to the Internet Age, an age where being connected is more important than how one is connected, where access to information from multiple devices—PCs, wireless devices of all types, set-top boxes for televisions, from our vehicles—is driving productivity and knowledge to new levels.

Computer Age incumbents such as Oracle and Microsoft are at war over the transition to the Internet Age for their software platforms. But the real question is, can they remake themselves into the vendors of choice for the Internet Age? In a recent interview, Peter Drucker stated that for many firms, their future has already been determined by the forces of the business environment and by their internal makeup. In other words, they have already been dealt the cards they will be able to play in this hand, and they have to do the best they can with what they have. Hardware platform vendors are struggling to remake themselves into the infrastructure providers of the Internet. These firms are all facing new competitors that were ready for the Internet and have established themselves as the new powerhouses. Commerce One, Ariba, BroadVision, Cisco, Nortel, EMC, and many others are the big dogs of the Internet Age.

We are becoming a society of data and information, a culture of technology and connectivity, a world of knowledge and electronic, real-time distribution and access to that knowledge. Only now are we close to realizing the dreams of Sarnoff when he envisioned the potential impact of radio and television on human society.

Ray Kurzweil comments on the acceleration of technology in his book *The Age of Spiritual Machines.*[17] Not only have humans evolved, but as physical evolution was replaced by cultural evolution (which is far more efficient as a process), and augmented cultural evolution with technological evolution (again, a cumulatively more efficient process), we have accelerated the rates of change. The potential is enormous for continuing advancements in technologies that will change society and human behaviors forever. The timing is right, our culture is so technologically driven, and the sizing is right—ever smaller packaging of technology for use by our increasingly mobile and connected society. We may soon be able to describe ourselves as *Homo technosapiens.* Perhaps that is what we will be called when the last chapter of the Computer Age is written.

END OF THE FIRST WAVE: RECENT TECHNOTRENDS

A recent *Boston Globe* article cited the following statistics for failed e-businesses[18]:

- 130 dot-coms have closed in 2000
- 100 consumer-oriented sites failed
- 26 B2B companies failed
- 21 e-businesses folded as of November 19, 2000
- 50 more may close before the end of 2000

Reading this section might cause readers mild concern over the state of the Internet for the business that emerged with the rise of the web, but as users and implementers of the Internet, we also have to be believers. I believe that the next wave of e-businesses will be battle hardened and wise to the ways of making a living over the Internet landscape. New marketspaces will continue to be created, and more experimentation will take place combined with more innovation. Our historical tour of invention and innovation should have demonstrated that each wave of technology, each innovation complex, brought with it waves of additional social and cultural changes of far-reaching impact. This will be the case in the Next Wave of the Internet.

BEGINNING OF THE NEXT WAVE

We are at the beginning of the Next Wave. The Next Wave will be characterized by the massive network effects of millions of users connected over the web. Sun Microsystems' marketing tag line was incredibly accurate: "The network is the computer." The Next Wave will be characterized by the real-time computing capabilities of the Internet. John Doerr, of venture capital firm Kleiner Perkins, refers to it as the *Evernet,* an "always on, high-speed, broadband, ubiquitous, multiformat Web."[19] Many analysts expect a 25 times increase in minutes per day of usage of the web, combined with a 5 times increase in the number of users at home and at work.[20] I believe this estimate is conservative. The number of users, combined with the amount of time they will spend online, will spur the convergence of industries already under way, such as entertainment and computing, computing and telecommunications, the Internet and telephony, and much more.

Access to the Internet will continue to grow and become a day-to-day feature of all human experience eventually. It will penetrate our lives in ways we have not completely imagined, and the useful aspects will survive, while the trivial or nonvalue-added facets will fade into insignificance. Not all technology finds a useful place in human history.

BUSINESS IMPLICATIONS

In *Blown to Bits,* Evans and Wurster state "Every business is an information business."[21] Even for firms that are not the typical information-intensive business, the role of information plays a surprisingly critical role. This reminds me of my first years in manufacturing. It was argued that the difference between manufacturing and service industries is an artificial one. Manufacturing firms have a large percentage of their operations tied up in services, from customer service to all the clerical functions and internal support functions; these are all services provided in support of manufacturing.

Similarly, the important point that Evans and Wurster[22] make is that companies—all companies—have significant information components. I would argue that the information business of today's corporations plays an increasingly critical role in day-to-day operations, as well as being largely a determinant of the firm's future. This makes information technology an important facet of a business. Many executives will reply that their IT budgets are only 2 to 3 percent of their business, whereas their property, plant, and equipment are the major cost elements of their makeup. This may be true; however, the value contribution that the information assets provide is far more valuable than the value of the other firm assets.

Davis and Meyer,[23] in their book *Blur,* compare the Industrial Age to the information economy. The first half of the information economy used computers as a number-crunching tool, focused on automating transactions and removing the variability and fatigue of human intervention from the mundane data entry tasks of the early Computer Age. This was an industrial-style approach to the use of computing technology. The emergence of the knowledge worker and the connectivity of the Internet Age have forever changed things in the business world.

The Internet is clearly an example of how the information technology assets and processes provide much more value to a firm's bottom line and, increasingly, its top line. The Internet is a special case of technology. It is the fastest known and most well-documented example of technology adoption in the history of humankind. When compared to other technologies or innovations, the Internet has been not only the fastest but also one of the most important innovations in its impact on society. And we mean society here as in the global society. All nations are part of this wave of technology. The brain-to-body ratios of today's corporations are increasing through the rapid adoption of IT as a key strategic driver of business strategy.

COMPETITIVE TECHNOLOGIES (FOR THE NEXT WAVE)

The adoption of the stirrup increased the warfare ability of horse-riding warriors. This increased fighting efficiency allowed mobile forces the ability to conquer numerically superior enemies. This technological advance can be likened to the use of digital technologies to compete. The winners will apply information technology as competitive weapons, to increase the fighting capabilities of their warriors against the competition. The differential application of information technology in support of superior business models is now a competitive requirement of the e-business age. But this is not the typical IT-departmental view of technology that many firms embrace. That is the old way—treating IT as a silo, as a separate function from the business. Firms that treat their technology portfolio this way will not be the leaders of the Next Wave. They are ignoring the obvious trends of the New Economy. This does not mean that they solve the problem by putting up a nice web site displaying brochureware to their prospective customers. This does not mean increasing the IT budget by 10 percent to leapfrog the technocompetitive advantage their competitors may have over them. It means much, much more than that.

It means redefining the firm around the concepts of Information Mastery discussed in Chapter 1. The following list summarizes what redefining the value of information entails in the context of Business Darwinism:

- *Information mastery.* Defining a new role of IT. Defining new value from the IT processes and core capabilities of a firm. Unleashing IT from its Industrial Age tethers and allowing new information value to spring forth. Building information mastery into corporate strategy, in the information-based business model, and in all core processes and capabilities.
- *Digital agility.* Investing in IT as a source of future business value means that IT cannot be a source of business replication friction. Business models must be transferable across generations of business change, business leadership, and technology changes in an industry.
- *Digital DNA.* Facilitation of information-based evolution, in effect increasing the corporate brain-to-body ratio, in order to execute information-based business models, which will lead to superior returns and the ability to transition a corporation from its current business model to a future business model.

DIGITAL DILEMMA: PREPARING FOR THE NEXT WAVE

The forces of change have placed today's firms in a precarious position. While they have been involved in the First Wave, and have benefited from the lessons of their own doing as well as from those of others, they are now wondering what to do next.

- What should we do with e-business?
- What will be the next frontier of e-business innovation?
- What will confer competitive advantage to my firm that we are not doing currently?
- How can we continue to compete using the same business model combined with the same basic technologies we have always used?
- What changes can we make to our business model, to our corporate strategy, to our operational model that will allow us to do more than incremental improvements?

Incrementalism is dead. Magnitudes of improvements are a must. The Next Wave is approaching, and many firms will be caught flat-footed. They are not prepared. They have not thought through the range of possibilities that may face their organization in the Next Wave. They must begin their preparations now or face the daunting reality of Darwinian selection: they may not be able to survive the Next Wave by continuing the same trajectory of action they have until now. But the tools do not exist, not for the fiercest competitor of all—change. Companies must increase their brain-to-body ratios by increasing their ability to create, harvest, and exploit information in support of fitness drivers of their particular firm, competing against others for the same scarce resources—customers and market share. The tools and techniques for competing in this fashion are explained in subsequent chapters.

LOOKING AHEAD TO THE NTH WAVE

This section has intentionally been left blank. See Chapter 9 for advice.

NOTES

1. Betsy Morris, "Can Michael Dell Escape the Box?" *Fortune* (October 16, 2000), pp. 93–120.
2. Charles H. Fine, *Clockspeed* (Reading, MA: Perseus Books, 1998).
3. Evan Schwartz, *Digital Darwinism* (New York: Broadway Books, 1999).
4. Jared Diamond, *Guns, Germs and Steel* (New York: W.W. Norton & Company, 1999), pp. 258–259.
5. Ibid., p. 259.
6. George Gilder, *Telecosm* (New York: The Free Press, 2000).
7. Ibid.
8. Diamond, *Guns, Germs and Steel,* p. 360.
9. Philip Evans and Thomas S. Wurster, *Blown to Bits* (Boston, MA: Harvard Business School Press, 2000).
10. Mary Ellen Papesh, *Frederick Winslow Taylor Business Biography* (www.stfrancis.edu/ba/ghkickul/stuwebs/bbios/biorgraph/fwtaylor.htm), 2000. Also see Paul Halsall's summary of Taylor's impact on business management in *Internet Modern History Sourcebook: Frederick W. Taylor: The Principles of Scientific Management, 1911* (www.fordham.edu/halsall/mod/1911taylor.html), July 1998.
11. T.R. Reid, "Inventor of the Microchip Gets His Due," *Boston Sunday Globe* (December 10, 2000), pp. A16–17 (originally in the *Washington Post*).
12. Schwartz, *Digital Darwinism*.
13. "A Look Back to When PC Power Took Off," *USA Today* (August 8, 2001), p. 3B.
14. Bernard H. Boar, *Strategic Thinking for Information Technology* (New York: John Wiley & Sons, 1997), p. 91.
15. Stan Davis and Christopher Meyer, *Blur* (Reading, MA: Addison-Wesley, 1998), p. 9.
16. David Rynecki, "What to Buy—or Sell—Now," *Fortune* (November 27, 2000), p. 108.
17. Ray Kurzweil, *The Age of Spiritual Machines* (New York: Penguin, 1999).

18. D.C. Denison and Beth Healy, "Dot Gone: Web Unravels," *Boston Sunday Globe* (November 19, 2000), p. A1.
19. John Doerr, "Smart People," *Fortune* (November 27, 2000), p. 95.
20. Bill Gross, CEO of Idealab, in ibid., p. 98.
21. Evans and Wurster, *Blown to Bits,* p. 9.
22. Ibid.
23. Davis and Meyer, *Blur,* p. 13.

3

EVOLUTIONARY METAPHORS FOR BUSINESS

In the natural world species evolve—that is, they change to meet new challenges—or they die. The same genetic imperative operates in business.

—Charles H. Fine, *Clockspeed*

The year 1848 was one of revolutions instigated by the social changes that followed the rise of manufacturing around the world. In France, Austria, Germany, and Hungary there was revolution and revolt, all pointing to the political and social turmoil that was to characterize the modern world. In Britain, though, the main upheaval was among the famous peppered moths. A report from Manchester noted the appearance of a black form of the peppered moth, an animal that previously was known only to be gray. By 1882, the year of Darwin's death, the black (or melanic) type of peppered moth was the most common form throughout most of industrial Britain.

The explanation for the disappearance of the lighter peppered moth in favor of the dark moths was simple. The dark forms could not be seen against the filthy trees on which they resided by the birds that preyed on them, making them much safer from attack than the original form, which had until then been camouflaged against the lichens of the rural woodlands. The dark moths appeared in London in 1897, and by then just one in 50 was of the original type of Manchester peppered moth. In rural areas of Britain, black moths were rare or even absent because of the lack of industrialization. The same phenomenon of the melanic moths occurred around the world in other industrial parts of Europe and the United States into the early 1900s. London still has black mallard ducks, black pigeons, and black squirrels because of the Industrial Revolution, carryovers from a time of rapid change not only for the region's animal and plant species, but for the corporate species as well that evolved during the Industrial Revolution.

The Industrial Revolution was a test of the theory of evolution in more ways than one. The rise and adaptation of the dark peppered moth over the lighter form, and then its eventual demise as pollution controls eliminated its temporary advantage, namely the soot-covered buildings and filthy trees, demonstrates how fleeting our fit to the environment can be. The story of the peppered moth, however, has as much relevance to the companies that caused the filthy, soot-covered trees and buildings to be a facilitator to natural selection's favoring the dark, melanic moth over the lighter form. The firms of then, like the firms of today, are subject to the same forces of natural selection and fitness to the particular environment in which they find themselves competing. Other variants of the same species, as well as other species, are competing for the same food or energy resources. They have their own predators preying on them as well, much as the peppered moths had the birds to contend with.

Evolutionary forces have carried on, bringing many new species and the demise of many others, as well as witnessing the eventual emergence of humans from our early ancestors. We have been through massive environmental shifts in hominid development as well: glaciations and interstitials, warming trends and cooling trends, radical and rapid (in geological time periods, that is) environmental changes, and gradual, relatively slow changes in the ambient conditions surrounding us. The same sorts of forces confront businesses as well, although the history of the modern corporation is extremely short.

The use of biological and evolutionary concepts in describing corporations and their behavior is popular these days. We already mentioned a few recent books that apply evolutionary concepts to business topics. Throughout the history of business strategy, from its early days beginning with Frederick Taylor to the most recent thinking by Gary Hamel and C.K. Prahalad, business strategists have sought input from many other disciplines, such as population ecology, organizational ecology, anthropology, economics, biology, and sociology. Hannan and Freeman were first to completely apply a biological analogy to corporations in 1977,[1] according to Rumelt, Schendel, and Teece.[2] In this work, Hannan and Freeman treated firms as individuals with a set of fixed genetic endowments and advocated the study of a population of firms over time.[3] This was clearly the "species" view of firms that we are striving for here. An exhaustive review of these approaches to business strategy is unnecessary here, since that has already been done. We will, however, attempt to further the use of biological and evolutionary metaphors to provide an explanatory framework for the present and to develop a more predictive framework for the future. Today's companies are faced with challenges unique to our time. As our technology review in Chapter 2 should have demonstrated, however, technology and change have been part of the human experience for hundreds of years. The salient difference of today is the *pace* of change, which can largely be attributed to the rapid adoption of technology by consumers in our everyday lives, by corporations in serving customers, and by corporations in competing with one another. The business landscape is a technology arms race. Those who can best adopt technology to serve customers better, compete better, and function better will win market share and be more profitable. Those who do not will, in Darwinian terms, be deselected.

EVOLUTION AS A GUIDE TO THE FUTURE

To begin our discussion of evolution as it applies to business, we must first describe the environment in which firms are operating. Much as the peppered moths had to contend with environmental change to survive, and equally so as humans devised new adaptive strategies to respond to new environments and geographies as we expanded into every continent, companies have to be placed into the context in which they are trying to survive. What are the major environmental conditions that companies have to face as they strive to survive the treacherous business landscape? How will firms interact with the ecosystem of competitors, predators, and prey as they engage in corporate survival?

Charles Darwin, in *Origin of Species,*[4] clearly described the notion of survival of the fittest. His ideas have been among the most important ever in describing how living organisms, including human beings, evolve and adapt to the environmental conditions around them. Darwin placed humans squarely within the domain of the animal kingdom, which was at the time completely revolutionary. In this chapter, corporations are treated as living organisms, subject to the same processes of evolution that all living organisms are. This concept will form the framework for describing how corporations—like humans in particular since they consist of humans—must follow the same path toward cultural evolution to increase their ability to compete in times of rapid environmental change and heightened intensity of competition. Natural selection and survival of the fittest surely apply to corporations today. Darwin's ideas can be summarized into the major concepts that follow.[5]

ENVIRONMENT, NATURAL SELECTION, AND SURVIVAL OF THE FITTEST

First, the environment is a filter for what will survive and what will not. It puts constant pressure on living organisms by limiting the available energy and resources for individuals to survive day to day. This struggle for existence is a part of the experience of any living creature. Natural selection is the process by which life-forms change to meet the challenges of day-to-day survival, or "the myriad opportunities afforded by the physical environment and by other life-forms."[6] Survival of the fittest, then, means that those who survive have the machinery to "make a living" better than others. The machinery consists of physical traits that allow an organism to "make a living" better than others. Those individuals who make a living better than others will have a better probability of passing their genetic makeup on to the next generation. Darwinian fitness, then, is the ability to "make a living" long enough to pass one's DNA on to the next generation.

EVOLUTION AND ADAPTATION

Adaptation is the ability of organisms to survive shifts in environmental conditions, over long time frames, by having enough variation built into their genome such that the physical manifestations, the phenotype, of their genetic "recipe" will confer an advantage over other competing species. Evolution is inevitable as a force. It depends on "mistakes" in reproduction, which supply the genetic variation required of evolutionary change. Descent always involves modification because any copy, whether a picture, a photocopy, or a gene, cannot be exact. As Jones notes, "Information cannot be transmitted without loss, and a duplicate of a copy is, in its turn, less perfect than what went before. To reproduce in succession an original again and again is to make—to evolve—something new."[7] Variation is created by the mutation rates inherent in the transcription and replication processes of RNA and DNA, respectively. This genetic variation manifests itself over time in a rich variety of physical characteristics that may or may not confer competitive advantage over others within the species and over other species competing for the same resources.

NATURAL SELECTION

Natural selection is simple, according to Jones.[8] It picks up the inherited differences in the capacity to reproduce. If one version multiplies itself better than others, it will take over and, in the end, a new form of life—a new species—will emerge. Natural selection is based on the differential survival of the set of physical characteristics that allow individuals of a species to harvest energy better, and ultimately breed, than the other members of their species. The differential survival of the physical traits that confer competitive advantage determines the possibility that the DNA from those individuals will be used to create the next generation of individuals of that species. Jones writes: "Variety is the raw material of evolution, used up as natural selection takes its course. Once it has been consumed, the Darwinian machine comes to a stop. Diversity is renewed by chemical errors—mutations—made as DNA is copied. Mutation is the fuel rather than the engine of biological advance." Evolution was driven by the simple, slow, and potent mechanism of natural selection. Because this acts solely by accumulating slight, successive, favorable variations, it can produce no great or sudden modification; it can act only by very short and slow steps.[9]

COMPETITION

Competition within the species is based on having traits and characteristics that allow differential reproductive success. Ultimately, as Richard Dawkins explains in *The Blind Watchmaker,* the competition boils down to the genetic level through two phenomena, arms races and coadapted genotypes. Coadapted genotypes are a result of genes teaming or collaborating in their competition against other genes for proliferation, through the life-forms they exist in and get passed on by. A successful gene does well in environments provided by other genes that it is likely to meet in lots of different bodies. Therefore, successful replication or survival is the equivalent to collaborating with other genes. Dawkins explains:

> In natural selection, genes are always selected for their capacity to flourish in the environment in which they find themselves. We often think of this environment as the outside world, the world of predators and climate. But from each gene's point of view, perhaps the most important part of its environment is all the other genes that it encounters. And where does a gene "encounter" other genes? Mostly in the cells of the successive individual bodies in which it finds itself. Each gene is selected for its capacity to cooperate successfully with the population of other genes that it is likely to meet in bodies.[10]

While our discussion of competition will remain at the company level, we can surmise that as cooperation of firm functions is enhanced, especially toward achieving company fitness, then the successful functions will grow in importance and the firm will succeed. We have seen this repeatedly as the leadership of automobile companies has shifted between "finance guys" and "engineering" or "car guys" over the years depending on which function was perceived as contributing more to the firm's success over a given period.

The notion of arms races also fits into our discussion of competition, and more appropriately describes firm-versus-firm competition. Arms races are evolutionary trends in lineages of populations that adapt to one another over geological time. As Dawkins states, "Lineages of animals and plants will, in evolutionary time, 'track' changes in their enemies no less assiduously than they track changes in average weather conditions."[11] Arms races are improvements in one lineage's survival equipment (prey species) as a direct consequence of improvements in another lineage's evolving equipment (a predator species). While the weather-tracking nature of evolution fluctuates, responding to cyclical changes over geological time frames, the arms race version helps explain the progressive directional improvements in predators and prey as they respond to one another. Dawkins uses the cheetah and the gazelle in his example, where the cheetah becomes faster, develops keen vision, and grows sharper teeth in response to the ability of the gazelle to detect threats through senses of smell, its vision systems, and its ability to outrun the cheetah. The arms race phenomenon also applies to plants. Herbivores in this sense are the enemies of plants, and plants are the enemies of herbivores. Plants, over time, develop thorns and bad-tasting chemicals that help ensure their survival against the creatures that consume them.

Arms races can take many forms. They in a sense can be summarized as symmetric and asymmetric arms races. A symmetric arms race is between competitors trying to do the same thing in a similar environment. They are competitors for the same resources (e.g., trees competing for sunlight in a dense forest). Success by one species means failure by another species. The arms race between the cheetah and the gazelle, or plants versus herbivores, is an asymmetric arms race. In this case, the two sides are trying to do different things to survive. Cheetahs are trying to eat gazelles; however, gazelles are not trying to eat cheetahs—they are trying to avoid being the prey of cheetahs. This competitive relationship results in interesting and complex adaptive weapons systems over time.

Competition among life-forms is for the same economic niche, the same energy sources, such as flora and fauna. The organisms that have the ability to extract energy from their ecological niche more efficiently than competing species will increase in numbers, forcing other species out. Competition is for survival, which means surviving long enough to reproduce. Jones comments: "Evolution is an examination with two papers. To succeed demands a pass in both. The first involves staying alive for long enough to have a chance to breed, while the mark in the second depends on the number of progeny."[12] In our discussion, we primarily focus on environmental pressures and predator-prey relationships, or in business terms firm-versus-firm competition.

One central law of competition explains how organizations and markets evolve: the expectation of profits attracts imitators.[13] As firms continually seek new sources of revenue, new markets, and new customers to service, they will always look for easier pathways to revenue and profits. Their ability to exploit these economic niches will vary based on inherent strategy and structure, core capabilities, and corporate culture, among many other things. Firms, like predators and nature's competitors, will seek survival through the conservation of energy and will operate in as efficient a manner as possible while trying to survive and compete.

These are the basic ideas of evolutionary theory that will be applied to corporations. Given this backdrop of facts, we must review the larger environment in which today's corporations find themselves. The ambient business climate, along with a firm's competition, in many ways determines the survival, evolution, and adaptive capabilities of the fittest via natural selection.

BUSINESS ENVIRONMENT

Corporations today deal with the same forces as living organisms. These forces include environmental changes, both gradual and dramatically sudden. They include interactions with other species, including plants, animals, and a myriad of others. The indomitable forces of evolution, namely natural selection and survival of the fittest, apply aptly to companies. Companies have to contend with external forces of the business environment and with other competitors. They, much like living species, have to survive a struggle for existence, much as Darwin described in *Origin of Species*. This struggle for existence pits corporations against the irrepressible forces of their environment, as well as the host of competitors, predators, and other corporations that surround them.

The environment a firm competes in is largely a determinant of its success. Michael Porter's work stands out in the analysis of industry structure and the competition within an industry.[14] Corporate performance is largely determined by the structure of the industry in which it competes. The factors of industry structure include the size of the industry, defined by the number of customers, the value of the industry by profit and revenue, and the number of competitors. An industry with few competitors will have higher margins than an industry with many competitors. Industry structure establishes the baseline conditions from which firms operate, make their decisions regarding how they compete, whether to remain in a particular industry or move elsewhere, and other related decisions. As evolutionary theory proves, however, changes in the surrounding environmental conditions force changes in participants in nature. In business, where change is constant and the pace is accelerating, this can be highly disruptive for corporations trying to survive.

PUNCTUATED EQUILIBRIUM AND CHANGE

In today's business environment, one overarching word can be used to describe things: change. The pace of change, the nature of the changes, and the responses to both have become the bane of many executives' existence. The pace of change in the world, and specifically in the business world, is akin to what Stephen Jay Gould meant when he developed the notion of "punctuated equilibrium" to describe evolution. His ideas on punctuated equilibrium challenged the long-standing idea that evolution was a slow, gradual process resulting in the manifestation of changes in all living species based on natural selection acting on populations, and ultimately their respective gene pools, over geological time. Punctuated equilibrium asserts that the history of evolution is concentrated in relatively rapid events of speciation rather than taking place gradually as slow, continuous transformations of established lineages. These speciation events sparked selection of traits and attributes of populations in a dramatic fashion, far faster than the gradual evolutionary changes originally postulated by Charles Darwin. Simply put, punctuated equilibrium is characterized by rapid evolutionary change. In geological time, this would have taken place over millions of years, minimally hundreds of thousands of years, but this is a short time in evolutionary terms.

In the spirit of being accurate and consistent with current evolutionary theory, the punctuated equilibrium analogy has some merit when discussing the rapid proliferation of firms based on the explosion of the Internet; however, it is not a suitable substitute for the original thinking in Charles Darwin's *Origin of Species*. All evolutionary tenets are Darwinian in nature, enhanced by new ideas from genetic research and other modern thinking, and still supporting the original premises of Charles Darwin. The compression of time and distance, as evidenced by the Internet, by the convergence of computing and communications technologies, catalyzes change and the emergence, and even the eventual demise, of corporations in this environment. Punctuated equilibrium captures the notion of time-compressed evolution based on our modern, high-change environments.

PUNCTUATED EQUILIBRIUM AND THE BUSINESS ENVIRONMENT

If we apply punctuated equilibrium to today's business environment, we can say with some degree of certainty that the pace of change has clearly accelerated over the last few years. With the explosion of the Internet, this pace has been ratcheted up even more. We now refer to Internet speed or web speed as the current benchmark. What does this mean? For business it means that every move a company makes—or does not make, as the case may be—exposes it to new competitors, new threats, and new customers and markets. These changes are real and maddeningly sudden for management teams that are struggling with the rigors of today's business environment.

The emphasis today is on speed and agility. These attributes are critical for firms because of the rapidly shifting business landscape. We have mentioned technology as a primary driver of massive societal change. This will continue to be the case for many decades to come, but other forces of change are also disrupting the business environment. Global expansion and new competition from abroad are placing new demands on corporate leaders. Shortening product life cycles create narrower windows of competitive advantage for firms, which then require the ability to create and launch new products and services faster than ever before. For technology products such as consumer electronics, personal computers, servers, routers, and other infrastructure products, Moore's law is driving prices down while computing power is continually rising. This situation places even more emphasis on delivering new products to market faster than ever. Charles Fine captures the essence of temporary competitive advantage in his book.[15] He describes the pace of change in various industries using the concept of clockspeeds. Technology industries have faster industry clockspeeds than, for example, the automotive industry. Therefore, depending on industry clockspeed, the duration of any competitive advantage will be longer or shorter. That notion forces companies into ever faster cycles of innovation to offset the shortening duration of competitive advantage. Based on selective evidence gathered from our short history as a species, I would argue that regardless of the industry, the advances of technology are permeating every industry, whether it be a fast-clockspeed industry or a slow-clockspeed industry. The automotive industry, as an example, is a slow-clockspeed industry compared to the electronics industry; however, automobiles are increasing in electronics content steadily, with high-end models from Mercedes, for example, carrying dozens of microprocessors to handle functions such as airbags, engine control, antilock brakes and other mission-critical functions. New models will come equipped with Internet access for online directions, real-time maps, and weather updates, all driven by global positioning satellite (GPS) technology. This means that the automotive industry is trending toward faster clockspeeds with a push from two forces: (1) the natural trend toward faster clockspeeds to offset the competition, and (2) the increased technology content from a fast-clockspeed industry, namely electronics.

There will be winners and there will be losers. Which will you or your organization be? How will firms prepare for the unknown forces that will surely confront them? How will organizations adapt to the changing business landscape in the face of rapid change, shifting markets, globalization, staffing shortfalls, technological obsolescence, and more?

Firms are facing these environmental conditions every day in their quest for survival. The survivors will be the firms that perform certain basic functions better than other firms. These functions allow some corporations to differentially win customers, gain and hold market share, and earn profits. Like living organisms, companies have to "make a living" to survive by performing the functions required to do so. But what are those basic functions? For organisms, it means taking in energy, or making a living, to hold off entropy and then reproducing, or passing their genetic material on to the next generation. For humans, it means working to make money to buy food, which allows us to survive, and eventually reproduce to pass our genes on to the next generation. For corporations, it means providing products and services to customers who value them, which earns the firm market share, revenues, and ultimately profits. This is how firms "make a living."

CORPORATIONS ARE LIVING ORGANISMS

Viewing corporations as living organisms is a useful analogy in describing the behavior of firms. Both are living systems focused on surviving by extracting energy from the environment in which they exist. In the animal world, species are equipped to extract energy from their environment to make a living or survive. Different species have similar equipment that may allow them to exploit the same or overlapping natural resources to make a living. These are competitors for food or energy. Companies in similar industries also compete for customers using similar competitive strategies, organizational structures, and core capabilities. Given finite numbers of customers, firms that compete better than their competitors will win more customers and drive their competitors out of that marketplace. The banished firms will either go extinct or move into other niches where they can survive. These forces also exist in nature.

Jeffrey R. Williams defines firms as "collections of evolving capabilities that are managed dynamically for the purpose of earning rents. Differences among firms arise from the interplay of capabilities, search behavior, and sustainability conditions. As firms attempt to attain their ends, robust differences arise, are nullified, and arise again."[16] This definition nicely summarizes what a firm is and what it does, with emphasis on the evolving differences among firms as they compete over time. A firm is an organization with a purpose, and can be broadly described by three related features:

1. Its strategy
2. Its structure
3. Its core capabilities[17]

The concept of strategy here describes a broad set of "commitments made by a firm that define and rationalize its objectives and how it intends to pursue them."[18] Firm structure, as it is defined by the strategy of a firm, involves how a firm is organized and governed, how decisions are made and carried out, and it therefore determines what a firm actually does given its broad strategy. Changes in strategy may require a change in structure for successful execution. A firm's core capabilities, or the things that a corporation is capable of doing well (better than on the outside by others), are defined and guided by the firm's strategy and structure. But these core capabilities change and evolve over time as dictated by strategy. "Simply producing a given set of products with a given set of processes in a competent way will not enable a firm to survive for long. To be successful for any length of time a firm must innovate."[19]

Corporations are for-profit enterprises. The decisions made by a firm's management, such as company strategy, structure, and core capabilities, are conscious decisions based on accumulated knowledge and experience of the management teams making the decisions. The extent of the collaboration of the management team on the decisions varies, as does the collective body of knowledge used to make those decisions. This is one major difference between human-based organizations and other species of life-forms: the conscious choices we, as humans, are capable of making in pursuing our livelihoods, or in "making a living."

When a corporation finds a potentially profitable economic niche, it thrives because of the lack of competitors for the same rents. Once other firms learn of the potential for profits from this new niche or marketplace, they may decide to enter. The addition of competitors to an industry structure tends to drive profits down first, as well as market share over time. The winners of these competitive battles are the corporations or the species that have the skills and machinery to differentially extract more energy or win more customers (market share) from their environment. The species that are not as well equipped will eventually cede that niche and move elsewhere for survival. The corporate battles for market share and profits are no different from the ecological battles for food resources, or energy, in the natural world. Competition among firms for customers and market share is similar to the day-to-day battles of living creatures for energy, for the fuel of life. The same competitive forces that pit species against species, country against country, or company against company have been around forever. Some would argue that these battles can be reduced to competition for energy or intake of calories for organisms. In ecology, these are called environmental niches. In business, these are known as markets or industries in which firms compete for market share or customers. In many cases, there was a known objective and a known competitor or incumbent that had to be dislodged in order for the conquering society to assume control of a given territory. The comparison of corporations to living organisms extends to all activities that firms engage in to survive and win in today's economy.

NATURE OF THE FIRM: HOW COMPANIES SURVIVE, COMPETE, REPLICATE, AND ADAPT

Why do firms exist? What makes a corporation "fit"? How do corporations survive or "make a living"? Companies, like organisms, do four basic things:

1. They "make a living" or survive. By survive, we mean that a company performs the basic functions that allow it to be a viable entity in its marketplace—win and service customers, gain and hold market share, generate revenue and be profitable.
2. They compete against other corporations for the available energy resources, or paying customers, in their marketplace or niche. This means having enough of the appropriate equipment, processes, and behavior to allow companies to harvest enough customers and market share versus their competitors to survive.
3. They reproduce or recreate in the face of business changes and competition. This means being able to replicate their business model in the same or similar industries, or with similar products in new industries. It may also mean transitioning corporations across major shifts in technology, in corporate leadership, in business conditions, and in the industry they originally served.
4. They adapt to change. Adaptation is the ultimate test of corporate skill and resolve, much as the struggle for existence is the ultimate, instinctive drive of all living species. The ability of corporations to position themselves for survival in high-change environments or against new competitors allows them to survive the business environment.

Exhibit 3.1 places these four evolutionary activities into the context of short-term, immediate company needs and longer-term company needs.

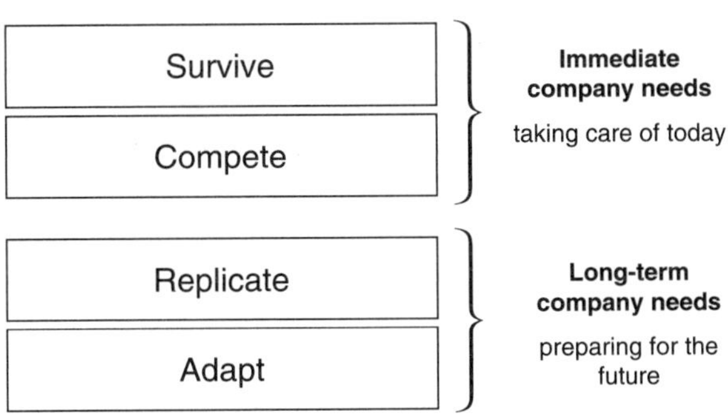

Exhibit 3.1 Business Evolutionary Process

As described previously, surviving and competing are short-term requirements of a firm for it to subsist and make a living. A firm must undertake these activities to support its core business franchise and revenue streams. These activities are the lifeblood of a firm and must be performed at least well enough to ensure the ongoing survival of the firm as a business entity. This means supporting the fitness levers of any business, which are revenue, profits, cash flow, and market share. Lack of fitness in these categories means that a firm will eventually perish, much like a living organism will perish without being able to secure food for its daily subsistence requirements.

The long-term needs of a corporation are replication and adaptation. These activities position the corporation for the future. Replication activities, as discussed, allow a firm to transition itself across generations of technological change and leadership changes. This is similar to reproduction in a living organism. Adaptation is the long-term process of surviving, competing, and replicating carried out across several generations of change.

HOW DID CORPORATIONS EVOLVE?

The history of modern corporations can be traced to the early stirrings of the Industrial Revolution, upon which the current Internet or Information Revolution is piggybacked.

The first factory was built to house the hydraulic cotton loom because the machine was simply too big to contain in the homes of the traditional artisans of the cotton industry. This machine required people to operate it as well as maintain it. Although division of labor has existed for thousands of years, the application of this organizational concept to corporations can be traced to the mid-1700s, as documented by Adam Smith in *Wealth of Nations* in his description of the typical pin factory of the time.[20] His principle of division of labor became the corporate organizational structure of the Industrial Age, which, Smith opined, would increase worker productivity by orders of magnitude. As the momentum of the Industrial Revolution accelerated, economies of scale emerged as the key to success. Managing huge factories staffed with vast numbers of specialized employees was a critical core competency, and mass production was the way to profits.

The next evolutionary wave of corporate organization and management came from the mass proliferation of railroads in the 1820s. As Hammer and Champy observe in their book *Reengineering the Corporation,* the railroad industry "not only extended and accelerated economic development, but also moved the evolution of business management technology forward. It was the railroad companies that invented the modern business bureaucracy—a significant innovation then and an essential one if industrial organizations were going to grow larger than the span of one person's control."[21] The creation of formal operating procedures, as well as the organizational structure and mechanisms to carry them out, were required to prevent train collisions on single-track lines that carried trains in both directions. This paradigm of command-and-control management has persisted into today's corporations despite its origins 150 years ago during the development of the early railroad industry.

The automobile industry was the source of the next major steps in the evolution of the modern corporation, thanks to Henry Ford and Alfred Sloan. Henry Ford's moving assembly line was predicated on an extended division-of-labor concept, whereby each worker would have only one task to complete in assembling a vehicle. Initially, each worker would walk from assembly line to assembly line, until the moving assembly line was developed. This incredibly efficient assembly operation based on job simplification required different management principles, because the coordination of the armies of assembly workers, as well as ensuring that their work efforts resulted in a completed and correct vehicle, became complex. Alfred Sloan's contribution to the modern corporation was to create smaller, decentralized divisions that corporate managers could oversee from a small corporate headquarters simply by monitoring production counts and financial results. Sloan's efforts resulted in the multidivisional corporation (MDC), where the managers did not need specific training in manufacturing or engineering; they simply had to know the financial results generated by each of the divisions to assess performance. The MDC structure extended the division of labor from the factory floor into the professional ranks of engineering, finance, and marketing.

The final evolutionary step in the development of the modern corporation resulted from the post–World War II expansion, a time of enormous economic growth. The MDC model matured into the portfolio model of management, where elaborate planning exercises conducted at corporate headquarters determined what businesses they wanted to be in, how much operating capital to allocate to each strategic business unit, and what financial returns the managers of these businesses were expected to pass back to the firm. This model of the corporation required large staffs of financial controllers, planners, and auditors to monitor and analyze divisional financial data and assess performance. During this expansion period, one overarching concern was managing capacity, which meant keeping up with the fast-growing postwar demand. Great emphasis was placed on planning, building, and managing capacity to demand, which created yet more elaborate procedures and systems for budgeting, planning, and control. This required a pyramid organization structure, which was suited to high-growth environments because of its scalable nature. To support more growth, a firm simply added staff on the bottom of the pyramid and filled in the management layers above. This resulted in the huge layers of middle managers, which forced the decision makers further away from the reality of their decisions, as well as from the customers and the products manufactured for the customers. This mode of management persisted until the information economy began to take hold, which is now the driver of the current management paradigms in corporate America. As we have seen from the Information Age and the Internet Age, however, imposing an Industrial Age management structure, organizational design, and physical infrastructure on an increasingly information-based product and service business model is a recipe for disaster.

But the question still remains: Why did corporations form to begin with? From an economics perspective, corporations emerge as the ability to execute transactions, to make and deliver products or services valued by customers, becomes cheaper within the boundaries of the firm than on the outside. Companies must have something of value to a collection of customers willing to pay for it. That something can consist of manufactured products, services, or a combination of both. The size of the market for the product or service determines how big the company can become, as well as the number of competitors vying for a share of that marketplace. Ronald Coase, as early as 1937, described the nature of corporations.[22] According to Coase, firms exist as long as they perform transactions more efficiently than they can be done outside of the company. This determines the size and configuration of the firm. In other words, as long as companies provide products and services that are valued in an efficient, affordable manner, they will continue to exist. Transaction costs are a set of "inefficiencies" in the market that should be added to the costs of goods and services in order to compare the performance of the market to the behavior of firms. Transaction costs are friction in the market that is a part of conducting business between firms and individuals. They add a "layer of complexity to market transactions."[23] Transaction costs exist in six basic forms:

1. *Search costs.* Buyers and sellers locating each other in the open market.
2. *Information costs.* For buyers, this is learning about products and services of sellers and their cost, quality, and profit margin; for sellers, information costs include understanding the legitimacy, financial health, and needs of the buyers, such as market and product research.
3. *Bargaining costs.* For both buyers and sellers, these involve the negotiations of a sale or contract for goods and services, which may include meetings, phone calls, letters, faxes, e-mails, sharing product and service information, legal costs, and the like.
4. *Decision costs.* For buyers, this means evaluating the seller's terms and conditions versus other sellers, as well as internal processes such as approvals from purchasing departments for compliance purposes; for

sellers, decision costs involve choosing whether to sell to this particular buyer over another, or not at all in some cases.

5. *Policing costs.* For both buyers and sellers, this includes the steps required to ensure that the goods and services actually meet the claims under which the sale was made, in effect making them the real goods and services exchanged. These costs include, for example, inspections, service charges on late shipments, or late payments, and the like.
6. *Enforcement costs.* For buyers and sellers, this means rectifying any satisfaction issues with the purchasing transaction, such as agreeing on a discount as a remedy, penalties, and litigation costs.

Coase argued that firms are created because the incremental cost of organizing and maintaining them is cheaper than the total transaction costs involved when individuals conduct business with one another using the market. A firm should only perform the functions internally that cannot be performed more cheaply in the market or by another competing firm.

The performance of transactions, then, can be likened to the notion of "making a living." As long as firms make a living as well as or better than their competitors, they will survive. If they do not, they eventually cease to exist as a viable business entity. "Firms exist as collections of evolving capabilities that are managed dynamically for the purpose of earning rents."[24]

Corporations are anti-entropy machines, similar to living organisms, in that they harvest energy from their environment, grow, and live to reproduce. Corporations, though, do this by processing transactions more efficiently than individuals or other corporations, which allows them to charge a rent for their services. Again, referring to Coase's transaction view of corporations, firms exist as long as it is cheaper to execute transactions within the firm than on the outside. When it is cheaper to perform transactions outside of the firm, the process is transferred outside of the firm. The firm contracts. Firms are manifestations of order. They are organized for a purpose. They are systems characterized by less entropy and therefore more information. Firms are a collection of intelligence assembled for the purpose of the firm—to make money or "make a living." Transactions are about conservation of energy. Firms that can execute their transactions more efficiently will overtake their less efficient competitors for the same customers and market share over time. A firm is an entropy-reducing organization, by virtue of being able to execute transactions and provide value to customers better than they are able themselves. Entropy and information are different sides of the same coin. This means that firms that have more efficient entropy-reducing, value-creating capabilities are better adapted species than their competitors, who may be less efficient at entropy-reducing, transaction-conducting, and value-creating functions.

Firms are collections of information. More information means less entropy. This collection of "order" is organized around the ability to make a living, to be fit in business fitness terms. This is the corporation's version of the struggle for survival. Making a living is simply holding at bay the natural forces of entropy. This takes constant intake of energy. For firms, the intake of energy is revenue. The more digital the content of a firm is, the better its ability to manage information, which makes a firm more able to win against entropy, other firms, and the unknown. The more digital a firm is, in its content, its strategies, and its execution, the better able it is to conduct transactions and dominate its economic milieu, or industry.

Porter views a firm as a collection of discrete but interrelated economic activities, such as products being assembled, sales calls by the sales force, or orders being processed internally.[25] The basic unit of competitive advantage, then, is the discrete activity. The economics of performing discrete activities determines a firm's costs relative to its competitors. These related views of corporations show that firms, in order to be viable, must perform some activity that is valued by customers. Firm activities must provide value such that others cannot easily copy its products or services. Whether one takes the transaction view of firmwide activities or the economic activity view of firm activities, it is clear that when a corporation is doing its business, it is performing services for customers who assign value to them.

HOW CORPORATIONS SURVIVE

The first and foremost activity of corporations, like life-forms, is to survive. The constant struggle for survival is a part of life and death in nature, and it is no different for corporations. The fundamental purpose of a for-profit company is to make money for its employees and shareholders. This means executing the processes of developing and delivering products and services to paying customers, and being able to charge prices such that profit remains after all the debt obligations are covered. Organisms first and foremost have to survive by taking in energy and staving off the forces of entropy, the constant onslaught of randomness that, ultimately, would result in death. The intake of energy by living organisms is necessary for survival or entropy avoidance. Their differential ability to survive is based on their ability to extract energy from their environmental niche, their ecological milieu. Those that do it better will survive better and will have better odds of reproducing or passing on their genetic formula to the next generation, which will survive in greater numbers because they are better at extracting energy from the environment. Companies that have the ability to survive based on a superior business model will continue as viable business entities. They will "reproduce" by extending their successful business model, or genetic blueprint, to a similar business or to new businesses. Before we continue this discussion, we must first discuss what makes companies "fit." Fitness for companies must parallel fitness for individuals of populations of living organisms if we are to apply our analogy completely.

BUSINESS DARWINISM: WHAT IS FITNESS FOR CORPORATIONS?

Darwinian fitness is the ability to survive the environment long enough to pass one's genes on to the next generation. Business Darwinism is the corporate equivalent of survival of the fittest. Survival of the fittest means that companies that survive in business are better able to win and maintain customers or market share, which provides revenues and cash flow, ultimately leading to profits for the corporation. Those that do these things better than other firms will survive and grow at the expense of their competitors. Fitness for corporations means having enough market share to derive revenues, which provides profit. Profit is a primary measure of fitness for corporations. Cash flow is another metric that is important, as well as market capitalization or stock valuation for public companies. Porter states that a firm's success is "manifested in attaining a competitive position or series of competitive positions that lead to superior and sustainable financial performance."[26] Corporate fitness and performance have to be tied to the mechanisms that allow a firm to extract profits from its industry. The day-to-day survival of a firm means that it is able to sustain enough paying customers, or market share, to generate the cash flow and profits required to sustain day-to-day operations and future growth. Corporate fitness, in the immediate term, requires the combination of strategy, structure, and capabilities that allow the firm to win enough customers, market share, and ultimately enough revenue and profits to sustain itself as a viable business entity.

The struggle for survival for corporations is the competition for customers or market share, revenue, cash flow, and profits. These equate to the constant struggle for existence that living organisms undergo in their quest to "make a living," or to survive long enough to reproduce. Those that are better equipped to survive will thrive and eventually dominate those species that are not as well equipped to compete in that environment.

HOW CORPORATIONS COMPETE

Companies must be able to compete against firms that are in the same industry, just as species of living organisms must compete against others that occupy the same ecological niche. Limited resources are available, generally, within a specific ecological niche, just as limited numbers of customers are available in a given industry. Competition can be considered from multiple perspectives. A species competes evolutionarily with environmental changes as well as with other species. The arms races described earlier capture the nature of the firm-versus-firm competition we are interested in here. These are most often symmetric arms races, where firms are competing for the same resources in their environment, customers, and market share in this case.

In new or emerging industries, the marketplace is wide open with abundant customers or resources available for the firms to compete for. The competition initially is limited to moderate in the early stages of market maturation. As the number of competitors increases, the competition intensifies, and only those with the tools and capabilities to compete more effectively, to win more often than the other firms, survive. Competition among firms is for the same economic niche, the same energy sources, or more accurately, the same customers. The companies that have the ability to win customers and market share (extract energy) from their industry or marketplace (ecological niche) more efficiently than competing companies will increase their market share, forcing other companies out over time.

According to Porter, firm success is based on two factors: (1) the attractiveness of the industry in which a firm competes, and (2) its relative position within that industry structure.[27] Competitive advantage, then, results from a firm's ability to perform required activities at a collectively lower cost than its competitors, or to perform activities in unique ways that allow the firm to command a premium price, hence to create more profit for the firm. The competition within an industry is for limited resources, or customers. The firms that are better able to win customers and market share, and ultimately profits, will eventually dominate that industry.

This is not unlike the evolutionary forces that make a challenger species able to move into and occupy an ecological niche more efficiently than an incumbent because of the manifestation of traits, through natural selection, that confer advantage on the upstart. Whatever the series of adaptations is that makes the challenger more able to exploit that particular ecological niche, the fact that the two or more species are competing for the same sources of energy means that one or more may eventually be doomed. Ecological niches are finite spaces that can accommodate finite occupants.

According to the Lanchester Strategy,[28] market share is warfare potential. In other words, market share gives a firm enough mass, enough potential energy, to compete. If a firm does not have sufficient market share, it will not be profitable, and more important, it will not have enough capability to compete in its industry. This supports the notion that competition for customers and market share ultimately has a direct affect on a firm's ability to compete in the long run.

Winning does not necessarily mean eliminating the competition, but it does mean demonstrating an ability to harvest energy or resources, or customers and market share in the business case, from a chosen competitive milieu. Those that do so better than their competitors will eventually dominate that competitive landscape. Surviving in intensely competitive industries may require elimination or absorption of a firm's smaller competitors in order to aggregate enough mass and market share to challenge the leaders.

REPLICATION: HOW DO CORPORATIONS REPRODUCE?

The notion of corporate reproduction can take many forms. Having developed the analogies for surviving, competing, and adapting, the next step is to describe how firms pass their genetic material—their genes—on to the next generation. Darwinian fitness is the ability to pass one's genes on to the next generation. This goes to the heart of the matter: fitness is the ability to survive long enough to reproduce. That is what living organisms do, period. For corporations to reproduce, the analogy is the ability to span a technology wave, such as the transition from the Computer Age to the Network/Internet Age, or the Industrial Age to the Information Age. Another aspect of a firm reproducing is its ability to successfully replicate its management or business model in another industry or in another firm.

For example, Microsoft is trying to become the major player of the Internet Age after it, along with Intel many argue, was one of the major drivers of the Computer Age. The rise of the PC based on Microsoft's operating systems made it a software powerhouse. Adding personal productivity software, word processing, spreadsheets, and office graphics to the mix allowed Microsoft to continue to dominate the PC software marketplace. The Internet ushered in a new paradigm of computing. Netscape outflanked Microsoft with its web browser, which opened up the world of the Internet to consumers around the world. This new market opportunity created a massive wave of new competition and a new way of using computers. They became devices for connecting and communicating more than they were for computing and programming. Microsoft saw this new market, realized that it was losing, and responded. The release of Microsoft's Internet Explorer and the subsequent bundling of its browser with its operating systems and office suite software spelled the demise of Netscape as a competitor to Microsoft, as well as signaling Microsoft's intent to be a leader of the Next Wave of the Internet Age.

Most recently, Microsoft has announced another major shift, from license revenues to subscription fees.[29] Microsoft's latest reinvention of itself comes in the form of its new operating system—Windows XP. Microsoft's Windows operating system runs 92 percent of the world's personal computers today, and Bill Gates and Steve Ballmer worked feverishly in 2001 to convince all of the existing Windows users to upgrade to Windows XP. Windows XP bundles many Microsoft-centric features and services into this version of its operating system so that users are automatically ushered into Microsoft's web services, such as its travel site Expedia, its passport authentication service, or its media player. These bundled services, according to many, are an extension of Microsoft's continued attempts to lock out other competitors to its products; however, Microsoft contends that bundling services makes using computers and software easier for users, exemplified by bundling Windows 95 with Internet Explorer, its web browser product.

The long-term goal of Windows XP, however, relates to Microsoft's announced initiative called .Net (dot-net), in which web sites can interact with one another as well as with wireless devices such as cell phones, pagers, and other web-ready devices. The first incarnation of .Net is the initiative dubbed HailStorm, which will include 14 services that will be activated through the XP operating system. Planned services include e-mail, instant messaging (similar to AOL's de facto standard), and calendar functions that will be served through XP using standard protocols that are accessible through any web-enabled devices such as those mentioned previously. Microsoft's passport authentication service is the segue to HailStorm, which will initially be free but is expected to become a subscription service once a critical mass of users is built up on the service. This is where Microsoft's business model transition begins to change.

Ultimately, Microsoft is transitioning all of its software licensing fees to subscription fee-based services. This means that corporations will pay a subscription fee to use Microsoft products rather than a one-time license fee, which will include upgrade services as well. Microsoft will be placed in a position of dictating when upgrades are required for a subscribed service as opposed to the license model, where a company can use a licensed piece of software as long as it wants without upgrading to new software. This model, which poses some risk, will force users and corporations to upgrade and pay to do so on Microsoft's schedule, not necessarily on the user's schedule. The benefit for Microsoft under the subscription-based business model is creating a steady stream of subscription revenues rather than the spiked demand for new software products when they are released as upgrades to existing products. Subscription fees will create a recurring revenue model based on services instead of discrete licenses of products.

In order for Microsoft to transition its business model to one based on subscription services versus licensing revenue, consider the actions that were required from a product development perspective as well as a fee collection and product distribution perspective. All of Microsoft's products will eventually have to be retooled to be sold and delivered on a subscription basis over the web. Collection of fees will be accomplished using credit card transactions from individual home users, as well as using traditional contracts for corporations. Product upgrades and software distribution will continue to be web-based as well. This is a very different model from the mass distribution of compact discs and floppies, and the revenue and profit generation of this business model are yet to be seen.

For the remainder of this chapter, we treat the notion of corporate reproduction as replication of a formula for success, or the business model. Given that we have defined a firm as consisting of the interplay of a firm's strategy, its structure, and its core capabilities, it makes sense that some or all of these aspects of the firm are "passed on to the next generation" in firm reproduction, or replication. What is the unit of corporate replication? How is it passed on? How can corporations replicate themselves in strategy, structure, and capabilities, and more important, in results? What are companies replicating when they, in effect, reproduce?

Possible answers include corporate culture, specific management methods, competitive capabilities, or proven formulas for running a business. But there has to be more to it than simply populating the new setting with the management from the parent company. The idea of corporate "reproduction" can take the following forms:

- Allowing a firm's business model to span generations of technology, such as the PC/database era to the network and Internet age, or generations of leadership changes, such as a new CEO or a new senior management team.
- Allowing a firm to replicate its business model in a different industry using the same management skills and business processes.
- Spinning off a division into a new corporation, which replicates in some form the management styles and corporate controls of the parent.
- Installing corporate leadership principles in a merger or an acquisition, as well as incorporating technologies and the intellectual property of an acquired firm.
- Replicating a business model or style of management that has been successful in other industries or geographies.
- Creating product or service innovations, which help the firm grow market share and profits, as well as prolong the firm's ability to continue to survive and service its market.

But in all cases, what exactly is the reproductive medium? In living organisms, it is the genetic content, fundamentally the genes and DNA of the individuals of the species. What is the DNA or gene equivalent for corporations?

CORPORATE DNA

When the book *Clockspeed*[30] hit the shelves, Charles Fine introduced the notion of corporate DNA, a fundamental set of building blocks on which a firm's competitive advantage is based. Fine treats corporate DNA as elements of companies' supply chains, which consist of three sets of interrelated links:

1. Organizational supply chains
2. Technology supply chains
3. Business capability

The *organizational supply chain* refers to the collection of other companies that a firm does business with in executing its business process. The *technology supply chain* is the mapping of the various technology components that are required by a firm in order to produce its products and services. *Business capability chains* are the various distinct business processes required to process a firm's inputs and convert them into outputs, or salable products and services for the firm's customers. Fine's analysis provides one view of what might comprise corporate DNA.

Other views treat corporate DNA as corporate culture or a particular management style. Hamel and Prahalad use the phrase "corporate genetics" to describe the collective knowledge and beliefs, biases and assumptions, and other similar knowledge of a particular industry.[31] They continue:

> Every manager carries around in his or her head a set of biases, assumptions, and presuppositions about the structure of the relevant "industry," about how one makes money in that industry, about who the competition is and isn't, about who the customers are and aren't, about what customers want or don't want, about which technologies are viable and which aren't, and so on. This genetic coding also encompasses beliefs, values, and norms about how best to motivate people; the right balance of internal cooperation and competition; the relative ranking of shareholder, customer, and employee interests; and what behaviors to encourage and discourage. These beliefs are, at least in part, the product of a particular industry environment. When that environment changes rapidly and radically, those beliefs may become a threat to survival.

Another possible view of corporate DNA can be found in resource-based views of firms, in which a company's resources and its core capabilities are sources of competitive advantage in its industry. These views were popularized by the work of Hamel and Prahalad. A core competence is a bundle of skills and technologies that enables a company to provide a particular benefit to customers.[32] Core competencies are difficult to copy. Building core competencies represents cumulative organization learning rather than great leaps of innovation. It is therefore difficult to time-compress competence building. Core competencies are not product-specific, but rather they contribute to the success of a range of products and services.[33] In fact, core competencies may even transcend a particular business unit of a large corporation, and they are longer lasting than any individual product or service. According to this view, the combination of core competencies might be construed as the corporate DNA of a firm.

We must identify the fundamental elements of a corporation's makeup—its strategy, structure, and core capabilities, its corporate culture, vision, values, and norms guiding behavior, all of which are somehow melded together to allow the business entity to survive and reproduce across generations of technological change, leadership change, and environmental change. Corporate DNA, to be consistent with genetic theory and research, must be the stored instructions of a firm that allow its survival within a given generation of technology or leadership, as well as across generations of technology and leadership. It is the total archived digital recipe for a company's development and reproduction. So if corporate DNA is the ROM instructions of a company's survival recipe, what constitutes the gene equivalent for a firm?

Genes in this case must be the core competencies and skills of a corporation. These are the building blocks of what a company does to survive and reproduce. Corporate DNA is the documentation or archival mechanism of the core capabilities of a firm, its history of skills and lessons of survival that are encoded in company lore. In the pure biological sense, DNA and genes are chemical processes that store genetic information in a digital fashion. DNA is the storage system, the equivalent of magnetic media used to store computer instructions or quantities of information. The archive of genetic information is the corporate DNA. But what is corporate culture? And what is the role of corporate culture in the survival and reproduction processes of a firm?

Culture in human beings has augmented our biological reproduction processes by allowing faster adaptive responses to change. Cultural evolution is information-based much like genetic evolution. The information processes of cultural evolution are more efficient and responsive than genetic evolution. In fact, cultural evolution can occur within the same generation as well as across generations, whereas genetic evolution occurs solely across generations. This is what makes cultural evolution such a potent adaptive mechanism for human beings. It augments the information-based nature of genetic evolution by allowing faster and more flexible responses to change, and it is inherently more efficient by leveraging language, writing systems, and information management capabilities in the larger sense of the phrase.

Of all the views considered, the one that best fits our analogy is a hybrid resource-based view that blends the core competence view of Hamel and Prahalad with the three-tiered supply chain view of Charles Fine in *Clockspeed*.[34] Corporate DNA is as much the unique bundle of skills and technologies that are uniquely perceived by customers as it is the configuration and execution of processes and procedures that are held in common by competing firms. For example, having great technology but a sales force that is incapable of selling does not a successful firm make; however, possession of a good enough technology combined with an outstanding sales force may well be enough to allow a particular firm to win in its industry.

Corporate DNA is the unique configuration of core competencies and core business processes, supported by corporate knowledge and organizational learning processes and encoded and enforced by the corporate culture of the firm. Organizational learning and corporate culture are replication mechanisms of firm competitive advantage. Two mandatory corporate DNA elements for today's environment are the information management and the innovation functions of a firm, which support corporate agility and variability maintenance of corporate core competencies. The closer the alignment of the core competencies and core business processes with the marketplace, the more fit the firm will be according to the fitness metrics of customer and market share, revenues, and profits.

CORPORATE DNA VERSUS CORPORATE CULTURE

Success of companies has also been explained by the notion of having certain core competencies, or "corporate DNA." The question about how corporate DNA arises is subject to further discussion in order to be accurate with our analogy. For example, in this case I would support the notion that corporate DNA and corporate culture are different. The difference between the two is important to our discussion of changes in corporate behavior in response to competitors or to changing business conditions.

Corporate DNA is the collection of unique skills, knowledge, or core competencies a firm possesses that distinguish it from its competitors, even though those competitors may be in the same industry. These persist longer than the executives and leadership of the firm, and, although they can be changed, they take a relatively long time to ingrain into the corporate fabric to manifest themselves by way of results. Results in this case must support the fitness levers of the corporation, which means profits, revenue growth, and market share. Corporate culture, however, is the collection of corporate behaviors and knowledge that is unique to a firm and distinguishes it from its competitors. These behaviors are more transient and more easily displaced by new behaviors deemed necessary or appropriate to the firm's success. Corporate culture is more easily modified to suit the needs of the firm's strategy or competitive landscape, and can be enforced by decree.

WHAT IS THE DIFFERENCE BETWEEN CORPORATE CULTURE AND CORPORATE DNA?

Corporate DNA includes the building blocks of skills and competencies that make a firm different, or unique, from its competitors. Some of these are customer-perceived, as in the core competencies described by Hamel and Prahalad. Some of these are not necessarily so, but they determine the customer impact of other core competencies. These include internal core business processes that are so well executed that, in their entirety, they might actually constitute a core competence. In this scenario, the configuration and execution of core business processes becomes a core competence. Corporate culture glues these together into the purpose of the organization, the mission and vision of what the firm does and how it does it, but within the broader goals of making a living by winning customers, gaining market share, and making a profit.

Corporate DNA supports the firm's organization and structure as the firm is configured to compete and provide products and services to the marketplace. Corporate DNA can be replicated in other industries or other companies, but it is difficult without the supporting corporate culture and organizational knowledge. Corporate culture binds the firm's vision, strategy, and objectives with its business model, structure, and core capabilities. The corporate culture guides the behavior of the firm in executing the functions of making a living. Corporate DNA is the basis of the competitive advantage of a firm, but it relies on corporate culture for execution of and belief in the vision and objectives of the firm. Organizational learning and knowledge differ from corporate culture in that it can be both an element of corporate DNA and a means of replicating itself. Culture is the sum total of ways of living built up by a group of human beings and transmitted from one generation to another. Organizational learning and knowledge is the repository of corporate culture and lessons that allow the knowledge to transition from generation to generation.

Corporate reproduction consists of the ability of a firm to replicate elements of its corporate DNA in new industries, new geographies, or by spinning out divisions or business units. Replication of corporate DNA cannot be done without the replication of knowledge, skills, and corporate culture.

HOW CORPORATIONS ADAPT (OR COMPETING AGAINST CHANGE)

We have discussed how firms emerged historically, how they have evolved over time in form and organizational structure, and how they have been forced to adapt to changes in their competitive environment. Corporations perform four basic functions: survive, compete, reproduce, and adapt. Corporate fitness, similar to Darwinian fitness, is the ability to survive long enough to reproduce. Survival and competition to corporations must be performed to remain a viable business entity. We then discussed some ways companies can replicate themselves. In the bigger picture, though, we are interested in long-term survival. What capabilities will allow a firm to survive multiple waves of change? How do firms transition themselves from one major age to the next? How did corporations transition from the Industrial Age to the Information Age? How are these firms surviving the transition into the Internet Age? Can fundamental strategies be employed to facilitate the transition across industry shifts?

CHANGE: THE COMPETITIVE CONSTANT

There is a competitor that no corporation is really prepared for—change. Although all corporate strategists indicate a fear or at least a wariness of the unknown, they are no more prepared for dealing with this unnamed competitor than the next person. Competing against a known enemy is one thing, and it is not the easiest of things to do; however, the unknown is much more nefarious that any known competitor, and all firms competing in the same ecological niche are forced to compete against the same force. But they are not prepared. The tools and techniques do not necessarily exist. Not many firms have been able to transcend massive shifts in the business landscape to survive into the Next Wave of technological advancement or business change. What is needed is a framework to address change and the unknown, and to begin the thought process leading to a business strategy of maximal fitness—the ability of corporations to rapidly adapt to changes in the business landscape. The ability to adapt to rapid changes in the business landscape and competitive landscape will separate survivors from the evolutionary junk heap. Many corporations have failed because they did not see the change happening all around them, and they were unable to reconfigure themselves to adjust to the changes.

ADAPTATION FOR SHORT AND LONG TIME FRAMES

Adaptation, for our purposes, must address two time scales, an immediate horizon and a longer-term horizon. The immediate horizon is competing day to day for market share and customers, modifying products and services in response to changes in customer preferences, and adjusting to competitors' product and service modifications, sales tactics, pricing strategies, and marketing themes. These can be characterized by the "OT" elements of the classic

Boston Consulting Group SWOT analysis: strengths, weaknesses, opportunities, and threats. Porter[35] captures some of the key points supporting the shorter-term, tactical actions that support adapting to changes posed by the environment or competitors. These include quick-response capabilities, such as a firm's capacity to react to moves by competitors or the ability to mount an immediate offensive thrust against a targeted competitor. In addition to quick-response capabilities, Porter also notes some key factors that enhance a firm's ability to adapt to change, such as cost structure, managing more complex product lines, adding new products and services, competing on service, escalating marketing activity, and mobilizing sales forces. Responding to outside forces is important as well, including responding to sustained high inflation rates, technological changes that make products or processes obsolete, recessions, increases in wages, and even government regulation. Other constraints to adapting to change must be understood in order to craft responses, such as shared facilities, sales forces, manufacturing capacity, distribution channels, or relationships with a corporate parent or a strategic partner. Again, these short-term adaptive issues need to be dealt with by the current leadership and structure of the firm.

But there is a more strategic time horizon. This is the generation-spanning survival of a firm across changes in industry structure, massive technological shifts, and even the wholesale replacement of core C-level executives of the firm. Johnson and Russo point out this difference in time horizons: "Although the evolutionary time scale is much, much longer than that granted to managers, it may be speedy, relative to the competition that is more salient."[36] They emphasize the race to adapt, stating that the organisms or firms that are first to recognize and then take advantage of opportunities presented to them by the environment, or by adaptive actions taken by competitors or customers, may win the race of adaptation.

PROACTIVE ADAPTATION: FUTURE-FOCUSED CHANGE

The discussion of short-term adaptive tactics and long-term adaptive strategies would be incomplete without positioning both sets of adaptive capabilities for the real challenge. The onslaught of technology-driven change, global markets, and global competitors has rendered previously stable industry structures amorphous and fluid. In times of high change, entrenched competitors cannot assume that their position in their industries will remain stable, or that their industry will even remain viable. As Hamel and Prahalad note, competition for the future is different from competition for the present in that it often takes place in unstructured arenas where the rules of competition have yet to be defined, and it is more like a triathlon than a 100-meter sprint. Competing for the future, or adapting to an unknown future, requires different skills from competing for today. But they also caution that "being adaptive is not good enough."[37] Even in tumultuous industry situations, executives have to make strategic choices and execute competitive tactics. Adaptive strategies for unknown futures can be managed proactively by building in the agility of response, as well as the ability to "command the high ground" in military terms. That means dictating the rules and the structure of the industries in which firms compete, as well as knowing when to change the industry itself, and the firm, in response to new opportunities. Proactive adaptation can be accomplished in a direction established by a firm, but agility and response capabilities must always be a part of the fabric of the firm. The strategy, structure, and core capabilities of any firm must include generating and maintaining variability as well as the ability to capitalize on the opportunities afforded the firm by changes in the environment, competitive strategies, and the marketplace.

NOTES

1. M.T. Hannan and J. Freeman, "The Population Ecology of Organizations," *American Journal of Sociology* 82 (1977), pp. 929–964.
2. Richard P. Rumelt, Dan E. Schendel, and David J. Teece, "Fundamental Issues in Strategy," *Fundamental Issues in Strategy* (Boston, MA: Harvard Business School Press, 1994), pp. 33–34.
3. Ibid.
4. Charles Darwin, *Origin of Species* (New York: Hurst & Company, 1860), reprinted from the Sixth London Edition, with additions and corrections.
5. This review is not meant to be a complete analysis of Darwin's work, nor is it an update of his work based on more current research. It merely captures some of the highlights of Darwinian thinking to extend the concepts to business evolution based on the original *Origin of Species,* as well as more recent thinking that shores up and updates the original, most notably Richard Dawkins' work, Steven Jones (*Darwin's Ghost*), and Matt Ridley (*Genome*).
6. Matt Ridley, *Genome* (New York: HarperCollins, 1999), p. 24.
7. Steve Jones, *Darwin's Ghost* (New York: Random House, 1999, 2000), p. xix.
8. Ibid.
9. Ibid., p. xxv.
10. Richard Dawkins, *The Blind Watchmaker* (New York: W.W. Norton & Company, 1996), p. 170.
11. Ibid., p. 180.
12. Jones, *Darwin's Ghost,* p. 76.

13. Jeffrey R. Williams, "Strategy and the Search for Rents: The Evolution of Diversity among Firms," *Fundamental Issues in Strategy* (Boston, MA: Harvard Business School Press, 1995), p. 237.
14. See Michael Porter's *Competitive Strategy: Techniques for Analyzing Industries and Competitors* (New York: The Free Press, 1980) and *Competitive Advantage: Creating and Sustaining Superior Performance* (New York: The Free Press, 1985) for his landmark work in business strategy.
15. Charles H. Fine, *Clockspeed* (Reading, MA: Perseus Books, 1998).
16. Williams, "Strategy and the Search for Rents," p. 229.
17. Richard R. Nelson, "Why Do Firms Differ, and Why Does It Matter?" *Fundamental Issues in Strategy* (Boston, MA: Harvard Business School Press, 1995), p. 258.
18. Ibid., p. 259.
19. Ibid., p. 260.
20. Adam Smith, *Wealth of Nations* (New York: Prometheus Books, 1991, orig. 1776), p. 10.
21. Michael Hammer and James Champy, *Reengineering the Corporation* (New York: HarperBusiness, 1993), p. 13.
22. Ronald H. Coase, "The Nature of the Firm," *The Firm, the Market and the Law* (Chicago: University of Chicago Press, 1988), pp. 33–56. See also Ronald H. Coase, *Essays on Economics and Economists* (Chicago: University of Chicago Press, 1994).
23. Larry Downes and Chunka Mui, *Unleashing the Killer App* (Boston, MA: Harvard Business School Press, 1998), pp. 37–38.
24. Williams, "Strategy and the Search for Rents," p. 229.
25. Michael Porter, "Toward a Dynamic Theory of Strategy," *Fundamental Issues in Strategy* (Boston, MA: Harvard Business School Press, 1995), p. 435.
26. Ibid., p. 425.
27. Ibid., p. 431.
28. Shinichi Yano, *Lanchester Strategy* (Sunnyvale, CA: Lanchester Press, 1990), p. 102. See also *New Lanchester Strategy: Sales and Marketing Strategy for the Weak (Volume 2)* and *New Lanchester Strategy: Sales and Marketing Strategy for the Strong (Volume 3),* also by Shinichi Yano.
29. "Microsoft Arms Itself to Conquer Net as It Did PCs," *USA Today* (June 1, 2001), pp. B1–2.
30. Fine, *Clockspeed.*
31. Gary Hamel and C.K. Prahalad, *Competing for the Future* (Boston, MA: Harvard Business School Press, 1994), p. 49.
32. Ibid., p. 199.
33. Ibid., p. 201.
34. Fine, *Clockspeed.*

35. Porter, *Competitive Strategy,* p. 66.
36. Eric J. Johnson and J. Edward Russo, "Coevolution: Toward a Third Frame for Analyzing Competitive Decision Making," *Wharton on Dynamic Competitive Strategy,* George S. Day and David J. Reibstein, eds., with Robert Gunther (New York: John Wiley & Sons, 1997), p. 196.
37. Hamel and Prahalad, *Competing for the Future,* pp. 37, 40.

4

EVOLUTION OF INFORMATION TECHNOLOGY ORGANIZATIONS AND STRATEGIES

The impact of information technology will be even more radical than the harnessing of steam and electricity in the 19th century. Rather it will be more akin to the discovery of fire by early ancestors, since it will prepare the way for a revolutionary leap into a new age that will profoundly transform human culture.

—Jacques Attali, *Millennium*

The first few chapters of this book established the evolutionary foundation for viewing corporations as living organizations. The objective for the remainder of the book is to describe how information technology (IT) has grown and evolved from its inception as a support function for accounting applications to the strategically focused discipline of today. The rise of strategic software applications is reviewed to show how the IT organizations of today are outgrowths of their Industrial Age roots. We show how the needs of an information-based business model demand different strategies, organizational structures, and core capabilities than asset-based business models. These will necessarily require software applications that allow agility and speed, and help prolong episodes of competitive advantage. As in evolution, the increase in the corporate brain-to-body ratio must be supported by the thinking and information-synthesizing capabilities of a firm. A review of major waves of software applications in business demonstrates how today's corporations fell into their present condition. We develop a strategy and a series of actions that will help them get out of it. In short, a more strategically oriented IT organization needs to evolve. This will be critical for avoiding deselection based on the Principle of Information Darwinism.

RISE OF INFORMATION TECHNOLOGY

My first years in the IT business were with Electronic Data Systems. The year was 1987.

Recall the changes that were about to take place. Compaq's DeskPro PC, based on Intel's 80386 chip, bundled with Microsoft's Windows operating system, was to create the Wintel duopoly that would dominate the PC marketplace for the next decade. This resulted ultimately, in 2001, in the appearance of Bill Gates in federal court for alleged monopolistic business practices. We marveled at the pace of change, at the new applications that were springing up all around us.

But while we were participating in one of the most exciting periods in IT history, the seeds had already been sown for the problems that corporations would face a decade later. In fact, most firms had already been suffering the ills of the mismatch between their business strategy and model and their ability to support them with IT. Consider the early days of business computing. IBM mainframes dominated the early years of IT, along with Amdahl, NEC, Fujitsu, Hitachi, and others. These machines were based on proprietary operating systems and were tremendously expensive. They required large staffs to support them in data centers reminiscent of NASA's mission control space centers. The programmers were housed in Dilbert-like hives of cubicles coding, testing, and promoting software applications into production.

The end of the mainframe era was signaled by two closely related innovations: the rise of minicomputers in the 1970s and the introduction of the IBM PC in 1981. These innovations allowed the shift from massively centralized mainframe architectures to distributed, decentralized client-server architectures that continue today. Minicomputers and PCs foreshadowed a "changing of the guard" in IT. Smaller computing devices packing more processing power, more storage capacity, and more random access memory (RAM) were far cheaper than mainframe computers. Because they were smaller, they could be kept in locations other than centralized data centers. These smaller minicomputers allowed departmental applications to be developed and maintained by IT resources under the oversight of divisional or departmental management, not the centralized IT support staffs affiliated with the mainframe paradigm of application development and support.

The evolution of various computer technologies is important because it helps explain the IT organizations that evolved to manage these burgeoning information enterprises. The mainframe era required large, centralized organizations with command-and-control management styles. These IT organizations were eerily similar to the manufacturing corporations of the time in that they were large physical assets requiring specialized facilities to house, protect, and control them. This is the economy-of-scale approach that values size—in fact, *demands* size—in order to be successful. This is a classic case of competing on physical asset intensity versus information asset intensity.

With the advent of client-server architectures, followed by n-tier Internet architectures, the process has in some ways come full circle back to a central server and a more or less "dumb" terminal running a web browser application. The salient difference now is that the Internet has engaged all business personnel in the firm's IT architecture and application selection dialogue. It has created a generation of IT-literate users and IT-literate leaders who are now in a position to change the ways that businesses deploy and leverage IT resources. Information technology is no longer viewed as the roadblock to obtaining a report, or blamed for expenses spiraling out of control, or the reason that business units of a corporation are losing their compass.

Information technology leaders often hear the comment, "We make widgets, dammit, not computer systems!" Information technology will henceforth be viewed as not only the enabler, but also the driver of enlightenment of market conditions, competitors, customer choices and desires, delivery of customer satisfaction, and repeat buyer behavior. Information technology will no longer languish as an overhead budget item. It cannot if today's corporations are to evolve into the next generation of information-based competition. The identification, valuation, and harvesting of information will be a significant facet of competitive advantage for leading firms of the Next Wave.

ORIGINS OF FINANCIAL APPLICATIONS

The first use of computing devices was purely for financial control purposes. The abacus, for example, was developed in Asia more than five thousand years ago to perform arithmetic computation using calculation techniques similar to those in modern computers. In 1642, Blaise Pascal invented the Pascaline, which was the world's first automatic calculating machine. It could perform simple addition and subtraction. Gottfried Wilhelm Leibniz, the inventor of the discipline of calculus, developed the Leibniz Computer in 1694. The Leibniz device performed multiplication using repetitive additions, which is the algorithm used in today's computers. In 1888, William Borroughs patented the first dependable key-driven adding machine, which was then modified four years later to perform subtraction and printing capabilities. Herman Hollerinth patented an electromechanical information machine in 1890 based on punch card instructions, which ushered in the use of electricity applied to a data processing endeavor. Hollerinth went on to found the Tabulating Machine Company, which eventually became today's IBM.

All of these early innovations in computing were based on executing basic mathematics. Fast-forward to 1950 and the introduction of the UNIVAC I by Eckert and Mauchley, the first commercially marketed computer. Its initial use was compiling the U.S. census for the first time. More interesting to this discussion is the first commercial use of the UNIVAC, which took place in 1954 at General Electric's (GE's) Major Appliance Division plant built in Louisville, Kentucky. On the heels of successfully predicting the outcome of the 1952 election (which Eisenhower won in a landslide) before the polls closed, the UNIVAC became a hit with businesses that suddenly realized that "If a computer could predict election results, why couldn't it forecast sales, lay out production schedules, simulate factory operations, perform 'what-if' analyses, and solve many business operations problems?"[1] One of the original programmers of the UNIVAC was Burton Grad, who embellishes on this first-time commercial programming effort conducted by the GE team:

> GE had constructed state-of-the-art manufacturing facilities in Louisville to produce washers and dryers, dishwashers and disposers, refrigerators and freezers and electric ranges and ovens. Expanding its plan to automate the production facilities and to help make Louisville a showcase plant, GE decided to use the UNIVAC I computer not only to process payroll, general ledger, accounts receivable and payable and other accounting functions, but also for manufacturing planning and control functions. GE Corporate Accounting Services took primary responsibility for designing and programming the first payroll system, which was to be initially used by the Washer and Dryer department. This design and programming team also had participants from UNIVAC. GE Corporate Manufacturing Services took responsibility for designing and programming the manufacturing control system for the Dishwasher and Disposal department.[2]

This GE effort represents one of the first uses of computers to automate the financial accounting functions of a major manufacturing firm, as well as the manufacturing planning and control functions. The GE projects demonstrated how companies could successfully use computers for solving real business problems. The GE model of software application development for accounting and manufacturing control became popular with other larger corporations, which dedicated large staffs of programmers to the task of creating accounting and financial control applications to support their business needs. As the GE example illustrates, their corporate accounting organization took the lead in developing the financial applications for their state-of-the-art appliance factory. The responsibility, ownership, and reporting structure were all into the financial organization, which is consistent with organizations of that time. Recall the evolution of corporations after World War II, in which large staffs of financial controllers were created to manage multiple units of multidivisional corporations (MDCs) in portfolio fashion from a small, centralized headquarters location. It was a simple extension of the management practices of the time to have the newly formed IT groups report to the financial organization. After all, they were developing financial accounting systems for them, so as the customer of those applications, it made sense for them to have oversight of these early IT projects. This organizational and reporting structure would continue for the next half-century as IT organizations remained under the oversight of the chief financial officer (CFO) and financial organizations of firms, even though the role of IT had changed dramatically.

CLIENT-SERVER ARCHITECTURE AND THE RISE OF THE DEPARTMENTAL APPLICATION

Fast-forwarding to the 1970s, the rise of multiple software and application innovations was taking place concurrent with the rapid advancements in computer technology on many fronts.

With Bell Labs' work in separating the computing hardware from the operating system, as well as leading the development in software programming tools such as C and C++, a host of software companies began cropping up. This period witnessed the rise of relational database technology, as well as a variety of software applications, including the early accounting systems such as payroll, accounts payable, and other financial packages.

Most software applications were primarily used for accounting and financial purposes. The rise of the PC and the PC-centric model of computing continued the rapidly evolving trend toward decentralized IT architectures. The shift to the client-server model of computing further segregated the software industry into the database vendors and the application software vendors.

The client-server model of computing created massive changes in the way that IT systems were developed, deployed, and supported by IT organizations. First, client-server changed the way applications were distributed. Concurrent with the PC adoption by businesses and home users, software applications were now being loaded at the end-user work site instead of remotely at data centers. This provided end-users more exposure to computing devices and functionality.

The combination of PC-based applications along with client-server distributed applications introduced new competitors to the computing world. IBM introduced the commercial PC in 1981, but Compaq, Gateway, and Dell would come to dominate the PC market in time. With DOS and eventually Windows, Microsoft Corporation would become the PC software leader. Intel, by virtue of the 80386, 80486, and the Pentium microprocessors, would assume a joint leadership with Microsoft as the increased processor horsepower and memory requirements of software applications drove demand for Intel's powerful microprocessors. The Wintel duopoly assumed a dominant position in the computing architecture of corporations based on Microsoft's Windows software franchise and Intel's chips. In a sense, the more distributed the IT and application architectures become, the more new competitors are introduced into the fray, followed by more innovation and more choices about how a given corporation may leverage its IT resources to attain competitive advantage.

MANUFACTURING MEETS THE WINTEL DUOPOLY

The evolution of computing and application architectures, as well as the IT organizations to support them, mirrored the corporate structures from which they emerged. Born of the desire to control MDCs from the central offices of large multinationals, the financial and accounting divisions needed the tools to remotely monitor corporate and divisional performance based on financial metrics. This spurred the development of early financial applications, exemplified by the GE example in its Louisville facility in the 1950s.

The IT organizations since these times have typically reported through and have been accountable to the financial organizations of the firm, and have been managed from a cost control and expense management point of view. This is generally true of all corporations; however, in manufacturing organizations there is an additional complication. Manufacturers have a dual information organization that arose to support two distinct functional needs—one for the typical business and financial processes and one to support manufacturing and production processes. These two computing paradigms emerged in parallel from completely different foundations and for completely different purposes, and yet the technology trends of today are forcing them to share many overlapping technologies and information management objectives.

As manufacturers seek new ways to improve their products and manufacturing processes, to control supply chains and inventory levels, and to shorten production cycle times, they understand that process information from the plant floor is crucial; however, the differences in the computing disciplines and architectures between manufacturing and business systems make obtaining and leveraging this information for strategic purposes difficult.

Manufacturing is representative of most industries in the sense that it has the same view of IT and has shared in the same evolution of computing platforms and architectures, as well as software applications; however, manufacturing also had dual silos of computing that derive from different legacies of purpose. The heritage of the traditional IT organization was from a financial control and accounting perspective. The heritage of the industrial automation department common to manufacturers stems from an engineering background. The computing platforms, tools, and objectives were far different from one another.

We have discussed how the historical development of IT caused its current perception problems in the business world today. The same phenomenon occurred in the parallel evolution of controls and IT in manufacturing organizations. The fact that they are now converging as a result of the adoption of common computing platforms and networking infrastructure is not that surprising. What is surprising is that organizations still have not taken complete advantage of the information opportunity that exists. While the need for more information about plant capacity, global inventory levels, throughput and product quality data, and on-time shipment has driven IT and controls closer together, much more opportunity exists for better performance of these assets in support of information-based competitive strategies.

ENTER THE ENTERPRISE APPLICATION

Several software companies emerged as the leaders of the client-server era. Enterprise software vendors were busily developing software applications that provided specific functionality for various departments of business enterprises. For example, SAP developed its enterprise resources planning (ERP) application initially for the mainframe, but when its client-server version was released, it took off. SAP's R/3 release contains functionality for purchasing departments, financial accounting, costing functions, materials management, production and capacity planning, sales and distribution, and most recently, Internet portal functionality called mySAP.com. SAP's market share of the ERP marketplace grew to a dominant portion of the client-server software marketplace. But all of these ERP applications had common features based around providing robust functionality to all departments and business functions. Importantly, these applications were not developed solely for manufacturing companies. They were also used for financial services firms, retailing firms and others as they too saw the need and the benefits of integrating all of their diverse business functions around a single database for the firm. This would allow huge benefits from common processes and common systems, as well as reducing application proliferation and the resulting higher support costs.

The strategic importance of enterprise applications had grown considerably, reaching into virtually every organization and function within global corporations. Nonetheless, they continued to develop more functionality as well as buying other firms to add needed functionality to help them continue their penetration into the enterprisewide operations of companies. They also expanded away from their manufacturing roots into other industries as their penetration into the large manufacturing firms deepened. This led them into financial services, banking, insurance, and many other industries over time. The tremendous growth in departmental and enterprise applications was enabled by the client-server distributed architecture as well as the massive adoption of the PC by both corporations and individuals.

The point of this discussion is that the client-server era enabled software vendors to begin selling their solutions to different buyers from the traditional IT organizations. This engaged others in the purchasing process for strategic software applications based on how they could improve specific operations of the business.

The Internet explosion of the late 1990s and early 2000s continued the wave of changes in IT architectures and support organizations. Life, as corporate IT departments had previously known it, was about to change. The early uses of the Internet involved posting marketing materials to a corporation's web site. These static web sites were created and maintained by the marketing organizations of these firms.

Soon more tools were available to sell to marketing organizations to develop and maintain web sites, as well as conduct business transactions on them. Online catalogs, product configurators, pricing applications, and personalization products started to appear, along with other e-commerce applications. Marketing organizations were in control of these early web sites because they were primarily used for marketing purposes. E-business consulting firms were calling on the marketing departments of major corporations to sell services for the first time. The web sites that were developed required more than technology support. They required the assistance of branding agencies and creative services firms and the software tools, infrastructure, and hardware to run them. Marketing had control over all of these decisions in the early years of the web. Again, this demonstrates the continued trend toward ubiquitous computing at all levels of a corporation.

All applications in business enterprises were now becoming web-enabled, with support for web browsers built into their product strategies. The e-business wave continued the trend of the client-server era of IT, except it extended it to virtually every organization of the firm. While the client-server enterprise applications clearly extended their reach into many areas of corporations, by no means had they completely penetrated the potential user base of their products.

The web, however, provided tools and information access to virtually all users with PCs on their desktops. If their role in their corporation did not require them to use the Internet for their job, then certainly they were able to access the Internet from home. Increasingly, the users of corporate software were using home PCs for Internet access, e-mail, online chats, and other communication functions. Internet telephony has taken off, although it has some maturing ahead of it.

The widespread corporate adoption of the Internet in all business functions will have similar, if not more dramatic, IT organizational implications than the other shifts in IT architecture and application distribution did. We have seen incremental adjustments to the Internet phenomenon by today's corporations, but the changes are extensions of the existing paradigm of managing IT as a function, not empowering IT as a strategic imperative. The main shift engendered by the Internet has been engaging all organizational functions and increasingly more PC and technology-literate executives and staff in the IT dialogue of the firm. More than ever, the value of the Internet to individuals has opened their thinking to the more strategic value of the IT functions of the firm. This will be a primary contributor to the ability of business professionals to participate in and drive the technology agenda for the corporations of the future. This is the beginning of the distributed CIO role in leading-edge corporations.

ORGANIZATIONAL STRUCTURES AND OUTCOMES

Today's IT organizations are largely structured along two dimensions: providing support to the business units, and the technology silos that are required to provide business unit support. At the macro level, IT has typically reported to the financial organization, frequently to the CFO. This is a derivative of IT's legacy of developing and supporting financial and accounting applications from the outset. This accounting control and orientation has led to the management of IT as an expense as opposed to viewing IT as an opportunity. As a management consultant, as soon as I notice on the organizational chart that IT reports to the financial organization rather than directly to the CEO of a firm, I can begin to make assumptions about how the IT function is viewed by the leaders of the firm.

Information technology is a strategic function, and it should always report directly to the CEO, regardless of the firm's industry, industry position, size, or structure. Information technology leaders of today must have access to the business vision, mission, and strategy in order to be a contributing force to achievement of the business objectives of the firm. This cannot be a filtered or interpreted viewpoint even one reporting layer removed. Information technology must participate in the creation and implementation of corporate strategy. The structure of the IT organization below its reporting relationship to the executive functions of a firm becomes the next issue to tackle. Depending on whether the organization is a large global firm or a midsized national or regional firm, the structure of the firm and the subsequent structure of the IT organization will vary.

This book does not tackle the issues of how best to organize IT to support the business organization. Rather, we focus on the principles of IT organization that, when implemented, will lead to a dynamic structure of IT that helps drive competitive advantage according to the business strategy and divisional or strategic business unit (SBU) objectives. This topic, however, merits at least some discussion.

The macrostructure of the firm may require a centrally organized structure; a divisional structure with shared central office functions such as human resources, marketing, and management; or an SBU structure with a central office with shared functions combined with these stand-alone businesses that have their own self-contained services. There are also hybrid structures depending on the firm size, geographic coverage, and other factors. These decisions, as most scholars would advocate, are based on corporate strategy.

The structure of the firm always follows the strategy of the firm. In fact, most theorists today believe that there is no one best way to organize a firm. What is important is that there be a fit between the organization's strategy and structure, its size, its technology, and the requirements of its environment. Other factors influence corporate organizations, such as pure size, supply chain structure, and even imitating other firms in the same or other industries.

There are performance implications from any macro-level organizational structure models as well. A recent *Wall Street Journal* piece summarizes the problem nicely: "As companies grow more global, they keep running into the same basic management dilemma . . . is it more efficient to organize by product line or organize by geography?"[3] Exide Corporation launched a restructuring initiative that changed its structure from a geographical, country manager business model to a product-based structure organized by product lines such as car batteries and industrial batteries for high-tech equipment. This restructuring was meant to eliminate the geographical business units competing with one another for business, which suboptimized margin attainment and overall revenue.

There are pros and cons for each structure, and performance implications of both. In fact, many firms find themselves swinging from one extreme to the other as they realize that there are positive aspects of each, but also downsides as well. For example, in the product model, efficiencies can be gained from standardizing manufacturing, launching products worldwide faster, coordinating global pricing, and eliminating redundant manufacturing capacity. Benefits of the geographic model include better product localization and regional customization, faster decision making, and pricing flexibility based on local needs.

Swinging too far either way can create chaos and impede performance overall based on the organizational upheaval that accompanies many change initiatives of this magnitude. Ford experienced these issues in the Ford 2000 reorganization that changed functional units, such as product development, and geographical units, and sales and marketing, into a global automotive operation.

While these changes saved some $5 billion during the first three years, the reorganization cost Ford market share in Europe.

Procter & Gamble's restructuring plan transformed it from a country organization structure to global business units based on product categories such as paper products, feminine protection, and beauty care.[4] The goals of this plan were to shore up sales and shift the firm to a global operation for its core brands and products, such as Tide laundry detergent, Crest toothpaste, and Pampers diapers. Similar to Ford and Exide, however, P&G's organizational makeover did not anticipate the massive organizational upheaval from moving thousands of employees into new jobs within new organizations.

Regardless of the structure chosen to support a given corporate strategy, executives must understand that the selected structure will have an indelible impact on the organization's ability to execute strategy.

These discussions demonstrate how the structure of a firm can play a determinant role in the behavior of its constituents. The IT function evolved in modern corporations out of Industrial Age corporate structures. These structures, as we traced in Chapter 2, have changed and adapted as corporations have changed and adapted, from the first division of labor in early factories to the MDC of the Industrial Age. Tracing the evolution of the early IT organizations from the 1950s through today has shown how they arose from the corporate finance organization to support the early financial and accounting applications. The behavior of the IT organization and the treatment of the IT function by the firm resulted in a mode of operation based on controlling costs and being managed as an overhead expense rather than as a value driver of the firm.

In order to break the historical paradigm of "controlling IT," we need to reconsider how it is structured in a New Economy firm. How should IT be structured for a large, geographically distributed organization? How should the technology silos that will inevitably continue to exist be maintained to retain necessary expertise while supporting an increasingly web-centric and horizontally integrated organizational and business processes?

ORGANIZING IT: PRINCIPLES FIRST

Organizing the IT function of a corporation in support of its macro-level structure is one of the more critical decisions executives face. It was not always this way, as we have learned. The Principle of Information Darwinism suggests that the melding of corporate strategy and IT strategy will necessitate a corporate structure that frees the information function from the tethers of its Industrial Age roots and truly enables information to be unleashed to drive the business model. Classical thinking suggests determining corporate strategy first, then deciding the organizational structure that will best implement that strategy. The IT organization would then, eventually, be mapped to support the corporate structure. Of course, conventional approaches would have an IT strategy developed after the corporate strategy was completed, with the IT function still held in a subservient role to the operational strategies of the business units.

But today's world is different. Because information strategy, in the broad sense that we have defined it, must now be a critical element of corporate strategy, the corporate organizational structure must be based on competing on information. The implications of this notion are far-reaching. Information technology strategy *is* corporate strategy. The corporate macro-level organizational design must build the information-enabling capabilities into all facets of the firm. This may require a radically different conceptualization of how to distribute the information functions in support of the information asset-intensive mode of competing.

But no matter how these organizations ultimately manifest their operating characteristics, their form and structure must always be dictated by the corporate strategy of the firm. Take this position one step further: IT must be structured and organized to help *drive* corporate strategy, as opposed to being constrained and managed by corporate finance objectives. Information technology in this sense cannot be structured the same way it always has following the legacy of reporting to the financial organization. Information technology must be structured, organized, and deployed much differently for the forward-thinking organization of the future. Information technology must be a key element of corporate strategy, and not a follow-on planning activity once the corporate strategy has been finalized. If IT is to be properly positioned in a modern corporation, the IT leaders have to be active contributors to shaping the agenda of the firm, the corporate strategy, the structure of the organization, the core capabilities required to compete in the chosen markets, and so on. There can no longer be a division between corporate strategy and IT strategy. That is what separates the Next Wave leaders from the firms of the Industrial Age: the defining of IT into the core activities of the firm, from strategy through execution of strategy and measurement of results. So, given the stated position that IT strategy is corporate strategy, much like e-business is really just business using the web, how do we structure the IT function of the modern corporation so that it supports the adaptive strategy required today?

There are many ways that IT can be organized to support the business structure of a firm. According to Bernard Boar, there are six basic IT designs, with multiple permutations and variations, that a firm may use to organize its information management functions:

1. *Functional structure.* Employees are organized into vertical groups based on functional skills and expertise.

2. *Matrix structure.* Employees are organized along two dimensions, with reporting and accountability to two sets of management.
3. *Product structure.* Employees are grouped into self-contained structures according to the production and end-to-end delivery of a family of products.
4. *Geography structure.* Employees are organized into self-contained units that deliver all the products and services to a specific geographical region.
5. *Front-end/back-end structure.* Employees are organized into customer-facing functions such as sales, product marketing, and customer service based on servicing customers using the products and services developed and supported by back-end functions such as product development, engineering, and R&D.
6. *Process structure.* Employees are grouped into horizontal units that deliver products and services according to the needs of specific business processes.[5]

According to Boar, most IT organizations tend to be a blend of functional and product structures. The organization of IT staff typically is structured according to technologies first, then by product teams serving specific internal customers second. For example, MVS teams supported the IBM mainframes; UNIX teams supported the Hewlett-Packard, Sun, and IBM flavors of UNIX; and PC support teams concentrated on the desktop hardware, software, peripherals, and LAN connectivity. At the same time, the software developers and application support staff were organized to support internal divisions or product groups. These teams needed the business knowledge of how the internal customers wanted to run their business with the chosen applications and functionality.

Information technology platforms were vertically segregated for better support of the users, and these functional concentrations of expertise provided stability, consistency of support services, and overall organizational stability. There was little need for cross-collaboration among these technology silos, and the development teams supporting the internal customers were largely unaffected by this vertical structure; however, this model no longer applies to the modern IT environment. There are two major issues with this IT organizational model. First, the Internet has created a massive wave of information sharing, with the content being largely rich media such as photos, music and other audio content, applications, and active web pages, among others. This is occurring across multiple heterogeneous computing platforms, which require collaboration across technologies and coordination among the support teams. The traditional vertical technology-based structures fostered loyalty to their particular technologies versus the types of cooperation and teamwork required in the Internet age of computing. The second issue with the industrial IT organizational model is that, according to Boar, it was "designed for stability and predictability. Its structure was designed to preserve rather than change." Boar continues:

> During the mainframe era of the industrial age, change was very slow and predictable. The smokestack structure took on a mechanistic and bureaucratic flavor as it would ponderously introduce or experiment with new technologies. Change was routinely viewed as a threat rather than an opportunity.[6]

From a technology perspective, IT organizations have had to maintain their focus on legacy technologies as mainframes and other legacy systems have persisted in some cases. While maintaining their legacy systems, however, firms have had to continue to adopt new architectures and technologies as they have emerged, including the adoption of PCs in corporate computing, the rise of microprocessor-based enterprise servers as alternatives to minicomputers and mainframes, the adoption of client-server architectures in all businesses, and now the widespread permeation of the Internet in all facets of corporate computing and personal computing. This is a natural evolution of technology. The sooner the legacy applications are migrated onto more modern hardware and software architectures, the sooner the organization can eliminate legacy platforms and retrain the associated support personnel.

The previous discussion serves as a primer for how IT has been organized in the past; however, the IT structures of the past have been held hostage to the corporate organizational structures of the Industrial Age. They have been subservient to the finance departments of firms, treated as overhead or as cost centers frequently, and have been "managed" from a cost containment perspective rather than from an investment perspective. This has led to many of the problems of business-to-IT alignment that are well documented in the literature. As hinted at throughout this chapter, IT can no longer have an alignment issue with the business units. That is not the problem. The problem now is driving the business units to an information-intensive competitive model. That is, the businesses must help drive their operations, their customer interfaces, and their production systems to an information-driven execution model. Information technology does not support the business. Information *is* the business. Information technology drives the execution of business processes, which are based on information. Corporate strategy does not dictate the IT strategy. The corporate strategy builds information-competitive strategies into the business model, which requires IT to drive revenue, cost reductions, execution of the strategy, and tracking of success. In this scenario, there is no correct IT organization and no correct way to deploy IT resources. Instead, we derive a set of principles that will be used to build the IT-based corporation of the Next Wave. This corporation will exemplify the Principle of Information Darwinism. These firms will win in the marketplace, and their executives will thrive as a result of using information in unique and strategic ways to survive, compete, reproduce, and adapt over the long haul.

WHY ALIGNMENT IS *NOT* THE PROBLEM

The classic "alignment" problem was not IT's fault. Rather, it was inevitable as the pace of change in industry and technology exposed fundamental weaknesses in many firms' business strategies, which further exposed weaknesses in their IT capabilities, along with many other functions.

Alignment is *not* the problem. Alignment is a symptom of the business placing blame on IT for not engaging in a dialogue, versus two independent monologues, about how technology can and should drive the competitive strategies of firms today. Business change is causing the problem of alignment. That is, the need to rapidly adjust business strategies because interludes of competitive advantage are more fleeting and because competitors are more able to quickly copy successful tactics and regain lost ground has forced business leaders into actions they are not necessarily trained for. It used to be that a strategy could remain absolute and fairly stable because the business landscape was stable and unchanging. Remember that evolutionary change can slow in response to a lack of change in the surrounding landscape. That does not mean that change is not occurring, or that the internal mutation rate of the particular species has slowed. It simply means that environmental conditions, and natural selection, have not changed the selection filters that make certain physical capabilities of life-forms more advantageous over others in their ability to survive, compete, and differentially reproduce. Over the long time frames of evolution, this means adapting across generations of change.

So in a sense, the alignment issue derives from the discomfort experienced by business leaders in trying to make sense of their world and being forced to change their tactics and strategies, sometimes radically, in order to remain a viable business enterprise and sustain their fitness levers of revenue growth, market share retention and growth, and profitability. The senior management angst has thus "rolled" downhill to the IT organizations as a reason for the problem. Again, this is simply pointing fingers at convenient targets based on gut reaction rather than analysis and careful study.

Alignment is also a logical outcome of underinvesting in IT historically, which created the need for increased IT spending in recent years. Executives today blanch when faced with a dramatic increase in their technology budgets, but what they fail to realize is that sooner or later, the underspending from the last 10 to 15 years has to catch up with them. This also leads to the "alignment" myth. This is what I affectionately refer to as the "Rip Van Winkle Syndrome," where a business fails to invest in its IT infrastructure and application portfolio over the years, then suddenly wakes up 20 years later to see that it now has to renovate its entire IT operation from top to bottom. This is an untenable situation in today's business world, where such a phenomenon would be considered a case of corporate malfeasance.

Alignment is a strategic business problem, not an IT problem. Blaming information technology for the shortsightedness of business leadership is only a reflection of a chosen paradigm, perhaps an inherited paradigm, of how the technology functions of the firm should be managed and controlled. It is an attitude deriving from the Industrial Age of IT management.

Alignment is an inevitable outcome of Industrial Age IT management, where the business makes its decisions independent of the role of technology in not merely supporting the business but also in driving the future value proposition of the firm's stated goals, objectives, and itinerant competitive advantage.

ROLE OF IT HAS CHANGED, BUT MANAGEMENT DID NOT REALIZE IT

Competing on information in the fashion posited by the Principle of Information Darwinism and the value discipline of Information Mastery, we need to expand our definition of information along with our definition of information management. The role of IT has changed more than the things IT management takes care of. It is the role of IT and how information value is defined and delivered that we are concerned with in this book. A broader treatment of information and its management will be a requirement of competing in the Information Age. A starting point is redefining the scope of what information management really is. Information management in all subsequent discussions includes all activities involved with information strategies, assets, systems, processes, organizations, and behaviors for both internal and external firm activities. Information management is not solely management of IT the way it has always been done. This is a cost-control approach, a vestigial carryover from the Industrial Age of IT management. This approach is not appropriate for today's economy. The approach advocated here is one not of control but of value, of releasing the information value contained in the firm already, as well as harnessing future information value that is yet unrealized.

IT ORGANIZATIONAL STRATEGIES AND PRINCIPLES

The roots of today's IT management structures and philosophies derive from the incipient IT applications of the 1950s, which were developed from a financial and accounting functional point of view. As demonstrated with the organizational structures and hierarchical management tenets of the first large MDCs, these also had tremendous legacies that stemmed from a financial control and accounting philosophy. These two sets of conditions created the current IT environment that corporations, despite their purported leading-edge thinking, have fostered into the new millennium. These IT management philosophies include the following:

- Manage and control IT costs, versus investing in IT opportunities.
- IT is an expense that must be controlled, as opposed to an opportunity that could be exploited.
- IT is an afterthought of corporate strategy, versus IT is a driver of corporate strategy.
- CIOs should report to the CFO/COO organization, versus CIOs reporting directly to the CEO.
- IT must be aligned with the business, versus IT must drive business alignment with the marketplace and customers.
- IT must support the business model, versus IT must drive the business model.
- IT must be viewed as an opportunity, not as a liability.
- IT must be used as a strategy lever, not as a strategy inhibitor.

Clearly, there has to be a better way. Perhaps the following IT strategy and organizational principles provide some hints:

IT Strategies

- Define the new value of information for the corporation.
- Define the new role of IT in the Information Age.
- Create new processes for managing information in the business enterprise.
- Develop new metrics for information-intensive competition, such as information conversion.

IT Organizational Principles

- IT must report directly to the top executive of a firm in order to participate in the creation and realization of corporate strategy.
- IT must be tightly linked to the business functions of the firm, which can be accomplished in a variety of ways; one clear link is holding IT accountable to profitability and cost reductions via information-based initiatives.
- IT must be allowed to participate in and in some cases drive the specific business strategies that will lead to competitive advantage.

- IT must be integrated into business operations in explicitly clear and visible ways.
- IT must be operated with a new charter: drive new value for the corporation.
- IT will define information management in a more strategic context, one that encompasses the core business processes of the firm.

NOTES

1. Burton Grad, *The First Commercial Univac I Installation,* 1997 (www.softwarehistory.org/Grad1.htm).
2. Ibid.
3. Joann S. Lublin, "Place vs. Product: It's Tough to Choose a Management Model," *Wall Street Journal* (June 27, 2001), p. A1.
4. Ibid.
5. Bernard H. Boar, *Strategic Thinking for Information Technology* (New York: John Wiley & Sons, 1997), pp. 217–218.
6. Ibid., p. 223.

5

INFORMATION MANAGEMENT IN BUSINESS EVOLUTION

Nearly every great discovery in science has come as the result of providing a new question rather than a new answer.

—Paul A. Meglitsch

Chapter 4 reviewed the evolution of information technology (IT) as we know it today. We have seen how the IT organization and structures of today derive from the corporate strategies and structures of the Industrial Age. In addition, by tracing the evolution of information technologies, from the hardware platforms to the variety of software applications that exist today, we can understand how IT has attempted to resolve the need to manage multiple technologies transparently to the needs of the business. The business, however, has no empathy for the challenges of IT. After all, the IT organization must be managed and controlled, at least by the tenets of Industrial Age thinking. Information technology's track record of managing the technology shifts of client-server and the desktop revolution was not so stellar according to many corporate managers. Look at how IT spending ballooned, how enterprise applications spun out of control—overbudget and months to years late. Some CEOs might exclaim: "How can we trust IT? They do not understand how to run this business, and I certainly would not trust them to do so."

But our review of the technology shifts and the rapid proliferation of software applications has demonstrated that, if anything, IT has managed this incredible rate of change quite well, all things considered. Now IT is in a position to add incredible value to today's corporations as a result of three fundamental developments: (1) the widespread adoption of personal computers (PCs) in homes and businesses, (2) the rapid adoption of the Internet by businesses and consumers in everyday use, and (3) the Year 2000 phenomenon, which created a new awareness of both the pervasiveness of computing throughout global corporate operations and the ability of IT to understand the business processes that employ IT in their day-to-day functions. Information technology rose to the challenge of Y2K, no matter how overhyped it may have been as an event, and made it a nonissue for virtually all corporations.

The software is why firms buy the hardware, not the reverse. In the new role of IT, the software must drive the hardware, which in this case is the corporation, the company's physical infrastructure. If the application needs of the corporation are defined concurrently with the strategy of the firm (merging IT and corporate strategy), the lag between the business and the IT will shrink.

Completing this analogy, when a firm announces a new strategy and a new organizational structure to support it, the IT organization is typically a secondary planning activity. Information technology strategy and IT organizational designs always lag behind the corporate strategy and corporate structure, but the IT organization is the "software application" of the firm, the adaptive mechanism that allows the firm to compete and survive, replicate and adapt over time.

Today, however, the role of IT is different from what it was during the Industrial Age of IT. The new role of IT is strategic enabling of corporate objectives through the application of technology in products, processes, and business execution. Information technology is *not* a support organization in accomplishing these tasks. Information technology is the driving capability of the Next Wave of digitally evolved corporations. This is a critical distinction and is essential to the Principle of Information Darwinism. The corporations and executives that are best able to apply technology to all aspects of their corporate operations will survive the inevitable evolutionary selection and deselection of firms by the business edition of natural selection.

In this chapter, we discuss the categories of IT spending to offer a framework for analysis of IT investments based on the Principle of Information Darwinism. What IT spending, for example, confers the advantages of agility on a corporation? What IT spending facilitates the replication functions of a firm? What IT investments will help a firm compete and survive day to day in its core franchises? What becomes apparent is that analyzing IT spending according to old categories of Industrial Age management is an old framework meant to control IT. We instead develop a framework that analyzes IT spending as an investment for the future growth of the corporation.

NEW ROLE OF IT

No longer solely managing today's information needs—IT must play a role in defining tomorrow's information value as revenue streams, as well as contributing actively to cost-saving opportunities. Information technology is now a proactive business discipline that positions a firm for future opportunities by ensuring enterprise agility and business value migration. Information technology, therefore, is an essential tool for business evolution, the ability of the corporation of today to adapt to changes in the business environment as the firm is confronted by them. We discuss IT management concepts to lay the groundwork for a new IT management philosophy. This new IT management philosophy is essential to drive the new value equation for IT, to help bridge the value gap between the Industrial Age method of managing IT and the Information Age method of managing IT.

ARCHITECTURE, ARCHITECTURE, ARCHITECTURE

One of the first questions I ask during an IT consulting engagement is "What is your IT architecture?" I attempt to get a concise description of the high-level decisions a particular firm has made with regard to the goals of the business, hardware and software platform choices, infrastructure decisions, enterprise software decisions, and, of course, application portfolio choices.

These architecture decisions are critical for firms trying to support the business strategy with a given IT budget and a set of constraints imposed on them from legacy systems and past investments. The architecture is a road map that can help the IT organization get from here to there within established spending guidelines. "Here" is the installed base of existing infrastructure, hardware and software platforms, and the portfolio of applications used to run the business. "There" is the indeterminate future based on where the business is going strategically and tactically, as well as where the IT world is going with increased rates of technological change, increased computing power at less cost, the rise of pure web-based solutions based on new tools and component technology, and more that is new to many IT shops. "There" is the unknown. The challenge for the IT organization is to define an architecture that is able to accomplish the "getting there" from "here" functions of the firm based on IT and the business strategy.

Managing a firm's IT architecture becomes a central task facing CIOs as an ongoing function of their organization. There are several ways to make sense of IT architecture. "The Zachman Framework," developed by John Zachman in 1987 while he was with IBM, was a sorely needed early attempt to define a "Framework for Information Systems Architecture."[1] Zachman observes that during the early 1980s, researchers recognized the notion of architecture, but the concept had not been defined or further developed into a set of principles and ideas for application to corporate information assets.

The Zachman Framework, in its enterprise form, was a logical structure for identifying, classifying, and organizing the elements of a business enterprise that are essential to the management of the business enterprise as well as the development of the information systems supporting the enterprise. The basis for the Zachman Framework comes from the disciplines of architecture and construction as well as from engineering and manufacturing.

Zachman recognized the fact that businesses were making systems design decisions "out of context," resulting in suboptimization and wasted costs and effort. The remediation of this situation—making the systems that were installed actually achieve their original design intent—was financially prohibitive after the fact. Many organizations found themselves in this situation "after about fifty years of building automated systems, out-of-context. They have a large inventory of 'current systems,' built out-of-context, not integrated, not supporting the Enterprise, that are too costly to replace." As a matter of fact, the inventory of existing systems has come to be referred to as "the legacy," a kind of "albatross," a penalty to be paid for the mistakes of the past.[2] Zachman's early work in creating a framework for documenting and analyzing a corporation's IT architecture set the stage for the wave of technological change that was to befall the IT professionals of that time.

Architecture can be described in many ways, but all the definitions converge around a set of common concepts. Weill and Broadbent define an architecture as "an integrated set of technical choices used to guide the organization in satisfying business needs."[3] An IT architecture then is a set of policies and rules that governs the use of IT and plots a path to the way business will be done in the future.[4] An architecture is not fixed, but rather must be constantly reviewed and updated as technology and business intent change. An architecture must cope with business uncertainty and technological change, which makes it one of the most challenging activities for a company. As stated previously, IT staffs had actually done a respectable job of navigating the intense rate of change that was hurled at them by the IT industry. A good architecture, as Weill and Broadbent observe, evolves over time and is documented and accessible to all managers in the firm, and consists of policies and guidance for the following types of technology choices[5]:

- *Computing,* such as the hardware and operating systems for desktops, servers, and other functions
- *Communications and networking,* including data and voice
- *Data,* such as data dictionaries, information repositories, database design, naming conventions, and how data will be shared by common users
- *Applications,* which actually run the business; the goal is to drive toward common systems and minimize application proliferation.

- *Work activities,* which means standard business processes, process definition and documentation, and the system and technology requirements to support these business processes. Some firms call this a "bill of process" similar to a bill of material for a manufactured product.

These policy guidelines lead to decisions regarding purchasing and vendor management, and standardization on specific hardware, software, and related components to help ensure compatibility, consistency, and economies of scale for the firm. They must all support the information requirements of the corporation first and foremost.

Boar defines IT architecture as "a series of principles, guidelines, or rules that guide an organization through acquiring, building, modifying, and interfacing IT resources throughout the enterprise."[6] Boar suggests using the concepts of reach, range, and maneuverability as three critical dimensions of IT capabilities. Information technology architecture reach describes the facets of the IT function that influence who can access information, from where, from what devices, as well as what specific information. This is the information distribution capability of a firm.

Information technology architecture range describes the formatting or contextualization of information with internal and external users, such as customers, suppliers, and partners. Range defines how information is structured for use by classes of users based on their needs and functions.

Finally, IT architecture maneuverability describes the factors that contribute to increasing the flexibility or agility of the architecture.

Lorin uses the following five statements to describe his view of architecture. According to Lorin, an architecture:

1. Is a statement of vision but also a statement of constraints. It must provide limits for design efforts (as design must limit development).
2. Must be costable within a broad range. Expenditure levels must be inferable from architectural standards.
3. Must identify industry standard parts to be used in development and construction.
4. Must provide support for a broad window of business strategies.
5. Must provide for the evolution and replacement of components over time. Migration costs must be built into the architecture.[7]

In fact, Lorin suggests that the concept of "architecture" used in reference to IT is a dangerous one. This building metaphor for IT management implies a fixed, unchanging structure rather than a fluid, amorphous, and flexible entity. While IT may take on the particular style of its time (e.g., centralized mainframe architectures versus client-server architectures compared to modern n-tier architectures), the intent of IT architecture is not to freeze IT investments permanently. The rates of change in the business of IT are too swift to be locked down in the sense of the building metaphor, and business strategies and tactics can change as quickly.

These discussions of IT architecture have common themes. All have a goal of supporting the business activities of the firm. They all state flexibility as a critical feature of IT architecture, but they are all artifacts of the Industrial Age of IT. While they properly state supporting change in both business strategy and in the technology itself, these views of IT architecture do not incorporate what seems to be clear from today's business environment: that information is far more valuable to a business than merely managing the IT functions of the firm. The IT architecture of an information-based competitor must be aggressively focused on changing the value equation of their results, from delivering information services to the business functions of a corporation to driving the information value of the firm as a basis of competition. This means using information to increase the value and competitive position of the firm relative to its peers. The role of the IT architecture must be different in order to accomplish these goals. The IT architecture must be mapped to the evolutionary goals of surviving, competing, replicating, and adapting over time. The information value in this model is substantially higher than the Industrial Age management techniques companies have been saddled with to date.

Weill and Broadbent characterize the IT portfolio of a firm as "its entire investment in information technology, including all the people dedicated to providing information technology services, whether centralized, decentralized, distributed, or outsourced."[8] In their treatment of IT, Weill and Broadbent treat IT as an investment in computing core capabilities, not as an expense to be managed. They expand on their views of IT:

> The concepts fundamental to managing information technology are those of business, not technology: portfolios, business value, investment, and alignment of resources with strategic goals. The objective of information technology investments is to provide business value in two related ways: to successfully implement current strategies and to use the technology to enable new strategies.[9]

Weill and Broadbent capture the essence of how IT could best be managed given the Industrial Age strategies of controlling cost of IT and relegating it to a support function. They clearly capture the notion of the strategic value of IT in helping implement current business strategies while enabling future, yet-to-be determined business strategies. Boar takes it a bit further in the following summary of the strategic nature of IT:

> In the information age, information technology is of strategic importance. In the industrial age, IT had only a support or factory/production role. In the information

> age, every business becomes dependent on IT. Information technology becomes the business because it defines the way goods and services are produced and exchanged in the marketspace.[10]

This quote clearly foreshadows what has occurred in the Internet Age. Information technology has clearly become strategic. Information technology is the system of production for firms today, even those that utilize physical assets, such as manufacturing plants and machines and equipment. Information is the engine that today makes a greater contribution to the market share, revenue, and profitability of corporations.

MAPPING IT ARCHITECTURE TO BUSINESS FITNESS

We have suggested that the IT architecture defines a set of choices a firm must make to match technology capabilities with the business direction of a firm; however, IT today takes on a much more critical role in fostering business evolution, the adaptation of corporations to the ever-changing business landscape. Weill and Broadbent's discussion of IT categories, with particular emphasis on infrastructure, sets up the mapping of IT spending to business fitness levers. Information technology spending falls into four main categories, according to Weill and Broadbent[11]:

1. *Infrastructure.* Ability to add applications and capabilities, shift strategies, launching pad for strategic intent
2. *Transactional systems.* Support current business, operational efficiency, drive costs down through automation; fine-tuning today's business model and short-term objectives
3. *Informational systems.* Provide the ability to learn, knowledge management, replication systems; enhance customer and product information; competitive assessments of other firms, other firms' products and services, marketing and sales management systems
4. *Strategic systems.* Compete, plan, position for three to five years out—positioning for the future

Exhibit 5.1 shows how these IT architecture components build on one another, beginning with the foundation of infrastructure, then adding transactional systems, followed by informational and strategic technologies.

INFRASTRUCTURE

Weill and Broadbent define infrastructure as the foundation of a firm's IT portfolio. Infrastructure is the "enabling information technology investments,

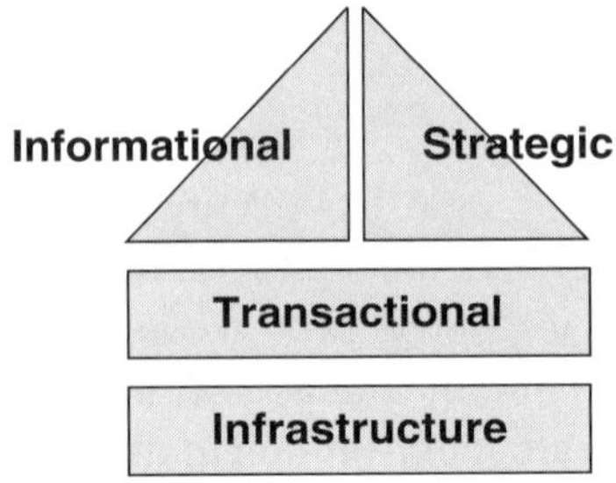

Exhibit 5.1 IT Architecture

Source: Adapted from Peter Weill and Marianne Broadbent, *Leveraging the New Infrastructure* (Boston, MA: Harvard Business School Press, 1998).

which are large, have long lives, are shared by multiple business areas, and support many applications."[12] Infrastructure is delivered as centrally managed shared services provided to the business units of a firm by the IT organization. Typical infrastructure elements include communications and networking for voice and data, data center management, provision and management of large-scale computing resources such as large enterprise servers and mainframe systems, management of large shared applications, firmwide web and intranet capabilities, and research and development of emerging technologies pertaining to infrastructure. The IT application portfolio, which actually performs business computing functions, resides on top of the infrastructure. Investing in infrastructure services increases the speed of application deployment in response to new corporate strategies, which enhances the firm's strategic agility and flexibility.

The value of infrastructure comes from its enabling role in the quick, economical implementation of new business applications, both within business units and enterprisewide. The business applications create business value for the firm, but the infrastructure enables business value to be realized. As Weill and Broadbent note, the advantages of a more robust and extensive infrastructure are the common services that can be provided to and leveraged by the business users in a corporation. These include shared voice and data networks and intranet systems for sharing various types of corporate data within the firm and, for close trading partners, outside of the firm. These are merely a few examples of the standard services that can be exploited from the infrastructure of a firm.

Infrastructure averages 58 percent of a firm's IT budget, representing 70 percent of a firm's centrally managed IT investment and 38 percent of a firm's business unit IT budget.[13] Firms that invested more aggressively in infrastructure services have shown increased benefits. Examples of these benefits include faster revenue growth per employee and more revenue per employee. Firms with more robust infrastructures also demonstrated more sales from new products and speedier time to market for new products. In fact, time to market for these firms, according to Weill and Broadbent, was especially sensitive to the breadth of their infrastructure. Faster time to market with new products was enabled by shared infrastructure by multiple business units and processes across business units. In addition, extending this infrastructure capability to suppliers and customers to share data, enable digital transactions, and collaborate on product designs also drives even more synergies; however, Weill and Broadbent note that firms with less investment in firmwide infrastructure, although more profitable in the short run, are less able to react to shifts in market needs than firms with greater investments in infrastructure.

This "agility" capability appears to be a clear benefit of greater expenditures in more robust, integrated infrastructure. This also highlights one of the main challenges of implementing infrastructure for a corporation: infrastructure must be specified, sized and scaled appropriately, and successfully implemented before the exact business application requirements are known. It is no surprise, then, that infrastructure investments facilitate agile responses to market and technology changes because there may often be excess capacity available for rapid deployment in support of emerging corporate strategies. Because by definition infrastructure has a long useful life span, these investments are planned to be in production for significant periods, often spanning multiple generations of commercial and homegrown applications. Therefore, the technology decisions must be made with an eye toward maintaining as many strategic degrees of freedom as possible for future business and application deployment requirements. A critical requirement of infrastructure planning is maintaining the future option portfolio of the firm. This means that those infrastructure investments must serve a dual purpose: (1) they must support the current business needs of the firm on par or better than their competitors, and (2) they must support a rich variety of competitive advantage options for the firm, allowing it to pursue alternative competitive strategies in response to both market and environmental conditions as well as competitive pressures.

Infrastructure has emerged as a mission-critical IT core competency in recent times, and particularly so as e-business initiatives rose to the forefront of management's attention during the late 1990s. Corporate leaders soon realized that their underinvestment in infrastructure and application portfolio now hampered their ability to migrate various business processes to a web-based execution model, either as pure e-business plays or as hybrid brick-and-mortar plays. This phenomenon occurred across the board in all industries, including manufacturing, financial services, and insurance. In some cases, recent investments in large, enterprisewide systems proved to be as inhibiting to e-business as the failure to invest in a more extensive and agile infrastructure.

Many manufacturers recently invested in enterprise resources planning (ERP) systems. Many did so as Year 2000 compliance initiatives. Others implemented them to take advantage of moving all of their diverse operations to a single business operations platform for the firm. Such systems typically require firms to completely reengineer themselves to fit the software application. This package-based reengineering approach, in my opinion, is not a formula for competitive advantage for a corporation, especially in today's fast-paced world. Investing in these software applications can drive savings by standardizing business processes, establishing a single logical view of the firm for conducting business transactions, and performing the financial rollups for quarterly and year-end reporting. These are all clear benefits from these applications.

The downside of these ERP implementations, though, can be serious. One of the most damning issues, in my opinion, is the fact that corporations are intentionally designing their business around a software application that several direct competitors are also implementing in the same way. In other words, firms in the same industry are implementing the same software solutions by altering their fundamental business processes to fit the requirements of the application. The outcome of this scenario is an industry filled with "me too" competitors who are unable to enrich their business models with new ideas and unique value propositions that may arise from developing and implementing new business processes that may provide competitive advantage. That result seems to be precisely the reason *not* to implement the same solution as a competitor. Many would argue that they customized their ERP implementations to fit the way they perform their business operations. In fact, virtually all of them spent additional millions of dollars to customize their "packaged" commercial off-the-shelf (COTS) application to fit their unique business needs. But if that was the case, why engineer your business to meet the requirements of the application? There is a fundamental problem with changing the core of a business to meet the demands of a software package that was designed by someone completely unfamiliar with the ways a particular firm's business processes are organized and designed to deliver value to its customers.

Another paradox of these ERP solutions derives from the misunderstanding of the value that these systems were ultimately delivering to the business enterprise. While they were sold as competitive advantage–enabling applications, they are actually more like infrastructure. Recall the definition of infrastructure from Weill and Broadbent: Infrastructure consists of the "enabling information technology investments, which are large, have long lives, are shared by multiple business areas, and support many applications."[14] ERP systems by definition are large. Because of the size of the financial and organizational investment, they will have long lives (no IT executive will scrap a $30 million SAP system after two years). Because ERP systems are multimodule solutions with functionality that targets nearly all functions of a business enterprise, they are therefore shared by multiple business areas. Finally, addressing the point about supporting many applications, I would argue that ERP systems *are* the "many applications" that our definition of infrastructure refers to. In every respect, ERP systems are infrastructure investments. Therefore, a business executive would have a difficult time constructing a business case from ERP systems based on clear business impact. Infrastructure is extremely difficult to evaluate on this type of business case. Infrastructure, because of the nature of the investment, *must* be able to support several applications over a long time span. Infrastructure investments are almost always sized and deployed without knowing precise business application requirements.

The paradox of ERP systems comes from the fact that they are infrastructure in all respects *except* in how they provide agility to an enterprise. Once implemented, these rigid and complex systems are difficult to change in response to changing business requirements. A corporation will find itself locked into a particular way of doing business that will require significant modifications to its complex ERP solution in order to change. Because of the single logical database view of the corporation, any changes to one module will potentially affect functionality of other modules. This makes modifying an ERP system a risky and time-consuming activity.

Infrastructure, however, is supposed to enable new business initiatives and new business applications to be deployed without fundamentally altering the underlying infrastructure. Infrastructure, again, is a flexibility and agility technology, an investment in future options for the firm. ERP systems, as discussed, tend to remove enterprise agility and limit future options for the firm. As Anderson observes in "Seven Levers for Guiding the Evolving Enterprise," ERP systems may freeze their adopters into a set of best practices from the 1980s and early 1990s, which may not be the best practices required of the current business environment. ERP systems are designed to "institutionalize and integrate a common set of best practices, not to change those practices in order to keep up with fast-paced shifts in the business environment."[15]

This situation was apparent when e-business captured the hearts and souls of business leaders. In manufacturing, for example, in order to perform simple transactions over a web site, such as ordering products and services, checking product availability, or confirming delivery dates, the interfaces of the web applications to the ERP system have to be developed. This is often not an easy task to accomplish because of the complexity of ERP systems.

The rapid rise of B2B exchanges, for example, similarly exposed the inadequacies of rigid enterprise systems in adapting to new models of business. Web-based business processes clearly demonstrated that the ERP architectures are not the most agile platforms for launching new business processes and supporting e-commerce capabilities. ERP systems are infrastructure solutions that do not behave like infrastructure. E-business initiatives have shown how inflexible ERP architectures are in supporting fluid and dynamic business processes.

Infrastructure's role in the business enterprise is one of enabling performance and ensuring flexibility. Again, infrastructure must support all current and planned business initiatives, but perhaps more important, it must allow all future strategic options to be pursued. Infrastructure is like the central nervous system of a living organism. It is the wiring that connects the moving parts of the living creature, allowing them to work together in a coordinated fashion. Infrastructure enables the physical components of the living organism—the bones, tendons, muscles, and all the complex organs managing their rich variety of unique functions—to work together to ensure the basic survival functions of the life-form. In businesses, this is how the transition from competing on physical asset intensity to competing on information asset intensity begins. The basic "wiring" of the physical enterprise must be accomplished so that the physical entity or entities can be coordinated to perform in a synergistic fashion, in a way such that the whole is greater than the sum of its parts.

Infrastructure is a critical element of an IT architecture. Clearly the Internet has shown how a poor infrastructure can inhibit a firm's ability to rapidly incorporate new business processes into its existing portfolio of skills and capabilities. Evolutionarily speaking, infrastructure is similar to the early development of central nervous systems in living organisms, and in humans, it is similar to the development of culture. These information processing and communication mechanisms help extend the physical structure of our bodies, help adaptation and differential reproduction, and help the basic processes of surviving, competing, reproducing, and adapting. The other elements of IT architecture are only enabled to deliver their contribution to business success based on the success of firmwide infrastructure investments.

TRANSACTIONAL SYSTEMS

Transactional technology consists of the tools and systems that automate repetitive transactions of a firm, such as accounting functions, accounts receivable, accounts payable, order processing, inventory control, electronic funds transfer, and other high- to medium-volume transactions. These technology assets help reduce the unit cost of handling fundamental transactions in higher volumes than is possible with manual human effort. Transactional systems typically utilize many infrastructure services in delivering their value to the enterprise, and in fact having the requisite infrastructure in place significantly reduces the time to benefit for implementing transactional systems. The epitome of transactional systems includes the large ERP systems used in manufacturing and other industry verticals. Typical vendors in this space include SAP, Oracle, and PeopleSoft. These systems are based on the notion of integrating all activities of the business enterprise, including order entry, manufacturing, shipping, finance and accounting, human resources, and more. These systems are able to unite all corporate operations around a single logical database view of the firm. These systems represent significant investments and can take years to implement. Although many purport that there is a clear value proposition behind these investments in transactional technology, the payback may actually be based on common business processes, common systems, and shared knowledge of how the firm conducts business on an operational level. In other words, the payback comes from standardizing the way a firm conducts operations in a repetitive, repeatable fashion.

Spending on transaction technology averaged 12 percent of a firm's total IT portfolio during the research conducted by Weill and Broadbent.[16] This broke down to 8 percent of the central IT budget and 20 percent of the business unit IT budget. Transaction technology, though, has a distinct return on the investment in business value. That value is in supporting productivity improvements, driving operational efficiency, and cutting costs through automation of repetitive transactions. Those benefits make transactional investments a solid business investment, with a payoff returning 25 to 40 percent on every dollar invested. As Weill and Broadbent observe from their research, transactional systems are consistently associated with greater business value and unsurpassed financial performance relative to the other types of IT investments. The more money invested in transactional IT by firms studied by Weill and Broadbent, the stronger the impact on performance. In fact, transaction solutions continued to demonstrate payback to the business for up to three years after the year of initial investment. This impact manifested itself in cutting costs through redesigned business processes and automation of business transactions. But according to Weill and Broadbent, an interesting fact emerged from their research: firms that invested more in transactional technology also had lower revenue growth. This, they surmise, was likely from the cost-cutting focus of firms that implemented transactional systems versus a top-line growth focus, which would have resulted in a different IT emphasis. The bottom-line impact of transaction technology makes these investments lower risk compared to other IT investments. They deliver solid returns with little risk, and as Weill and Broadbent note, they are an important element of a firm's overall IT architecture.

INFORMATIONAL TECHNOLOGY

This set of systems and tools is targeted at managing and controlling a corporation. Typical examples of informational technology include decision support systems, knowledge management systems, product data management systems, customer relationship management (CRM) systems, and the enterprise reporting capabilities of the firm. The "product" of informational systems is a combination of "data, information, and knowledge as an input to decision making and control."[17] Executive information systems fall into this category by providing a single dashboard view of the performance of key business operations across the entire enterprise. These systems typically use both the infrastructure and transactional elements of a firm's IT portfolio to gather, summarize, and contextualize the information for its users.

Informational technology represents on average 16 percent of the IT budget of firms in Weill and Broadbent's analysis; it represented 14 percent of the centrally managed IT budgets and 18 percent of business unit IT investments. Firms that invested heavily in this segment of their IT architecture had business strategies that depended highly on information for their execution. These strategies tended to (1) rely on detailed marketing data; (2) emphasize knowledge management and organizational learning; (3) rely on product and process control with an emphasis on quality; (4) enforce strong cost management practices and employ reporting tools to monitor spending; and (5) conduct vigorous market analysis and competitive intelligence-gathering efforts to spot potential product and service opportunities.[18]

While the payback on infrastructure and transactional technology was largely incontrovertible, the payback on informational technology investments in Weill and Broadbent's study was inconsistent. Firms have always talked a good game with regard to their collection and harvesting of information, but when it comes to demonstrating the results of these efforts, they sometimes tend to fall short of claims. The firms that did invest more in informational technologies demonstrated faster time to market with new products and services, higher product quality, and higher margins on products by being able to charge a premium for them. Informational investments showed more effectiveness when they were implemented at the business unit level. Although evidence strongly suggests that informational technology investments can significantly improve operational results at the business unit level—more so than firm-wide—no financial results were consistently derived from informational investments. Weill and Broadbent conclude that while more information does positively impact operational performance, its impact was not sufficient to influence the bottom line. More and better information does not necessarily generate financial returns to the business, and some corporations are clearly better at deploying and exploiting informational assets. The critical success factor for making informational investments pay off is having clear management processes and measurement systems that collect, analyze, and drive improvements based on informational systems. Dell Computer, for example, and General Electric drive their businesses based on information-based metrics. Treacy and Wiersema also note the almost fanatical data collection and analysis capabilities of firms they cite as demonstrating the value discipline of operational excellence.[19]

STRATEGIC TECHNOLOGY

The final category of IT spending in the framework advocated by Weill and Broadbent is called *strategic technology*. Strategic technologies are meant to deliver competitive advantage to the firm by increasing market share and sales, reducing costs and improving profits, or by providing superior customer service to enhance customer loyalty and reduce customer acquisition costs. As Weill and Broadbent note, firms that have successfully implemented strategic technology projects usually have found a new use of IT for their industry at a particular point in time. This provides first-mover advantage to that particular firm, which, if the technology was developed internally versus commercially, can be difficult for competitors to imitate. This opacity of strategy helps firms extend periods of competitive advantage for longer durations than if they had purchased and implemented commercially available software or technology.

Strategic technology averaged 14 percent of the IT portfolio, which broke down into 8 percent of central IT budgets and 24 percent of business unit spending; however, strategic IT spending has no guaranteed return because it tends to be risky. Weill and Broadbent observed a failure rate of roughly 50 percent with strategic initiatives, with a few selected projects considered successful and the rest merely breaking even financially, retaining competitive position rather than delivering the anticipated positive impact.[20] These initiatives tend to deliver competitive advantage for two to three years before competitors copy them, if they so choose and are able. Their ability to copy these strategic initiatives depends on the sophistication and investment levels in firmwide infrastructure. Without the necessary baseline infrastructure capabilities, strategic applications cannot be successfully launched in response to a competitive move.

Strategic investments demonstrated significant performance payback for the firms that invested successfully and reaped the benefits. Firms that expended more of their IT portfolio on strategic technology demonstrated faster time to market with new products and services, could charge a premium for their products, delivered the perception of higher-quality products, and had higher revenues per employee. The firms that realize these benefits know how to implement strategic technology; in fact, they rely on it for competitive advantage. These firms exploit IT more than their peers, they are the highly differentiated competitors of their industries, and they are more innovative with new products and services. Clearly, there is a pattern of IT investment here that separates these competitors from the others in a particular industry. These firms understand the value of IT investments as a competitive advantage, and they are willing to bear more risk in order to gain competitive advantage. Technology investments such as this begin to behave like research and development (R&D) investments for innovative product companies. The firms are actually developing a portfolio of future products and intellectual property that may pay off in the future, which represents an investment by the firm. Strategic IT investments are similar to R&D expenditures. Some are successful and result in proven competitive advantage, some break even and merely maintain a firm's position relative to its peers, and others are failures. Again, according to Weill and Broadbent, roughly 50 percent of the strategic information technology investments they studied resulted in failure, at least by financial return metrics.

For example, Citibank was able to gain tremendous first-mover advantage when it launched the use of automated teller machines (ATMs) in the 1980s, which changed the face of banking forever.[21] Citibank was able to triple market share based on this two-pronged strategy of reducing costs with electronic banking as well as providing 24-hour service to its customers. As Weill and Broadbent observe, the ATM strategy was initially a strategic system initiative based on its impact on customer service and market share, but it eventually became a transactional system by reducing costs of servicing typical banking transactions with human tellers.[22] Furthermore, with the consolidation of banking and the increasing overlap of ATM networks, banks are now able to share the infrastructure in order to provide ATM service away from their own bank's network of ATMs. By charging fees at both ends of the transaction, banks are making more profit off ATM fees while charging transaction fees to other banks that utilize their shared infrastructure services.

DEVELOPING AN EVOLUTIONARY IT PORTFOLIO

The Weill and Broadbent framework aids the identification of IT functions and their value contribution to a business enterprise. The categories of infrastructure, transactional, informational, and strategic technologies have varying contributions to the organization based on how a firm desires to use them in pursuit of various strategic objectives. The next task is to map these IT architecture elements to the survival requirements of corporations. From the previous discussion, we can already begin to see how aspects of IT investments have direct bearing on the evolutionary capabilities of corporations. For example, infrastructure technology is a major contributor to the agility of a firm. Agility and the ability to launch diverse IT applications to attack competitors or deliver increased value to customers is directly attributable to IT infrastructure investments. Therefore, evolutionarily speaking, IT infrastructure becomes an evolutionary enabler for a firm. Transactional technology is a key investment for driving costs out of a business enterprise through automation of repetitive business transactions. These low-risk, cost-saving investments almost always have a solid payback to the firms that implement them. The ability to take excess costs out of business processes has a direct impact on the bottom-line performance of firms and can reduce process cycle times and improve process quality. Informational and strategic investments contribute their own measures of value to a business enterprise in the unique ways discussed previously. They, too, have evolutionary impact on the survival, competitiveness, replication, and long-term adaptation of corporations to the business environment and to their competitors.

The current challenge is not one of balancing the IT portfolio or optimizing the IT expenditures to gain "alignment" with the business. The ultimate objective is to enable long-term business survival through the use of information in ways that have heretofore not been explored by corporations. The IT organization and structure, the role of IT in the modern business enterprise, and the IT architecture and technology portfolio must serve a much higher purpose in today's global business community. Information technology must drive the business to performance levels that have been constrained by the Industrial Age practices of the past. The modern IT portfolio must be tasked with the direct positive execution of competitive tactics, capable of corporate survival through basic business process execution, and linked to the ability of firms to replicate their business execution models, as well as evolve new models, across generations of disruptive change, discontinuities in technology innovations, and generations of corporate leaders. In the long run, these elements of evolutionary survival result in a firm being adaptable over long periods to business change. Change for corporations is the most often encountered competitor to their business franchises and their competitive landscape. It is constant and accelerating, and hence an evolutionary business model, driven increasingly by information, that will separate the most Darwinian fit firms from their less fit peers.

PATTERNS OF EVOLUTIONARY IT ARCHITECTURE MANAGEMENT

Based on the IT architecture framework, IT investment patterns will vary depending on the evolutionary needs of the corporation and its relative adaptive fit to its business landscape. In times of good corporate health, or high business fitness, IT investments will tend to be different from those in times of poor corporate health or poor business fitness. Recall the business fitness levers of revenue, cash flow, profit, and market share. If corporate performance according to these metrics is suffering, then the company will have poor business fitness. Exhibit 5.2 depicts the interplay among the evolutionary activities of a firm and its IT architecture and application portfolio. This simple illustration shows that the evolutionary goals of a firm will place different demands on its IT architecture and application portfolio.

For example, if a firm's primary objectives are related to survival initiatives, then the IT architecture will tend to emphasize cost-saving initiatives and operating efficiency. Survival goals of a firm relate to protecting core revenue streams by nurturing the core revenue generating customers and ensuring highly efficient business execution processes that support these customers. Given the previous discussion, this means potentially implementing transactional technologies to drive standardization of processes and efficient execution of

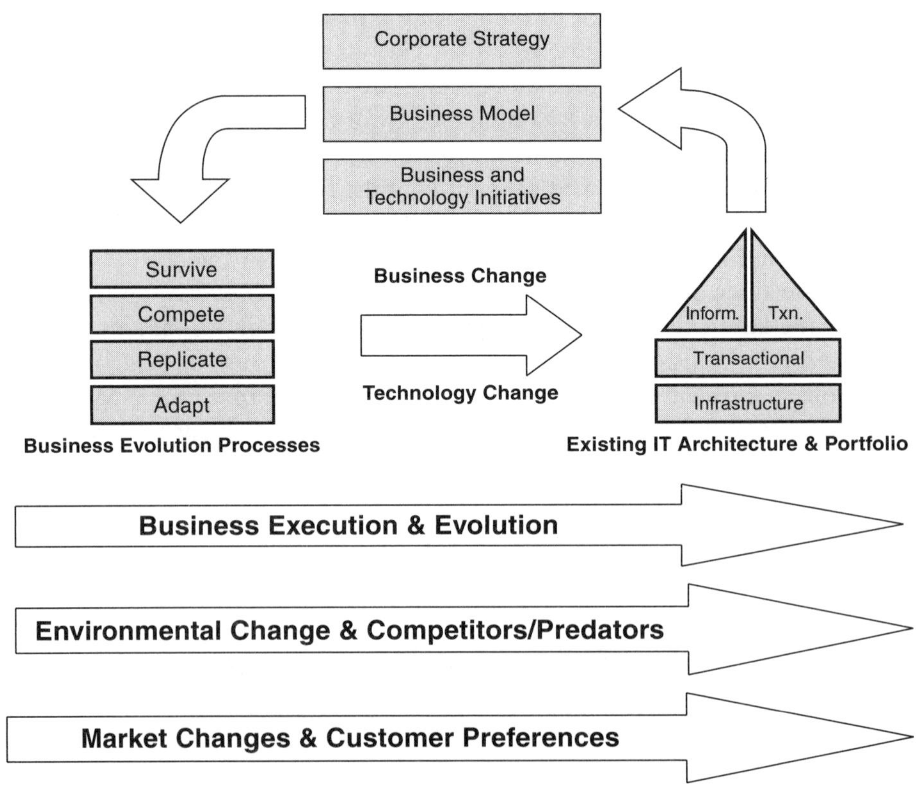

Exhibit 5.2 The Evolutionary Impact on IT Architecture

processes across the enterprise. Survival goals may also require support from informational technologies to provide necessary reporting information and other business management tools to assess performance in operations in order to make better decisions about how to improve them.

Competitive evolutionary goals may require different IT architecture investments to improve a firm's competitive posture versus its direct and indirect competitors. For example, competing better in an industry may require higher investments in strategic and informational technologies. Critical technologies in this case might include CRM and sales force automation technologies to drive better sales performance and customer loyalty. This may require enhancing product development processes, which will allow stronger competitive capabilities by virtue of the products and services offered by a firm. Additionally, informational technology may support competitive goals by providing new data and market research on customer needs and market trends, which will enable a firm to compete better by addressing these needs in unique new ways.

Replication activities of a firm relate to transitioning its business model and processes into new markets, based on new products, and requiring new processes to support both. Replication refers to the innovation processes of a firm that allow it to provide new products and new value to existing markets and customers, as well as create new value to deliver to new markets and new customers. Replication activities are those that help transition a firm to a new generation of technology or corporate leadership. These activities allow a firm to "pass its DNA" onto the next generation of the firm, which may require transitions in technology, leadership, processes, and other factors. The IT architecture elements that support replication activities include strategic investments, informational investments, and pure infrastructure investments, which provide the agility platform for the previous two IT architecture elements. Knowledge capture and organizational learning play a large role in replication, as well as innovation processes of a firm. Rapidly developing and exploiting new technology and tapping into new markets require all elements of the IT architecture to be utilized.

Finally, adaptive activities of a firm will necessitate "working" the IT architecture and application portfolio over longer periods of a corporation's history. This means that alternately spending in all four categories of IT in support of survival, competitive, and replication activities will be required; however, a higher emphasis will be placed on infrastructure, and the associated business flexibility and agility will pay off in a firm's adaptive fitness and its ability to respond to environmental and competitive threats. The infrastructure of a firm's IT architecture will allow it to be more agile and adaptive in information-based responses to market conditions and customer preferences, as well as competitive threats and environmental changes.

Information technology investments should be considered as future options to be potentially exercised given a variety of potential company futures. Exhibit 5.3 shows how patterns of IT investments will cause the IT architecture to evolve in response to corporate strategy and the business model, as well as environmental influences, over time. Environmental influences include market changes and customer preferences, as well as competitors and new entrants. As business and technology changes, the IT architecture will naturally be changed or evolved not only to meet the challenges of the business environment, but also to anticipate the challenges of multiple, unknown business futures.

The evolution of the IT architecture to anticipate business and technological change is a vital requirement of doing business today. As shown in the exhibit, launching business and technology initiatives will place demands on the IT architecture, whether it is to upgrade the infrastructure to allow more flexibility, or whether the needs are a rapid implementation and rollout of a strategic technology that will provide competitive advantage in a particular way

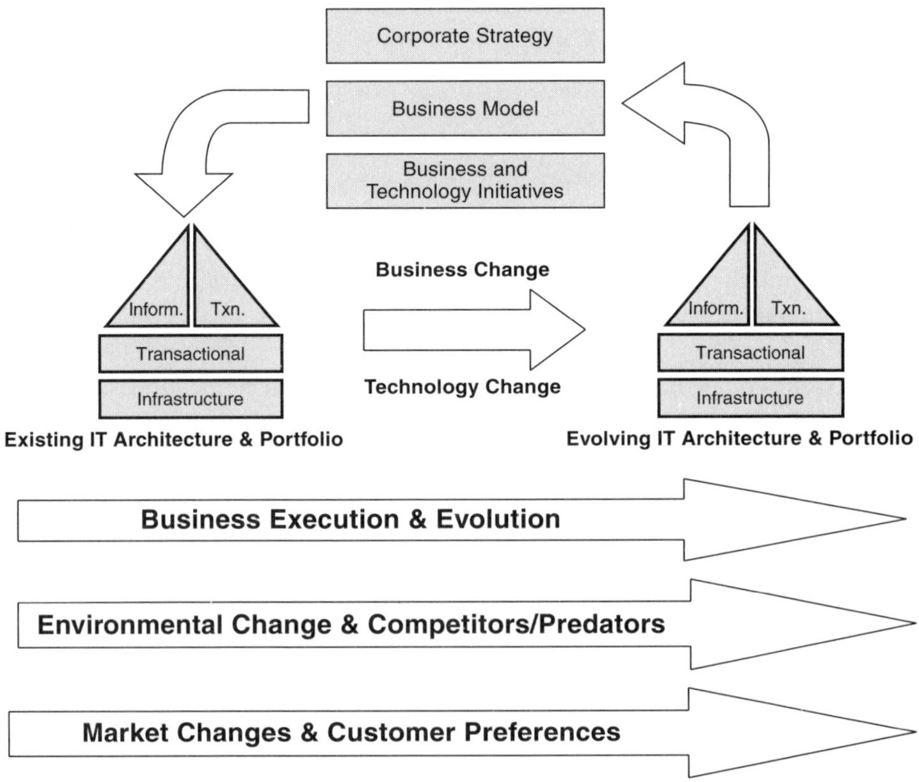

Exhibit 5.3 The Evolving IT Architecture

along a specific dimension of customer-perceived value. In Chapter 6, we place the IT architecture into a business evolution model that demonstrates the critical nature of this "flexing" of the IT architecture. Flexing the IT architecture is not only done in response to corporate strategy and the business model, along with their attendant business and technology initiatives; it is also performed in anticipation of the business and technology changes that are inevitable in today's highly uncertain business environment.

The following list summarizes key elements required of an IT architecture that supports the business evolutionary needs of a firm within the context of business evolution:

- Flexing the IT architecture is a critical capability for a firm, and the ability to use the IT architecture as a competitive weapon in and of itself in driving the business is essential.
- Developing an evolutionary IT architecture means investing in IT architecture elements differentially depending on the evolutionary goals and needs of the firm.
  - Investments in infrastructure, for example, should be an ongoing expenditure of corporate IT dollars based on its importance in launching new initiatives and new strategic applications and in sharing corporate information.
  - Investments in infrastructure should be done *before* the agility is required by the firm in performing its replication and adaptive activities, for example, during times of relative organizational stability and higher adaptive fit to the business landscape.
  - Investments in strategic technology will often map to compete initiatives, which are intended to provide some advantage against head-to-head competition in the marketplace.
  - Investments in transactional technology will often correlate with survive initiatives based on driving efficiency and repeatability of the core business model.
  - Investments in informational technology will often support survive and compete initiatives by facilitating better decisions based on information and reporting capabilities from core processes and operations.

Mapping the information management needs of the business to the business needs of the business involves two exercises: (1) ensuring that the IT architecture can be flexed to support the necessary business and technology initiatives, and (2) evolving the IT architecture so that it can be used as a weapon in conjunction with the selected business and technology initiatives. Flexing the IT architecture, as demonstrated in Chapter 7, will enlist IT as a mission-critical value discipline that is mandatory for business survival today and in the future.

IMPLICATIONS FOR INFORMATION MASTERY

The IT architecture frameworks we have discussed raise important questions for business leaders. Based on the needs of the business and the technology organization, what actions should be taken with regard to an IT portfolio and IT architecture to allow better corporate fitness? The value discipline we have dubbed Information Mastery is necessary for today's business environment. Information Mastery, as depicted in Exhibit 5.4, requires new capabilities and new roles for information management. The IT organization and structure, the role of IT in the modern business enterprise, and the IT architecture and technology portfolio must serve a much higher purpose in today's global business community.

Information Mastery as a new information-based value discipline allows a corporation to pursue multiple strategic options with its corporate strategy and business model. Similar to the value disciplines identified by Treacy and Wiersema,[23] Information Mastery has its own value proposition, operating model, and necessary processes and capabilities for execution. As shown in Exhibit

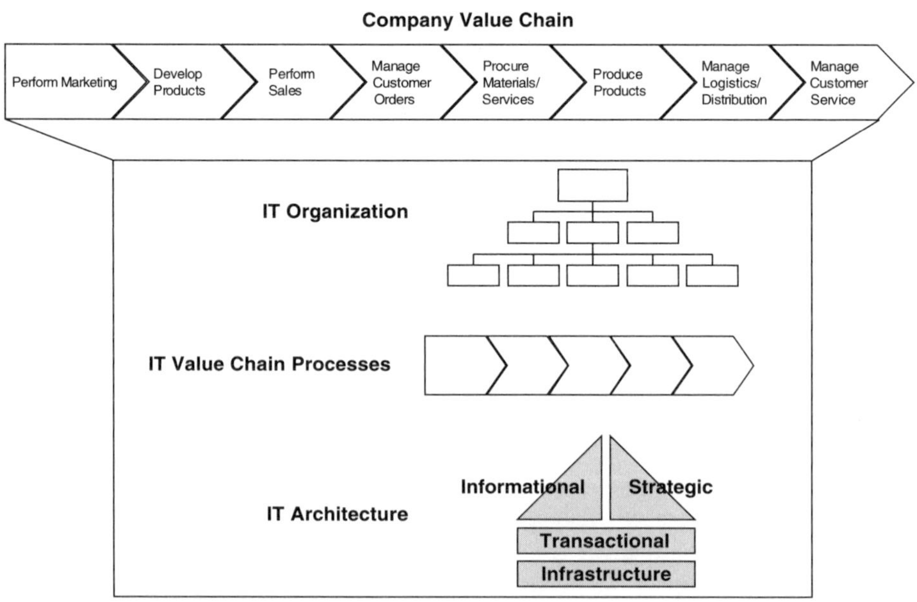

Exhibit 5.4 Information Mastery Essentials

5.4, there are clearly strategy, organizational, and structural requirements for Information Mastery, as well as the value chain and processes needed to deliver information value. In order to achieve Information Mastery, a firm must unleash IT from its Industrial Age constraints and allow it to flourish, to deliver the kinds of value it is capable of in today's business environment. The firm must cultivate the particular bundle of Information Mastery processes and capabilities in order to fully and repeatedly deliver the total value demanded of competing on an information-intensive basis.

The placement of a company value chain in Exhibit 5.4 is intentional. The value discipline of Information Mastery can deliver superior results to the business in and of itself, but even more so by driving superior business execution based on information. This places high importance on the ability to embed information processes and capabilities into all business processes and capabilities. This requires a new technique of business design, which means simply building business processes to be driven by information-based capabilities. Reviewing many of the breakthrough strategic ideas over the years reveals one clear pattern: information processes have always played a supporting role in business strategy and business process execution. How many of these strategic choices could really have been operationally effective without information-based organization, processes, and tools? A review of any of the major business strategy ideas over the last decade will show that information has always been considered after the grand corporate strategy thinking was completed by the powers that be. Eventually, in the Industrial Age information management philosophy we have become used to, the CIO and IT professionals would be consulted about how they would manage their allocation of the 1 to 2 percent of sales that would be their budget for the year.

Today, Industrial Age IT management still persists in most companies. The examples of companies that "get it" are few and far between, and the ones that do "get it" will be the big winners over time. The companies that continue their Industrial Age IT management tenets will be deselected by the forces of business change, technological progress, and the business environment and competitors. The leaders of those companies that subscribe to the Industrial Age IT management philosophies will be deselected as well if they fail to deliver superior results because they have missed tremendous opportunities to take advantage of new sources of information value.

What tools can we offer to these executives and companies to help them change the way they use information in their businesses? How can they learn to embed information in all business activities and processes? How can they build business models that are based on a new equation for information value and new levels of corporate performance? The answer is information-based business modeling.

NOTES

1. John A. Zachman, *The Framework for Enterprise Architecture: Background, Description and Utility.* See also John A. Zachman, "A Framework for Information Systems Architecture," *IBM Systems Journal,* Vol. 26, no. 3 (1987), IBM Publication G321-5298, and J.F. Sowa and J.A. Zachman, "Extending and Formalizing the Framework for Information Systems Architecture," *IBM Systems Journal,* Vol. 31, no. 3 (1992), IBM Publication G321-5488.
2. Zachman, "A Framework for Information Systems Architecture," p. 3.
3. Peter Weill and Marianne Broadbent, *Leveraging the New Infrastructure* (Boston, MA: Harvard Business School Press, 1998), pp. 14–15.
4. Ibid., p. 15.
5. Ibid., p. 15.
6. Bernard H. Boar, *Strategic Thinking for Information Technology* (New York: John Wiley & Sons, 1997), p. 171.
7. Harold Lorin, *Doing IT Right* (Greenwich, CT: Manning, 1996), pp. 40–41.
8. Weill and Broadbent, *Leveraging the New Infrastructure,* p. 24.
9. Ibid.
10. Boar, *Strategic Thinking for Information Technology,* p. 56.
11. Weill and Broadbent, *Leveraging the New Infrastructure,* pp. 26–29.
12. Ibid., p. 25.
13. Ibid., p. 58.
14. Ibid., p. 25.
15. Andersen, "Seven Levers for Guiding the Evolving Enterprise," in *The Biology of Business,* John Henry Clippinger III, ed. (San Francisco: Jossey-Bass, 1999), p. 117.
16. Weill and Broadbent, *Leveraging the New Infrastructure,* p. 53.
17. Ibid., p. 27.
18. Ibid., p. 54.
19. Michael Treacy and Fred Wiersema, *Discipline of Market Leaders* (Reading, MA: Addison-Wesley, 1995), p. 56.
20. Weill and Broadbent, *Leveraging the New Infrastructure,* p. 56.
21. Ibid., p. 28.
22. Ibid., pp. 28–29.
23. Michael Treacy and Fred Wiersema, *Discipline of Market Leaders* (Reading, MA: Addison-Wesley, 1995).

6

INFORMATION-BASED BUSINESS MODELING

We realized that the objects of strategy—such as business units, industries, supply chains, customer relationships, organizational structure, and so forth—are held together by a "glue," and that glue is essentially information.

—Philip Evans and Thomas Wurster,
Blown to Bits

Chapter 5 established a framework for understanding information technology (IT) architectures and IT portfolios based on the views of several IT strategists and practitioners. The IT categories established in Chapter 5—infrastructure, transactional, informational, and strategic technology—must now be mapped to the fitness levers and evolutionary capabilities that are required of firms today. The question is, how to guide the technology investment decisions for optimal business performance as well as evolutionary fitness. A framework for making decisions is developed in this chapter, with examples to show viable ways to navigate a path forward for leading-edge firms. We have reviewed how the IT strategy and the business strategy must be linked in new ways to drive increased value from company assets by using information differently. The framework developed explicitly incorporates IT decisions and thought processes into the essence of business models and corporate strategy. It can be no other way in the information economy.

CORPORATE STRATEGIES AND BUSINESS INITIATIVES

Surviving and competing in the corporate world relate to execution of the core business model or models and sustaining the firm's competitive position in its chosen markets. Of course, maintaining competitive position is not enough. Firms must always strive to compete better and to take market share from competitors if possible, because they are attempting to do the same thing. This section explores some current and past strategic themes and attempts to incorporate them into a new view of the corporation and information technology. This new view will thread strategic information management concepts into these strategic themes to show how they can be better implemented and exploited using information as a new competitive weapon. Exhibit 6.1 shows a business model framework adapted from Gary Hamel's latest book, *Leading the Revolution.*[1]

This framework describes the concepts and activities to consider when devising corporate strategy and is a framework I have employed in corporate strategy projects since Hamel's book was published. The simplicity of the model makes it powerful, and the clarity of what a business model is quickly emerges from the application of this business model approach. This framework serves as the basis for our discussion of strategic initiatives because it is simple, yet powerful for describing how various strategic initiatives fit into the overall corporate goals and the way the firm is organized to achieve them.

We will, however, add one more element to Hamel's model—information strategy. The information strategy component is a horizontal element that threads across all the others in the framework, and it will address how information strategies must be embedded in the business model to drive higher value and increased profitability for the firm in all activities. In this brief overview of Hamel's business model framework, the information elements of a forward-thinking corporation will be added to the business model to develop the structure of the business model based on information-based competition. But unlike business models of the past, this business model concept will incorporate IT into the fabric of the business model in all activities. This will lead to new performance levels heretofore unattained by the sequential business strategy

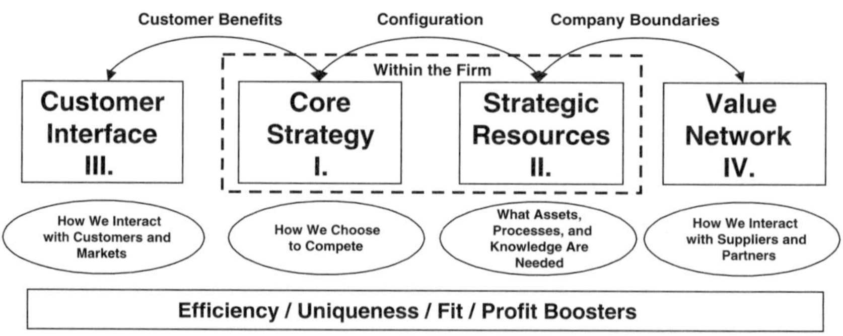

Exhibit 6.1 Unpacking the Business Model

Source: Adapted from Gary Hamel, *Leading the Revolution* (Boston, MA: Harvard Business School Press, 2000).

approaches of the past, where the corporate strategy and organization structures are defined first, and only then are the IT needs confronted. This has led to the traditional suboptimization of information value creation and the subjugation of the IT functions and role to the financial organization. Exhibit 6.2 shows the Hamel business modeling framework with information strategy added—the value discipline of Information Mastery.

A brief overview of Hamel's business model is needed here in order to develop the framework of a business model that is capable of incorporating information value creation as a core competency.[2] Hamel breaks down a business model into four major components (see Exhibit 6.1).

Two points must be emphasized before we review this model. First, we have dubbed this approach information-based business modeling. This was done to emphasize the heightened role of information in defining and executing a business model in today's information-driven business environment. This also helps avoid the classic "alignment" problem that has plagued corporations in recent years because of the poor fit of the business strategy and business model to the IT organization's capability to implement the requisite information processes and tools to drive the business appropriately. Again, and I will always emphasize this fact, this was not necessarily IT's fault. It was an inevitable outcome of managing the IT organization in an Industrial Age fashion. Based on this discussion, it is hoped that firms will understand that their strategy and business model concepts must have information-based competitive elements explicitly embedded in them in order to drive superior performance from the business model.

The second point of emphasis is that at the bottom of Exhibit 6.1, we have added a new element called Information Mastery: Competing with Information.

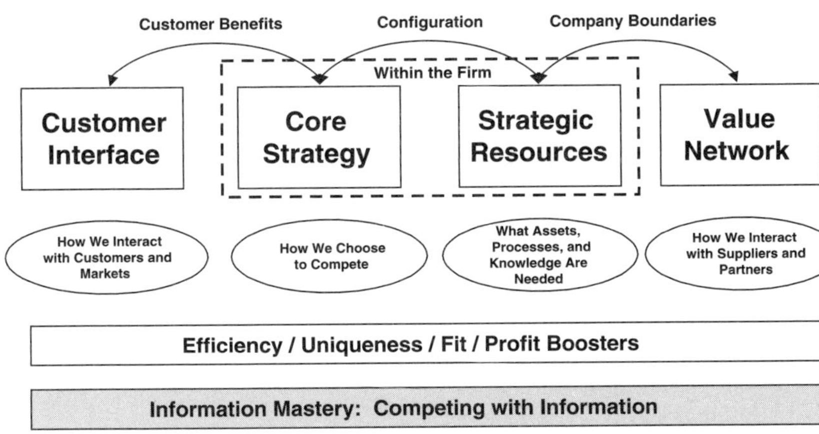

Exhibit 6.2 Adding Information to the Business Model

This again is an explicit addition to ensure that a firm's business model incorporates thinking about how the use of IT concepts can serve as a force multiplier, which can in effect push a corporation's business execution to new levels of performance far beyond those of its competitors.

This use of information can act as a force multiplier in many ways: (1) improving weapons efficiency, which means improving a firm's competitive arsenal by improving market intelligence, (2) embedding market intelligence into superior products, by deploying sales personnel more strategically, or (3) by managing operations more effectively. These are only a few examples. Using information as a force multiplier can also improve a firm's competitive posture by, in effect, increasing the size of its "army" through better deployment and more flexible organizational logistics. Finally, the notion of information-based value drivers is added to show how information-based concepts can add superior value to an organization if they are built into the foundation of the business model and not treated as an afterthought. Clearly, if information-based concepts are omitted from the business model, the organization will suffer as a consequence, which means negative information value being returned to the firm. This is critical because the lack of information tools can be as detrimental to a firm as solid execution of a poor business model, or even poor execution of a good business model.

Hamel's basic business model framework is comprised of four main components:

1. Core strategy
2. Strategic resources
3. Customer interface
4. Value network

In addition, three linking elements make the business model work. They are:

1. Configuration
2. Customer benefits
3. Company boundaries

These three bridging components tie the four major elements of the business model together in unique ways that add value for the customers. The linking activities make the corporate strategy fit together to develop synergies between business functions and ensure that all the "moving parts" interoperate to deliver the intended results. Finally, four foundational factors drive the profit potential of the business model:

1. Efficiency
2. Uniqueness
3. Fit
4. Profit boosters

This overview serves as a macro-level analysis framework for determining how various business initiatives will deliver superior value to a corporation, as well as how the IT demands of the business model will ensure execution of the initiatives in support of the corporate strategy.

Within each of Hamel's model components, we have added an information element unique to that particular component. This is to demonstrate that in all phases of devising corporate strategy and the operating business model, information today must be a central element of those thought processes. Exhibit 6.3 shows how information planning activities must be embedded in the business modeling process explicitly, in every element of corporate planning, business model development, and business model execution. We have dubbed this process information-based business modeling. Information-based business modeling makes clear that devising an Information Mastery agenda for the firm is essential to delivering the corporate performance that leads to evolutionary fitness in an increasingly fickle business landscape.

As reinforced throughout this book, information management occupies a far more strategic position in firms of today than it did in Industrial Age firms, and it must therefore be treated accordingly. Following the discussion of the business model framework, we show how various business initiatives map both to the Hamel framework and to the IT portfolio framework discussed in Chapter 5. These two analytical frameworks together provide a way to make sense of the business model and operationalize its execution using information assets in new and unique ways. This provides a powerful mechanism for competing on information asset intensity in conjunction with the traditional corporate strategy and business model concepts. As with any analytical framework, the operationalization of corporate strategy through various business initiatives, filtered through the prioritization and requirements imposed by the business

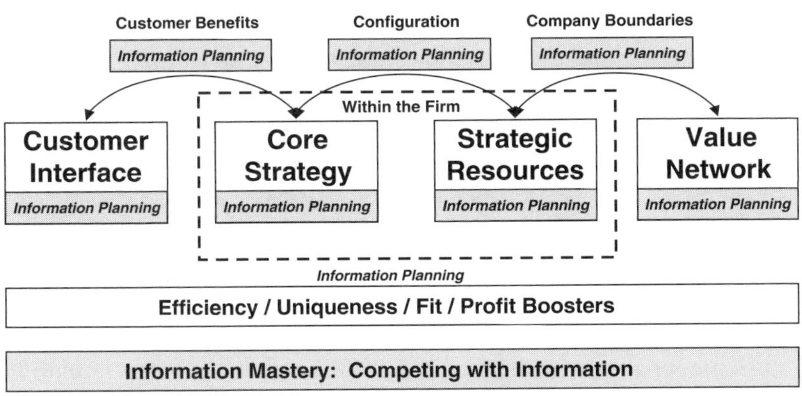

Exhibit 6.3 Information-Based Business Modeling

model, makes the strategy tangible and translatable into tactics and actions of the firm. Those actions can be grouped into survival, competition, replication, and long-term adaptation.

CORE STRATEGY

Everything begins with core strategy. Core strategy for a firm involves defining the central idea of how the firm will compete. The following elements define the core strategy of a firm:

- *Business mission.* This defines the overall objective of the firm's strategy, or what the business model will achieve or deliver to the firm. Issues to consider include strategic intent, the value proposition, the purpose or business idea of the firm, and overall performance objectives.
- *Product/market scope.* This describes *where* a firm chooses to compete as well as where it does not compete, and what it will compete with in product and service terms. It captures the target customers, geographies, and the products and services to be purveyed to those customers.
- *Basis for differentiation.* This category defines how a firm will compete and, equally important, how it will compete differently from its direct competitors. The basis for differentiation should clearly distinguish what makes your firm different from a customer-perceived perspective, not from an internal or artificial perspective. The basis for differentiation must be real and unique.
- *Core information strategy.* This is an addition to Hamel's model and is placed within the core strategy section to explicitly build the core information requirements of the core strategy into the business model. The core information strategy must define how information can drive new value propositions as part of the strategic intent of the firm, as well as support the achievement of performance objectives of the core strategy. Information value must also be built into the definition of product and market scope. Where a firm chooses to compete has a clear impact on the information needs of the organization as well as the products and services delivered, whether within a region or between continents. Finally, the basis for differentiation can be dramatically enhanced using information as a weapon. The use of information can deliver clear superiority in new product development, research and development, process control, logistics and distribution management, and many other ways. Information strategies as sources of differentiation and uniqueness in the business model are particularly interesting because they can remain opaque to competitors. A competitor may realize it is losing on a particular dimension of its business model, but the information systems involved

in driving that winning strategy can be difficult to copy, not to mention really understanding the exact functionality and value being delivered by those systems. But the definition and delivery of the value based on information-intensive rules of competition mean that the information value must be built into the core strategy of the firm.

Defining these elements of the core strategy helps clarify what makes the business idea valid and different from other business ideas. These basic steps help determine the requirements for the strategic resources needed to accomplish the core strategy.

STRATEGIC RESOURCES

The ability to deliver on the core strategy requires the right assemblage of knowledge, processes, and assets. These strategic resources fall into the following categories:

- *Core competencies.* These are the unique knowledge base of the firm, or what it knows. It encompasses the unique skills and capabilities possessed by the firm. By definition, core competencies are unique, valuable to customers, and transferable to new business opportunities.[3]
- *Strategic assets.* These are things that a firm owns, such as patents, brands, proprietary standards, customer data, and anything else that is valuable and not widely available to competitors. These can be employed to drive business concept innovation.
- *Core processes.* Core processes are the conversion activities of the firm that transform inputs into outputs. They are what firm employees do using the core processes, methodologies, and assets of the firm. This collection of activities converts competencies, assets, and other firm inputs into value for the customers in the form of goods and services. How these are combined into efficient, value-added processes determines the differences among firms.
- *Information competencies, assets, and processes.* Similar to core strategy, the strategic resources of the firm must also include those that relate to information. This is the value discipline of Information Mastery. A firm today must clearly identify the information competencies that will enable it to compete on an information-intensive basis. This is a different model of competing and requires new ways of leveraging technology. New goals, metrics, skills, and knowledge are required in order to use information competencies, assets, and processes to bring unforeseen levels of IT performance to the firm. New sources of value, new competitive moves, and new ways to creatively win will be enabled by the information-intensive competitors of the New Economy. Information assets will be

even more of the asset base of the firm under this approach, but the assets will be much more than mainframe computers, servers, data centers, and software licenses. The assets will also include patents and information and knowledge gathered from web sites, customers, market research, and other sources. Information culled from internal processes and research will also be added to the asset base of the leading-edge firm. Again, information management of the New Economy is more than managing systems, data centers, and networks. Information management in the modern age means delivering new sources of value.

CONFIGURATION: LINKING CORE STRATEGY TO STRATEGIC RESOURCES

The first linking element is configuration, which describes how the strategic resources of the firm are organized, structured, and combined to support the particular core strategy chosen by the firm's leadership. The core competencies, firm assets, and core processes must be sufficient to achieve the selected strategy, or the strategy will fail. Good strategy will identify the gaps between current competencies, assets, and processes and the needs of the organization over time. These gaps must either be developed in house or acquired to support the strategy, or the strategy must be altered to leverage existing competencies, assets, and processes.

The combination of core strategy and strategic resources defines the structure of the firm, its makeup, and its core business processes. This is the basic business unit of the corporation, which then services the customers and markets on the output side of the firm, as well as interacting with suppliers and partners on the input side. The decisions regarding the core strategy and its fit with available strategic resources dictate the degree of success that can be achieved in the near term.

INFORMATION'S ROLE IN CONFIGURING THE CORPORATION

As with other core components of the Hamel business model framework, there is a heavy information management element in configuration. Here is where the basic considerations of the structure of IT become important. What will the corporation look like organizationally and functionally? What are the basic IT requirements of the organizational structure? What is the IT organization and role in this structure? How can IT best provide services to the corporate organization and support the strategic information needs of the firm? Information

Mastery begins to assert its importance in this area of information-based business modeling. Defining the new role of information in configuring a corporation might begin with some of the following thoughts that are part of achieving Information Mastery:

- *New role of IT.* This is where the role of IT must clearly be articulated in conjunction with the core strategy. The role and value to be delivered by IT are different than in the Industrial Age of IT management.
- *New IT organization.* This is where the organization of IT must also be considered as it relates to the business as an entity. This discussion should not be one of how to organize IT to support the business's functional and geographical organization. This discussion should begin with "How can we structure IT to best execute the business strategy, while creating and delivering information value to the customers, both internal and external, using new and innovative ideas?"
- *New definition of information value.* This is where the value of information must be defined. The value of information in this structure requires new thinking and a new perspective. Information technology management cannot be deployed and valued using Industrial Age thinking. Information technology must be deployed and valued from an Information Age viewpoint. Information has new and strategic value to the firm if it can be allowed to perform unfettered by Industrial Age assumptions and paradigms of financial control and accounting.
- *New metrics of IT success.* The definition of success for IT has always been difficult to understand. Information technology is usually allocated a set budget to keep mission-critical business systems and infrastructure running, to perform maintenance on systems that require ongoing modifications and enhancements, and to deliver new IT initiatives on time and within their specific project budgets. Given this set of generic performance measures, it is no wonder that IT has been severely misunderstood. The IT organization has not been challenged to define itself in terms of real business value. Information technology has never been measured in market share per millions of instructions per second (MIPS), or return on net IT assets employed, or similar business metrics. This is the opportunity for IT leaders to take the initiative and create new metrics for the organization based on delivering new value—strategic value—to the business enterprise. The following examples are possible ways to value the information contribution to a business enterprise.
  - — Return on information (ROI of the Next Wave)
  - — Return on net IT assets employed (RONITAE)
  - — Return on Infrastructure (Return on Agility)
  - — Revenue per MIPS, per CPU, per client or user

Clearly, the value of IT in these examples is being expressed as a function of revenue and profits, not as a budgetary expense that must be controlled and, if possible, minimized. Information can deliver superior returns given the opportunity to treat the assets, processes, and capabilities as strategic corporate needs, not as an overhead function reporting to the financial organization for oversight purposes. But this requires a new management paradigm as well as new ways of valuing the contribution information makes to a business.

CUSTOMER INTERFACES

The third core component of the business model devised by Hamel is the customer interface. The customer interface involves five elements that relate to the ways in which the corporation engages with its customers and markets to sell products and services, what the selling dynamics are using various channel strategies, the pricing decisions and profit margins, as well as the overall market knowledge that leads to providing value to the customers. The five customer interface elements are:

- *Fulfillment and support.* This element describes how the corporation actually reaches customers with products and services. It includes channels, customer support, and customer service levels. For example, this element might include the number of retail outlets required to provide market coverage for the firm as well as convenience to the customers. Will direct sales be used or indirect via distributors, value-added resellers, and the like?
- *Information and insight.* This element covers the market and customer knowledge that is collected and leveraged to provide increased value to customers. This consists of specific customer data, such as personalization of customers using cookie technology on web sites, as well as customer relationship management (CRM) systems, which document all the interaction of a firm with its customers by managing contact data such as birthdays, historical logs of past transactions, and more. In addition, this element includes market research data that is used to create new value in the form of new products and services, as well as providing more information to the market and to customers regarding the firm and its products and services.
- *Relationship dynamics.* This element determines how a firm interacts with its customers. How do salespeople reach their targeted audience? Decisions regarding direct sales models, indirect sales models, and telesales/telemarketing all create different access paths to customers, as well as different perceptions of the firm by its targeted customers. This

element covers the relative ease that customers experience from conducting business transactions with the firm, such as search time, number of distributors or retail outlets, the number of sales personnel, and their knowledge level of products and customer needs.

- *Pricing structure.* This element determines the pricing structure for the products and services of the firm, which depends on the configuration of the other customer interface elements. Software products can be acquired on a license-fee basis, for example, or on a rental basis from hosting firms or application service providers (ASPs). The software and hardware can be identical, but the cash flow differences among these delivery models makes all the difference in how customers buy and benefit from the software.
- *Customer-facing information management.* This new element has become among the hottest application categories in the IT space. It includes CRM, call centers, web site personalization and content management, and a host of customer-facing information needs for today's corporations. These technologies provide significant opportunities for cross-selling and upselling of the firm's products and services, which are predicated on knowledge of a particular customer, buying preferences and patterns, and knowing what sales pathways lead to new selling opportunities. This provides additional value to customers by anticipating potential needs, and it provides revenue and enhanced relationship opportunities for the company by maximizing the sales process through bundled transactions. This supports a dramatic shift to the front by corporations in support of customer intimacy initiatives and customer service.

All of the elements of the customer interface business model component have clear IT and information needs. Some examples of the IT needs are:

- *Fulfillment and support* requires a clear definition of how IT and services can be used to bring customers and channel partners closer to the firm, or at least as close as desired by the firm. Regardless of the channel structure, for example, IT initiatives should contemplate how to provide a single company view to the end customers regardless of whether the products and services were delivered by the firm itself or by a network of channel partners.
- *Customer self-service* and related customer-facing service initiatives provide ways for customers to bypass the product and service delivery channels in order to extract information value from the firm on their own without customer service representative intervention. Providing the tools and processes for customers to access the firm's information content on

their own lowers transaction costs for customer service, while providing higher perceived value to the customer. When customers do require additional assistance, there may be the option to have a call center representative facilitate the transaction. This is another example of driving the value of the customer interface using information processes and tools, which has a dramatic impact on the customer relationship.

- Equally fraught with IT implications is the *information and insight* element. This element is clearly based on gathering market and customer information and knowledge, which can be leveraged to provide new sources of value back to the marketplace. This information may consist of individual buyer behavior, aggregated views of market behavior, market segment analysis, and even focus groups. This element should also incorporate competitive intelligence and environmental monitoring activities so that the firm knows how to compete more effectively, as well as anticipating changes in customer preferences and regulatory intervention by the government, standards bodies, and other coalitions and organizations. This body of data is important for new product development, for ascertaining competitive thrusts and parries, and for sensing what tactics and strategies competitors are employing while competing for market share, revenue growth, and profits.
- Similarly, *relationship dynamics* requires deep consideration about how information can support the customer interaction with a firm. The initial customer experience with a firm these days often begins with its web site. I have seen companies eliminated from bid lists because their web sites were crude and difficult to navigate. The relative ease of conducting business transactions among firms will lead to more customers and more loyalty from them over the long run. Information technology can play a central role in streamlining buying and interaction transactions, as well as speeding their processing. Relationship dynamics can be good or bad as a result of the IT processes that underlie this business model element.
- Sales force interactions with customers are also highly imbued with information strategy. Again, this relates to how sales and distribution channels are configured to provide products and services to target markets and selected customers. Technology plays a vital role in integrating all of these members of the sales channel into a seamless customer interface that represents the company's values and spirit, culture and esprit de corps, and even its brands and reputation for established customer service levels. Wal-Mart greeters at the entrance of its stores create a warm and welcoming atmosphere, plus they help customers locate products they are seeking; however, Wal-Mart greeters primarily perform an important

function for Wal-Mart: theft prevention. Posting a Wal-Mart greeter at the store entrance serves as a subtle warning that shoplifters will not succeed despite the warm, welcoming image that the customers perceive. The greeters have become a part of Wal-Mart's relationship dynamic with its customers. Similarly, how can information be used to drive efficiency and customer knowledge acquisition, while making a firm easy to do business with and adding to the overall positive relationship of a firm with its customers? Information can have a dual effect like Wal-Mart greeters do—helping customers and helping the company at the same time.

CUSTOMER BENEFITS: LINKING CORE STRATEGY TO CUSTOMER INTERFACE

The next set of decisions to be made introduces the second linking element of the Hamel business model framework: customer benefits. The customer benefits link helps align the core strategy of the business with its value delivery processes. This ensures that the bundle of products and services being delivered are truly valued by customers. The benefits, of course, have to be based on a customer-based definition of value. This linking element determines the value bundle provided to customers and provides assurance that the bundle is what the market needs and wants. There may be opportunities to provide more value or different value that will differentiate one firm from another, resulting in market share gains and more profits.

INFORMATION ROLE IN BENEFIT CREATION AND DELIVERY

The information role supporting and enhancing the linkage of a firm's core strategy to the customer interface is important. Information plays a critical role in delivery of customer benefits as well as providing customer support and service to ensure the delivery of benefits to the customer. In some cases, IT can provide compelling results in delivering benefits to customers. Ford's Internet-enabled vehicles, for example, represent a multifaceted use of information in its value proposition to its customers. First, convenient access to the web to obtain driving directions and to perform basic research functions from within a vehicle is an excellent innovation and clearly fits into the lifestyles of today's consumers. In addition, using the same web capabilities to perform customer service functions, such as scheduling vehicle maintenance, performing system monitoring functions on the vehicle, and sending instant messages or e-mail to alert the vehicle operator of pending performance problems or maintenance issues, provides additional value to consumers in the form of convenience, time savings, and delivering an overall superior vehicle ownership experience. These are creative ways of delivering benefits to customers using information value embedded within the product, as well as wrapping the product with an information-based service delivery and maintenance guarantee. This is enhanced benefit through strategic use of information delivery and value creation processes. Firms should consider how information processes and content can facilitate the basic delivery of the product and its associated benefits to customers. In addition, firms should consider how the information and product bundle provides value to customers in new ways. In many cases, the information bundled with the product becomes more important to the customer by virtue of convenience and connection to the firm. The firm's relationship for service, product information, and warranty assurance connects customers to it and contributes to loyalty. Finally, the information processes provide a two-way link to customers. This dialogue with customers one to one, en masse, is how a firm can connect with its marketplace for market intelligence and customer insights that can provide competitive advantage in the form of new products and services that are valued highly by customers.

VALUE NETWORK

The value network is the fourth core component of Hamel's business model framework, and it relates to how the firm engages with its suppliers, strategic partners, and coalitions to augment the firm's internal capabilities as well as provide critical inputs, materials, and knowledge to the conversion processes. The elements of the value network are:

- *Suppliers.* How a firm interacts with its suppliers has a tremendous impact on pricing structure and cost buildup of the value chain, as well as the quality of the inputs from suppliers. In addition, depending on the supply chain of the industry as a whole, deep relationships with suppliers of critical components can be a source of competitive advantage for the firm by locking up long-term sourcing deals with choke-point resources. In addition, outsourcing agreements and contract manufacturing models in electronics can have a dramatic impact on profitability and the competitive posture of a firm.
- *Partners.* Recruiting strategic partners and allies can also be a source of competitive advantage to the firm. In many cases, these partners can provide a complementary technology or component that completes a firm's "whole" product, or provides access to a new market segment for

the firm's products and services by virtue of the alliance. Partnerships and alliances have become increasingly important for accessing new technology because of the pace of change as well as the inability of a single firm to track all technological developments related to its particular industry.

- *Coalitions.* A firm can also partner with its competitors via coalitions, which can ally the firm for some period to stave off other more aggressive competitors or foreign competitors. This is common where research and development (R&D) investments or capital equipment investments are too high for one firm to bear alone.
- *Supplier-facing information management.* Supplier-facing information management processes and tools have been around for a long time. Electronic data interchange (EDI) has been a popular standard for execution of business-to-business (B2B) transactions across many industries, including most manufacturing verticals, financial services, insurance, and more. EDI is being updated by many standards organizations to take advantage of eXtensible Markup Language (XML), the emerging standard driven by the vast reach and power of the Internet in managing B2B transactions from purchasing and electronic funds transfer to complex forms and other information exchange. B2B exchanges and online marketplaces have been launched to consolidate buyers and sellers of goods and services for various verticals such as automotive, electronics, and consumer packaged goods (CPGs). The technology required to establish these online marketplaces includes automation of the procurement processes, forecast, inventory and procurement collaboration, and supply chain management, as well as supporting technology for online catalogs, payment, and transaction execution. Collaboration with suppliers, strategic partners, and other complementary vendors may allow corporations to extend their R&D capabilities by managing relationships with their partners as opposed to investing in potentially costly research and development and new product development on their own. This collaboration can be managed closely using various technologies that drive the execution of the collaboration processes between these firms. A new acronym has even been created to capture this supplier-facing collaboration and relationship network: supplier relationship management (SRM). While procurement and collaboration have been around for some time, the enabling technologies combined with the vision of an extended enterprise for procurement collaboration, R&D collaboration, and new product development collaboration will increasingly provide new ways to drive competitive advantage from the back end of the value chain to the customer.

COMPANY BOUNDARIES: LINKING STRATEGIC RESOURCES TO THE VALUE NETWORK

The final linking element is defining the firm's boundaries, which are based on what the firm does in-house versus sourcing to suppliers and partners. This comes back to the notion of business transactions discussed earlier based on Ronald Coase's research (see Chapter 3). If the activity can be done cheaper outside the firm than inside, and it is not vital to the core corporate strategy to own the resources or the processes, then it may be outsourced to the value network. The way a firm determines what remains core and what is noncore can have serious implications for strategy achievement as well as the cost structure of the value chain. This becomes a vital linking element, especially given the information processes that must be implemented to achieve it.

INFORMATION ROLE IN DEFINING COMPANY BOUNDARIES

As discussed in the value network section, information management has a clear role in establishing the boundaries of the firm, or what will be core, in-house activities and processes versus the processes and capabilities that will be outsourced to the value network to suppliers, strategic partners, and other value network members. This will be a fluid boundary depending on the geography, the product line, and the nature of the industry as a whole. The new generation of supply chain management tools now provides to corporations the ability to quickly reconfigure themselves, and their supply chains, around market penetration strategies, new product lines, and new sourcing relationships with their value network. The ability to dynamically reconfigure and manage the relationships of the value network with respect to markets, products, and suppliers offers the true back-end agility for firms that understand how critical the back end can be in delivering on the front-end customer processes and delivery functions. Online collaboration for forecasts, inventory visibility, warehouse and transportation processes, and in-plant operating capacities and order status become tools for managing a highly distributed network of suppliers and partners. Some industries demand these kinds of information and processes management capabilities even though they do not entirely exist yet.

The electronics industry has been in the forefront of finding new ways of gaining competitive advantage through vendor-managed inventory (VMI) programs, outsourcing of manufacturing, and even selling noncore manufacturing capacity to outsourcing partners in return for long-term supply contracts; however, the ability to manage a virtual warehouse of inventory across trading partners whose relationships to electronics firms vary can make this situation difficult to manage. The information tools and processes do not exist to provide the complete supply chain with visibility across a multitiered outsourced manufacturing model. Add to this the complexities of managing the transactions with several transportation and logistics companies, and there is clearly an opportunity for supply chain dislocation and "mystery inventory" issues to arise.

The information requirements for managing these extended enterprise business models have never been more complex. Product development collaboration, which requires the exchange of design data, product specifications, prototype and modeling information, and production process information will require a new level of infrastructure and strategic application investment by manufacturing firms. Management of the day-to-day supply chain and distributed manufacturing operations and processes will demand new ways of managing information, and distributing it to various tiers of trading partners will become more complex. As the host of online exchanges and marketplaces have demonstrated, the network of trading partners will only become more complex as firms extend their sales and distribution channels beyond their traditional physical infrastructure to these hybrid models based on blended channels consisting of the Internet and online marketplaces, retail and distribution outlets, and other trading partners and marketing alliances. Firm boundaries will be porous and dynamic as these hybrid supply models take hold. Managing the information capture, value creation, and eventual distribution in support of this model will be mission critical for the corporation.

WEALTH POTENTIAL OF THE BUSINESS MODEL

Finally, in order to devise a viable business model, the notion of wealth potential must be considered. As Hamel states, an executive must be able to describe how the business is going to make money by producing above-average profits. Four issues must be considered to understand the wealth potential of a business model:

1. *Efficiency.* The business model must contemplate how efficiently the firm delivers customer value and benefit. Efficiency determines relative pricing as well as company boundaries. The customers must value the delivered benefits sufficiently to pay the premium over what it costs the firm to create and deliver them. The IT role in executing repeatable business processes and driving transactional efficiency is well documented. Leveraging technology to reduce the internal friction of business processes and produce high-quality, low-cost business transactions will inevitably drive higher efficiency and reduce costs. As with the other core components of the business model, a firm should strive to employ IT creatively to produce new value from information as well as automating processes that rely on information. This can create cost

advantages as well as produce higher margins for the corporation, both of which positively drive the fitness levers for a company's long-term survival.

2. *Uniqueness.* The uniqueness of the business model differentiates one firm from another. The closer the resemblance of business models, the lower the relative profit margin in that industry, whereas a more unique business concept allows for easier differentiation and the potential to charge a premium for goods and services produced by that business model. Information technology can produce dramatic results in the creation and execution of a unique business model. Information-based competition has one clear advantage over many other competitive moves by corporations because of its relative opacity. Information technology initiatives can be implemented such that they produce efficiency and transactional benefits without being apparent to the competition. Information-based initiatives are opaque because they are difficult to observe, except by their effects, and they can be difficult to imitate because of the complexities of IT systems initiatives as well as from *time compression diseconomies.*[4] This phrase refers to the fact that certain skills or core competencies can only be attained over long periods through accumulated cycles of corporate learning. Information technology business initiatives, because they necessarily are bound to their respective business processes, can be complex and difficult to implement. Some firms are simply better at performing the process design work, the system development, integration, deployment and rollout activities, and the associated change management to ensure that these initiatives achieve maximal value for the organization. In addition, the opacity of information-based initiatives can be enhanced if the software is developed in-house as opposed to buying commercially available software. Enterprise resource planning (ERP) strategies of many manufacturing corporations were imitative strategies that were limited in their strategic value and competitive advantage impact because *all* corporations were implementing them at the same time. The results varied among firms because some were more capable of absorbing these information solutions into their business processes than others, but by and large, these ERP initiatives were easily imitated by competitors; therefore, any potential competitive advantage was mitigated within a short time. Higher strategic opacity arises from keeping software initiatives in-house, or at least maintaining the intellectual property in-house long enough to achieve strategic advantage. Then the technology might be licensed to produce new sources of revenue for the firm. Clearly, uniqueness of the business model can be augmented through the use of information-based strategies,

particularly when opacity of strategy can be a source of more lasting competitive advantage.

3. *Fit.* This means that the various elements of the business model have to work together. When they do, the business will generate more profits than otherwise. The components of the business model should be mutually reinforcing and aligned with the objectives of the overall strategy. One role of IT in this context comes from the clear contribution of infrastructure technology to business operations, especially across large, distributed organizations where horizontal systems are deployed across business units for sharing core processes, relaying common customer information, and achieving the cost savings that come from shared infrastructure. The infrastructure clearly helps business units and functional organizations within the firm work together toward the greater good of the firm, which enhances the fit in the business model framework.
4. *Profit boosters.* These substrategy elements can, if embedded into the business concept, really drive the company business model to high levels of return and superior profits. We do not cover profit boosters here, but they fall under the following categories (for a detailed discussion, see *Leading the Revolution*):
   — *Increasing returns.* Includes the notions of network effects, positive feedback effects, and learning effects (such as experience curve).
   — *Competitor lock-out.* This includes the notions of preemption or first-mover advantage, controlling key supply chain choke points, and customer lock-in techniques.
   — *Strategic economies.* This addresses competing with scale (Industrial Age competition model), competing on focus or specialization, and scope, where a firm leverages resources across a spectrum of opportunities.
   — *Strategic flexibility.* This is an important concept for the remainder of this book, so we expand this discussion as follows.

STRATEGIC FLEXIBILITY

This profit booster, as Hamel points out, can help a firm generate greater revenue and profits by fostering a company's adaptive fit to the market and its ability to avoid getting trapped into dead-end business models. Hamel identifies three ways of creating strategic flexibility:

- Portfolio breadth
- Operating agility
- Lower breakevens

PORTFOLIO BREADTH

Simply put, this strategic flexibility enabler comes from hedging corporate strategy by expanding the corporation's focus from a single product line or a single market to multiple product lines, multiple businesses, multiple markets, or multiple geographies. Portfolio breadth can even begin with enhancing core competencies, which can enable a business unit to develop new products and processes, new skills and knowledge, and new market opportunities. Expanding a firm's portfolio breadth provides a hedge against the vagaries of concentrating in one particular area of market opportunity. It is common for insurance carriers to transition from monoline policy writing (e.g., focusing solely on workers' compensation) to multilines of business by adding new lines of business, such as general liability, or bundles of coverages, such as commercial multiperil or business owner's policies. This provides a way to insulate a company from changes in insurance regulations from state to state, as well as offsetting poor loss experiences from one line of business. Additionally, expanding into new states provides additional hedging for insurance firms. Manufacturing companies hedge in similar ways by expanding into new regions globally, adding new product lines and manufacturing capacity in far-reaching global locations to take advantage of outsourcing opportunities and labor rates.

Evolutionary theory provides ample evidence for the advantages of variety in a gene pool of a species. In fact, the source of variety comes from mutation rates inherent in a particular species. Variety maintains species' strategic degrees of freedom with respect to changes in the environment and in the other species—both competitors and predators. Portfolio breadth is a corporate example of mutation, where variety is created organically through internal firm replication and experimentation processes. Portfolio breadth can also arise from strategic use of mergers and acquisitions (M&A), which add to the firm the assets, processes, or intellectual property developed by another firm or a coalition. Mergers and acquisitions are a rapid way of adding strategic diversification to the firm to rapidly create competitive distance from nearby competitors, or to attempt to catch up with other competitors with perceived advantages. This was clearly the case with the pattern of acquisitions by Lucent Technologies in response to the leadership established by Nortel in the optical networking market. This proved to be the only way that Lucent could attempt to compete with Nortel, despite the apparent R&D advantage that Lucent has traditionally enjoyed from the Bell Labs' research capabilities. Information technology plays a critical role in the integration of an acquired firm into the information architecture of the corporation. This requires the ability to understand the information assets of the acquisition target during the due diligence phase, and then devising strategies to quickly plug it into the financial and operations systems of the combined entity. The quicker this task can be accomplished, the faster the payoff will be realized. If these integration issues are not managed well, the acquisition can become a drain, and its value to the acquiring firm will diminish.

Along with portfolio breadth are related diversification strategies involving core competencies, physical assets, and information assets. Information assets include information management capabilities as well as patents and the R&D pipeline, which can be tremendous sources of competitive advantage in industries such as pharmaceuticals and biotechnology. Portfolio breadth can be augmented in several ways using information-based tools and processes, depending on how a firm elects to broaden its portfolio and in what areas.

OPERATING AGILITY

Operating agility provides a firm with the ability to quickly refocus its strategy and resources in response to new opportunities or new threats. This allows a firm to balance out margin erosion in its core markets or product lines by quickly adjusting and providing new products, adding new value to existing products, or driving costs out of the current production processes and current products. A firm might invest in flexibility in several ways. Manufacturing firms spent hundreds of millions investing in robotics and programmable logic controllers (PLCs), as well as flexible tooling. All of these assets were reusable for new products and manufacturing lines because of their ability to be reprogrammed based on the design data from new products.

A key premise throughout this book is that investing in IT, particularly infrastructure technologies, provides the adaptive framework and agility for firms in today's environment. Clearly, the IT capabilities of a firm provide enhanced operational agility above and beyond the scope that even Hamel identifies. Infrastructure technology spending is especially critical for firms that value their operational agility. The IT infrastructure allows sharing of large-scale computing assets, as well as e-mail and other messaging services. Riding on top of the infrastructure are the transactional, informational, and strategic technology assets, all of which are deployed more quickly and easily with a more robust portfolio of infrastructure assets. This provides the firm the often-unappreciated capability of quickly launching new IT solutions that tip the competitive advantage scales in favor of the investing firm. This is where operational agility is not an option for today's business environment—it is a must-have capability for firms planning on surviving the turbulence of the new millennium.

LOWER BREAKEVENS

All businesses have a breakeven point beyond which the firm can begin to make money. Breakeven points are inherently built into the business model and relate to the systems of production, customer acquisition costs, and the other factors required to make or deliver a unit of value to customers. Certain businesses have higher breakeven points than others. For example, capital-intensive business models of process industries such as petrochemicals, refineries, and others are asset intensive. Their breakeven point is higher than firms that have outsourced their systems of production, such as the electronics industry. These firms have essentially decapitalized their business models. This gives the firm more strategic degrees of freedom to pursue other businesses, because it has reduced its exit barriers. The cost to exit the business is less once a firm has decapitalized its business model. There are multiple ways of lowering the breakeven point for a business. For example, outsourcing strategies typical of electronics in effect reduce the asset intensity of their business model and replace it with a more information-intensive business model. Because the manufacturing conversion processes and inventory management processes are not owned and controlled by the firm, they must replace these physical assets with information about those assets. The information about their inventory can be referred to as "meta-inventory," and information about their outsourced manufacturing as "meta-capacity." Outsourced manufacturing models lower the breakeven point of their business model, but only if their information systems and processes can replace physical capacity and inventory with meta-capacity and meta-inventory. Information can play a vital role in helping reduce the asset intensity of a business model either by replacing physical assets with information and outsourcing aspects of the production base or by driving higher asset productivity by using IT to imbue these assets with more flexibility to handle more products in more efficient ways. All of these options open up strategic degrees of freedom for a firm and may allow it to pursue other industries and business alternatives by lowering the exit barriers from a money-losing or hypercompetitive market.

The final element of the business model is one that we have added. It is the information-based competition component that, I suggest, is on par with the four core components advanced by Hamel in his business concept framework. It is called information-based force multipliers.

INFORMATION-BASED FORCE MULTIPLIERS

Information-based force multipliers relate to how information strategies, processes and assets, and core capabilities can deliver superior performance to the business simply by building them into the core business model of the firm. This is not the alignment issue that is written about in all the IT magazines. This is a true melding and integration of information-based competitive levers into the core business operations of the firm. This is the implementation of the new role of IT, where the information value of firm activities is defined as an integral platform of corporate competitiveness. Information technology is not merely the supporting activity of the past; it is the opportunity of the future for the leading-edge firms, and it must be interwoven into the strategic fabric of the firm.

As shown in the business model framework, information strategies must be considered as a primary mechanism for business strategy execution. From the four core components of core strategy, strategic assets, customer interface, and the value network to the linking elements and the wealth enhancers, information can potentially play a mission-critical role in executing many elements of a firm's business model. Only when the business model is broken down into a simple framework such as Hamel's can the information potential of a business model be identified and understood. Once the understanding of how information strategies can become a primary lever of business model execution is developed, the creation of an information agenda can begin.

CREATING THE INFORMATION MASTERY AGENDA IN AN EVOLVING CORPORATION

The Information Mastery agenda for a firm begins with corporate strategy and the business model. We have built a framework for bringing the IT dialogue into the fiber of a business model in previous sections. We have provided some simple examples of the power of IT and its pervasiveness in all elements of a business model.

Exhibit 6.4 shows the big picture of how corporate strategy, the business model, and business initiatives all must fit into a broader context of adapting to environmental changes as well as competitors and predators. Business initiatives in this model are of two types: business initiatives supported by IT and business technology initiatives, which are primarily information-based. The diagram shows how the IT architecture and IT portfolio will evolve based on the needs of the corporate strategy and the business model. Again, the framework presented provides a mechanism for embedding the information needs of the business model into all aspects of the business model. This is important because of the real-time needs of today's businesses. There can be no traditional time lag between decisions of corporate strategy and the development of the business model, followed sometime in the future by the IT strategy managed in the old Industrial Age fashion. The modified Hamel model provides for *high-speed business modeling* and *rapid change adoption,* which are clearly required to compete today.

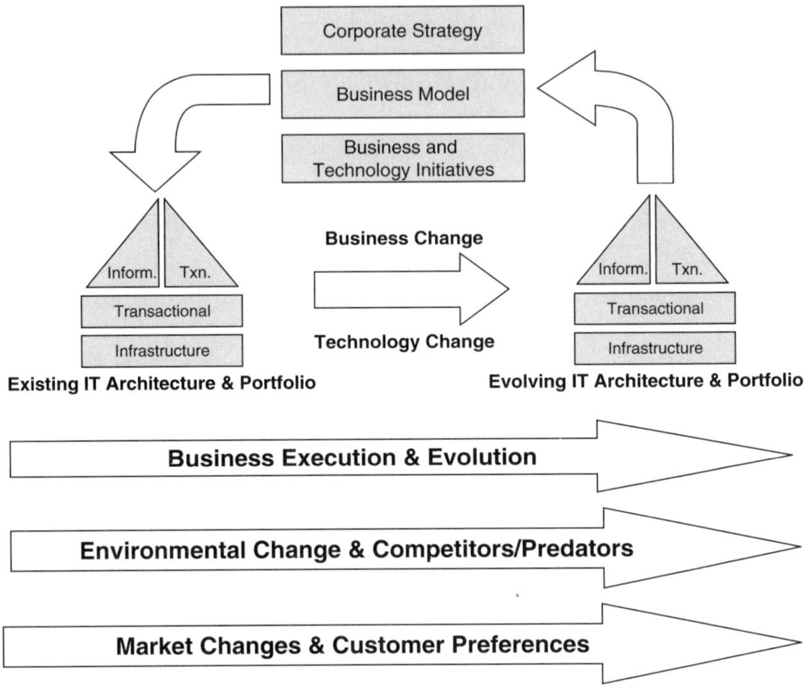

Exhibit 6.4 Evolving IT Architecture in Business Evolution

There are information implications for all business initiatives in today's corporation. The planning efforts for the supporting IT role and the planning for the information-based execution role must be built into the corporate strategy and the business model. That is what the modified Hamel framework helps us do—inject the IT planning and execution into the formulation and execution of the business model. This eliminates the classic alignment issue by explicitly defining the information needs of business initiatives up front, not after the fact.

Changes in markets and customer preferences demand vigilant monitoring for potential changes to the value proposition that firms create and deliver. The pace of change is fast and becoming faster, and the ability of firms to manage change and aggressively build adaptive capabilities into their business models will facilitate their survival. Information management strategies play a vital role in the high-speed business model required in today's environment. High-speed business modeling and rapid change adoption will become differentiators for firms in all industries, regardless of the inherent change rates and clock-speeds of their industries. Most strategy theorists today emphasize the criticality of innovation in crafting corporate strategy. Gary Hamel,[5] Constantinos

Markides in *All the Right Moves,*[6] Day and Ribstein,[7] and a host of others all emphasize the role of business innovation and creative nonlinear thinking in corporate strategy. Nobody would agree more; however, the position taken here is twofold: (1) explicitly incorporate the role of IT and the value-creating capabilities of information management into the essence of corporate strategy and business model development; and (2) give IT the role of innovation in the uses of information to drive new value for the corporation.

Exhibit 6.5 illustrates how many incumbent firms compete today versus how they should try to compete.

The column on the left of the exhibit represents the incremental thinking of established firms that are competing with known competitors in an industry with known rules. Most firms determine where they are versus their competitors in relative market share and profitability, and then formulate their strategies and initiatives from that starting point. This only leads to incremental

Playing the Game Better	**Playing the Game Differently**	**Playing a Different Game**
Focus on your existing strategic position.	Try to identify new or unexploited customer segments to focus on (a new *who*).	Find new businesses and markets the firm is capable of succeeding in regardless of current capabilities, assets, and customers (a new *game*).
Try to improve that position.	Try to identify new customer needs that no competitor is currently satisfying (a new *what*).	Craft a business model around the new business concept and test it on a limited basis; obtain capabilities and assets required to test the new business model (a new *way*).
To accomplish this, engage in practices such as restructuring, refocusing, process engineering, quality programs, employee empowerment, and so on.	Try to identify new ways of producing, delivering, selling, or distributing your products or services (a new *how*).	Win new customers and market share in the new business; execute fast cycles of corporate learning to shore up successes or learn from failure and adjust; this is a process of business development and execution, not a single-step solution (a new *result*).

Exhibit 6.5 The End Game: Creating New Games

Source: Adapted from Constantinos C. Markides, *All the Right Moves* (Boston: Harvard Business School Press, 2000), p. 14.

thinking and can only produce incremental results. As Markides observes, "Most firms take their current position and established rules of the game as givens and pour their energy into bettering each other at that same old game . . ."[8] This leads to an inevitable convergence of strategies and results.

The center column of the exhibit represents the minority of firms. These firms do not hold their current position as the central platform for business improvement. They concentrate their efforts on making themselves different from their competitors. These firms innovate their strategies by breaking the established rules of the game and experimenting with new ways of performing their business operations. What is important about this exhibit, though, is that one or the other is not sufficient. A successful corporation must be able to do both of these sets of activities well—maintain its core business franchise and seek incremental continuous improvements in its current competitive position, as well as looking for new ways of doing business, new customers, and new value to provide to the market. We have added a third column to those offered by Markides: playing a new game.

This column emphasizes the need to be capable not only of improving a firm's current position in its current industry, and not only of creating new ways of competing in its current industry. The new column emphasizes *creating a new game*; however, moving into a different game may require different core capabilities, new assets, and new ways of creating and delivering value. This is not always the case, but in most cases there will be clear needs for different assets, processes, and skills in order to succeed. In order to be in a position to explore new strategic opportunities, a firm must be able to incorporate new ideas into its strategic framework, new goals and objectives, new assets, processes, and skills.

A corporation must have the ability to nurture its core business model and sustain its core revenue-generating processes. This is the lifeblood of the firm and allows a corporation to continue to survive and compete in its current industry against the current competitors. This crucial element of a business must not be ignored. As Markides observes, firms must be able to sustain and continually improve their business in their core markets as well as inject change into the business model, seeking new customers, new products and services to provide to them, using new ways of creating and delivering them. Successful firms will perform both activities well and ultimately separate themselves from their competition by creating new sources of competitive advantage.

Continuing with this strategic theme, the same innovation infusion that corporate strategy requires must similarly be applied to the role and value of IT strategy. There clearly needs to be a dramatic shift in how IT is viewed, chartered, and measured in modern corporations. Given the strategic options discussed previously, the role of IT in all three strategic approaches might be summarized as follows:

- *Play better.* Define the role of IT and information-based competition in playing the current game better and driving performance improvements for the firm.
- *Play by different rules.* Define the role of IT and information-based competition in playing the current game by new rules, delivering new sources of value, and servicing new customers.
- *Play a new game.* Define the role of IT and information-based competition in seeking out and winning in an entirely new game.

All three strategic options for a company can be pursued and driven to higher levels of performance if the information strategy of the firm positions IT to play a more central role in their execution. But fundamentally a firm has to assess what evolutionary trajectory it is pursuing. For example, based on earlier discussions, corporate survival can be reduced to four biological activities: surviving, competing, replicating, and adapting. These four general biological functions have business equivalents in the everyday operation of a company. For any corporate strategy, business model, and collection of business initiatives, they can be mapped to these core biological processes such that they can be prioritized for action.

Survive and compete activities are targeted at playing the current game, to optimize the existing core business franchise of a business unit or a corporation. They are oriented at playing the existing game better. Compete activities facilitate competitive advantage within the current business model and core business franchise. Replication activities are required to help a corporation find and play a new game. They transition the firm's business model to a new competitive arena. Finally, adaptive activities are long-term processes targeted at searching for multiple potential new games for the firm to play. Adaptive activities help not only create new games, but they also should develop the core capabilities required to be in a position to play multiple new games. Exhibit 6.6 summarizes these evolutionary activities and their role in business evolution.

The key to assessing the priorities for business initiatives is the need for change. The following questions will help focus the change efforts and prioritize the business and technology initiatives required to support the business:

- What business evolutionary needs are being met with the particular business strategy?
- How do these fit into the corporate strategy and the business model framework?

Activity	Time Frame	Function	Information Goals
Survive	Immediate	• Continue basic functions of the firm	• Operational excellence • Conservation of energy
Compete	Immediate and medium term	• Sustain the firm by winning versus competitors and fending off predators	• Compete more effectively for customers and market share • Gather market and competitive intelligence
Replicate	Medium term; within generations of leadership and technology	• Reposition the firm; transition to the "next" future • Preserve firm best practices and core competencies • Innovation of new capabilities, new products, and services	• Corporate knowledge management • Intellectual property management • Innovation and new value creation
Adapt	Long term; across multiple generations of leadership and technology	• Ensure variability of firm capabilities and skills • Preserve agility and flexibility of corporate response • Preposition the firm for multiple futures	• Corporate and organizational flexibility • Corporate learning and organizational memory

Exhibit 6.6 Evolutionary Activities and Their Role in Business Evolution

- What business initiatives will lead to company survival, a better ability to compete and win, firm replication, and long-term adaptability of the company?
- What business initiatives are required to support the short-term company survival needs and the current business model?
- What short-term initiatives will facilitate competing for today's customers and market share in the currently targeted markets?
- What capabilities, assets, and skills will help the firm compete today as well as position the firm for the vagaries of tomorrow?

- How can company successes be replicated in new markets with new customer needs and new value requirements?
- What combinations of these evolutionary capabilities will allow the firm to survive across generations of technology change and leadership transitions?

Exhibit 6.7 places the four core requirements of a company into the same environmental context shown earlier. The four activities of survive, compete, replicate, and adapt are outgrowths of corporate strategy, the resulting business model, and the series of business initiatives required for execution of the business model. As shown in the exhibit, depending on what the evolutionary process is, the technology requirements will differ and the resulting IT architecture and IT portfolio will differ as well. The IT architecture must support all four evolutionary functions well. The business initiatives that drive the survival activities of the firm will differ from those that drive the ability to compete and win. Both of these functions, however, are closely related because they are tactical, shorter-term needs of the firm. Any company has to have the basic ability to

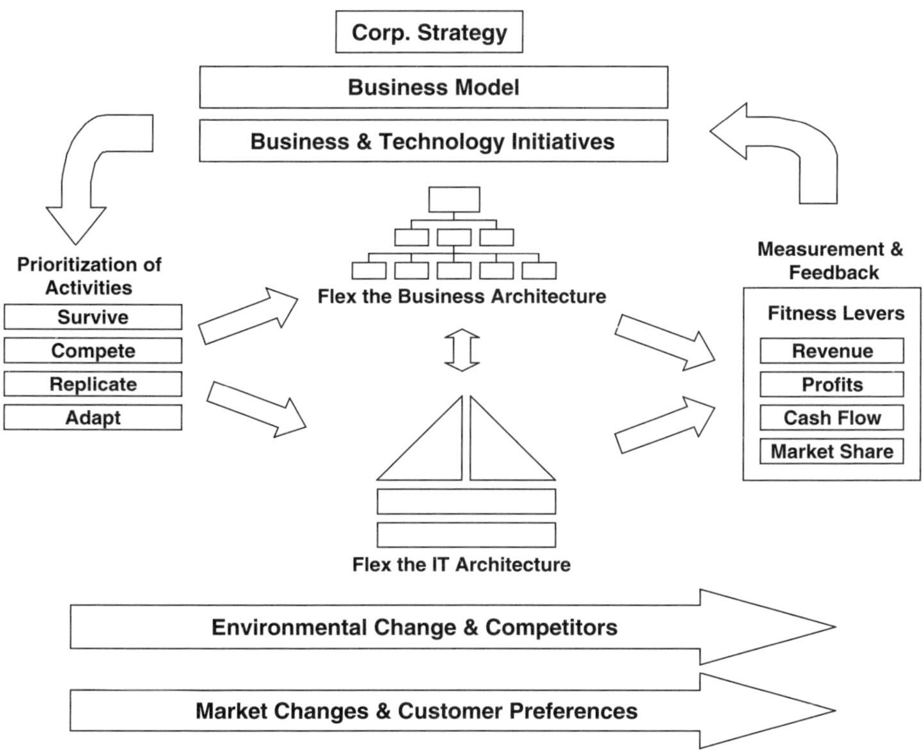

Exhibit 6.7 Change Initiatives in Business Evolution

survive and compete against the current competition. If there is little competition, then the competitive situation will be less, but the survival requirements do not disappear. Companies need to have existing customers who value their products and services enough to continue buying them. This provides the revenue and cash flow to sustain ongoing company functions and support other firm processes. In order to win customers against the competition, the firm needs to have at least a similar set of competitive weapons to support the ongoing operations.

Exhibit 6.7 shows how the corporate strategy and business model generate a series of business and technology initiatives that drive the implementation and achievement of strategic and tactical goals. The business initiatives fall into the four categories discussed previously:

- *Survival initiatives.* Survival initiatives are projects that are intended to shore up the core revenue-generating activities of the corporation. These projects include initiatives focused on core business processes, core production, and conversion assets such as manufacturing facilities, information systems, and others, as well as core business operations. Survival initiatives can include cost-reduction initiatives, implementation of transactional technology to achieve operational efficiencies, and quality initiatives that make business processes less variable and increase consistency of excellence as perceived by customers.

  Spending on survival initiatives will largely be constant investments in technology infrastructure and transactional systems in the architecture described in Chapter 5. Firms that are underinvested in these architecture elements will have to invest to bring these aspects of their portfolio up to par with their strategic objectives and their core business franchise needs. This may necessitate a rapid acceleration of spending in infrastructure and transactional systems to bring them up to the needs of the core business franchise, followed by a decline to normal spending rates. It is important to note that core business needs must be met with current IT systems and capabilities and must not be hampered by a lack of informational capabilities.
- *Competitive initiatives.* Competitive initiatives are those that help the firm either respond to a competitive threat or help achieve a superior competitive position versus the competition through preemptive moves. These initiatives are closely related to survival initiatives because a key requirement of business survival is to be able to compete effectively for market share and customers, and ultimately revenue and profit. Competitive initiatives are essential for maintaining the core business franchise as well as positioning for future viability through customer and market

proximity, and may involve sales and marketing initiatives, competitive intelligence initiatives, and market research initiatives as examples.

Spending on competitive initiatives will not be a steady investment stream of corporate dollars but, rather, intermittent bursts of spending to provide competitive advantage initially or to catch up to competitive moves by predators or other competitors for the same markets and customers. Preemptive moves by a firm may be costly initially, and may also require a steady stream of investment for a short to medium time frame in order to shore up and protect the duration of the competitive advantage episode. If a preemptive move does result in a sustained competitive advantage, it would be wise to continue investing to create more distance. Overall, spending on competitive initiatives will be in spikes and bursts rather than a steady investment stream.

- *Replication initiatives.* Replication initiatives are those focused on reproducing the firm's success in its core businesses as well as creating the possibility for success in future businesses. Replication activities include capturing the organizational knowledge of the firm for historical reference as well as for operational excellence. Capturing the organization's recipe for its current success and passing it on to new employees as well as applying successful processes and managerial techniques to new businesses is the corporate equivalent of evolution and adaptation through both genetic evolution and cultural evolution. Both processes involve replication of and improvement of the body of information that controls how we develop and what we do as a species. Documentation of the mission-critical conversion processes of the firm, such as a "bill of process," helps a firm sustain its core processes by having a reference base from which to inculcate new employees as well as a baseline process guide for continuous improvements. Replication initiatives also include those processes and systems that ensure organizational learning and adjustment to local conditions within short- to medium-term time frames. Replication initiatives can include knowledge management projects, process documentation and improvement initiatives, and processes for organizational learning and information capture. Corporate data repositories for customer information, product information, and process information also represent replication-oriented tools for retaining "organizational reproductive memory" of the firm.

Spending on replication initiatives will also be intermittent, but on a regular cycle for the firm. Corporate efforts to remake itself and to transition to new business models and new leadership paradigms require investments in knowledge capture; in product, process, and production information; and in customer and market information. Although these initiatives can and should be an ongoing part of the information processes and business processes of any world-class corporation, these efforts must be maintained and nurtured to feed the innovation engines of corporations. These innovation engines provide new ways of building on corporate knowledge and capabilities by making this replication information available to all members of the firm. Expect investments in replication technology to be cyclic on shorter cycles than competitive initiatives.

- *Adaptive initiatives.* Adaptive initiatives are the collection of activities and processes that facilitate the long-term survival, competitiveness, and reproductive success of a firm. Adaptive initiatives are often long-range business initiatives focused on transitioning the firm across generations of leadership regimes and generations of technological change. Adaptive initiatives are focused on organizational agility or the ability to shift strategic directions quickly to reach new markets, new customers, and new geographies. Adaptive initiatives incorporate rapid cycles of learning and organizational knowledge capture to facilitate transfer of corporate success to other businesses, business initiatives, and markets. Again, though, the time frames for adaptive initiatives are longer than those of survival initiatives, competitive initiatives, and replication initiatives. Examples of adaptive initiatives include long-range R&D activities that do not have immediate commercial pressures, as well as M&A and other business variation initiatives that augment the variability of the company portfolio of businesses. Adaptive initiatives are similar to replication initiatives in one critical aspect: they both generate variability for the firm. In the replication case, the variability is an internally driven change through internal processes and activities, continuous improvement activities, and product- and process-focused R&D. In the adaptive case, the variability is accomplished through a variety of external enrichment activities, such as merging with or acquiring another firm, or spinning off a division as a separate company. In human organizational terms, this was historically accomplished through colonization activities, warfare, and empire building. The magnitude of the variability enhancement is much greater than the mutationlike change that is driven by internal firm processes and activities and that resembles the mutation rates of living species.

Spending on adaptive initiatives should result in an aggregate pattern of increasing IT spending. As mentioned earlier, most firms are underinvested in IT spending to meet their needs, yet they continue to constrain IT budgets to historical levels rather than investing to allow greater performance and delivery of IT value. Adaptive initiatives will be concentrated in infrastructure to allow corporate agility and quicker response to environmental and competitive changes. Infrastructure represents the preponderance of IT spending, and these investments enable organizations to rapidly roll out new competitive and survival initiatives, as well as supporting the replication initiatives.

CONCLUSION

This chapter offered a framework for devising an information-based business model. This information-based business modeling framework eliminates the possibility of the classic alignment issue that has typically been blamed on IT for the last decade. We show how to overcome this problem by building information-intensive processes and capabilities into the fiber of a business model. The outputs of the business model process become a series of business initiatives and technology initiatives that must be implemented to achieve the goals and objectives of the company strategy and business model.

NOTES

1. Gary Hamel, *Leading the Revolution* (Boston, MA: Harvard Business School Press, 2000), p. 71.
2. This segment is from *Leading the Revolution,* pp. 70–113, with permission from Mr. Hamel and Harvard Business School Press.
3. See *Competing for the Future* and *Core Competencies of the Corporation* for the original thinking by Gary Hamel and C.K. Prahalad (Boston, MA: Harvard Business School Press, 1994).
4. Pankaj Ghemewat, *Commitment* (New York: The Free Press, 1991).
5. Hamel, *Leading the Revolution.*
6. Constantinos C. Markides, *All the Right Moves* (Boston, MA: Harvard Business School Press, 2000).
7. George S. Day and David J. Reibstein, eds., with Robert Gunther, *Wharton on Dynamic Competitive Strategy* (New York: John Wiley & Sons, 1997).
8. Markides, *All the Right Moves,* p. 13.

7

BUSINESS EVOLUTIONARY STRATEGIES

Change is no modern invention. It is as old as time and as unlikely to disappear. It has always to be counted on as of the essence of human experience.

—James Rowland Angell

The information-based business modeling framework established in Chapter 6 demonstrates how to avoid the pitfalls of defining corporate strategy and the associated business model separate from the information strategy. This has led to the years of blame and antipathy over information technology (IT) and its lack of alignment with the business. In reality, IT has been doing all that it could to manage the new and rapidly evolving technology platforms while supporting a business environment that has also been accelerating its rate of change. Also shown in Chapter 6 was how the business initiatives that stem from the development of a business model fall into the four evolutionary categories of survive, compete, replicate, and adapt. Implementing the necessary business initiatives to achieve both short- and long-term corporate objectives becomes a challenging endeavor. The short-term objectives using evolutionary tenets developed previously are to compete and survive as a viable business entity. These types of corporate initiatives are oriented around core business fitness levers of a company: bring in revenue by winning customers with the core business franchise. Short-term business objectives will most often be focused on ensuring success of the core business processes and core revenue streams.

There are also the longer-term activities of a firm. These involve the necessary corporate activities involved with corporate replication and long-term adaptability of the firm to its business environment. Replication activities can be ongoing knowledge capture and management processes as well as more sporadic activities involved in corporate renewal initiatives. Corporate renewal efforts can take place during periods of poor adaptive fit to the business environment, whereby the firm initiates corporate changes in order to rapidly respond to the business landscape. For example, the classic response to poor adaptive fit is a corporate restructuring and reorganization. These classic responses to poor corporate fitness are often knee-jerk reactions based on not knowing what precisely to do as a leader. The excuse is that by "shaking things up" the organization will perform better than in the cozy status quo mode of the prereorganization firm structure. Remember that corporations, unlike living organisms, have the ability to choose their adaptive responses and implement them using a variety of actions. This directional evolution of firms is a unique feature of human organizations and is implemented by processes similar to culture—organization learning and corporate culture. This body of knowledge represents the cumulative knowledge base of the company, much as the gene pool of a species represents the sum total accumulated evolutionary history of that particular species. In addition to replication activities, the long-term execution of survival, competition, and replication results in overall adaptive fit to the business environment through cycles of replication and business selection.

This chapter shows how the balancing of short- and long-term corporate activities must be accomplished using an evolutionary framework. This framework shows how a corporate strategy and business model are implemented and actualized using information-based business modeling and evolutionary thinking. We show that information will always be a critical element of a corporation's adaptive calculus, and that information also supports the non-IT elements of a firm's adaptive capabilities. Two important concepts help explain how a corporation should prioritize its business and technology initiatives to facilitate its business fitness and adaptive capabilities. They are flexing the IT architecture and flexing the business architecture. These concepts are developed to show how they contribute to adaptive response to both short- and long-term business needs of a corporation. Flexing the business and IT architectures, though, requires the ability to introduce and manage change in an organization. A discussion of change is required to set the stage for flexing corporate muscle in response to change or to preempt change. The business evolution framework must help prioritize change and manage change so that the business entity remains viable in the short term, but yet is able to replicate its success across generations of leadership, technology, and environmental change.

MACRO-MODEL OF BUSINESS EVOLUTION: ORCHESTRATING CHANGE

A corporation, as discussed previously, can be described by its strategy, its structure, and its core capabilities. These three features play a determinant role in what a firm does and how it goes about doing it. These factors determine how a firm makes a living. While each of these traits is somewhat pliable, changing the structure and core capabilities of a firm can involve considerable costs compared to changing the firm's strategy. This means that the structure and core capabilities of a corporation impart a stabilizing effect on the firm regardless of changes to its strategy. The structure and core capabilities exert an organizational drag that, while not actively resisting change, represents inertia and requires extensive and costly efforts to change. While the firm's strategy generally defines its corporate identity and what businesses it intends to pursue at a high level, it does so without precise details. Strategy in these terms frames a "broad set of commitments made by a firm that define and rationalize its objectives and how it intends to pursue them. Some of this may be written down; some may not be but is in the management culture of the firm."[1] The details of a company's strategy—the activities and choices that actually operationalize it—are contained in the business model and are then carried out in how the firm is structured to operate while executing the business model.

The corporate structure is how the firm really carries out its directives within the broad statements of corporate strategy, according to Richard Nelson. Nelson notes that "strategy tends to define a desired firm structure in a general way, without giving the details. Structure involves how a firm is organized and governed, and how decisions are made and carried out, and thus largely determines what the firm actually does, given the broad strategy."[2]

Changes to the structure and core capabilities of a firm occur in two fundamental ways within the business model: (1) flexing the IT architecture, and (2) flexing the business architecture. While strategy can be changed in its definition and articulation in several ways, including changes in senior management of the firm, the structure and core capabilities are far more difficult to alter in response to a new strategy. These are the flesh and bones of the organization, the physical and metaphysical infrastructure that allow the firm to pursue its strategic objectives by innovating, developing, and delivering superior products and services to its customers in ways that provide value to the customers and result in revenue for the firm. Changing the fundamental business processes of a firm, which include the personnel, critical skills, and physical assets, as well as the information personnel, skills, and information assets, is no mean feat. But in order to fundamentally alter the makeup of a firm, these issues have to be addressed and engaged in the process of corporate change for it to be successful. How can this be accomplished? The answer lies in flexing the corporate muscle to respond to the changes in strategy that, ultimately, should enable a firm to be more fit and well adapted to its business environment.

Exhibit 7.1 depicts a Business Evolution Model, which integrates corporate strategy and business models into a process—an internal selection process—for adapting to change. As discussed previously, the corporate strategy sets a high-level agenda for the firm about what objectives it intends to pursue and how it will do so. The business model, based on the Hamel framework reviewed in Chapter 6, articulates the details of how corporate strategy will be operationalized by the firm. Core strategy, strategic assets, configuration of the firm's internal processes, and core capabilities are all elements of the business model. Out of the business model should fall a series of initiatives that either implement the desired business model or change elements of the existing business model to fit the target business model. These initiatives must be filtered according to what allows the firm to be a viable, sustaining business entity. This *internal selection mechanism* is a filter comprising the fundamental evolutionary activities that a firm must perform to remain viable: survive, compete,

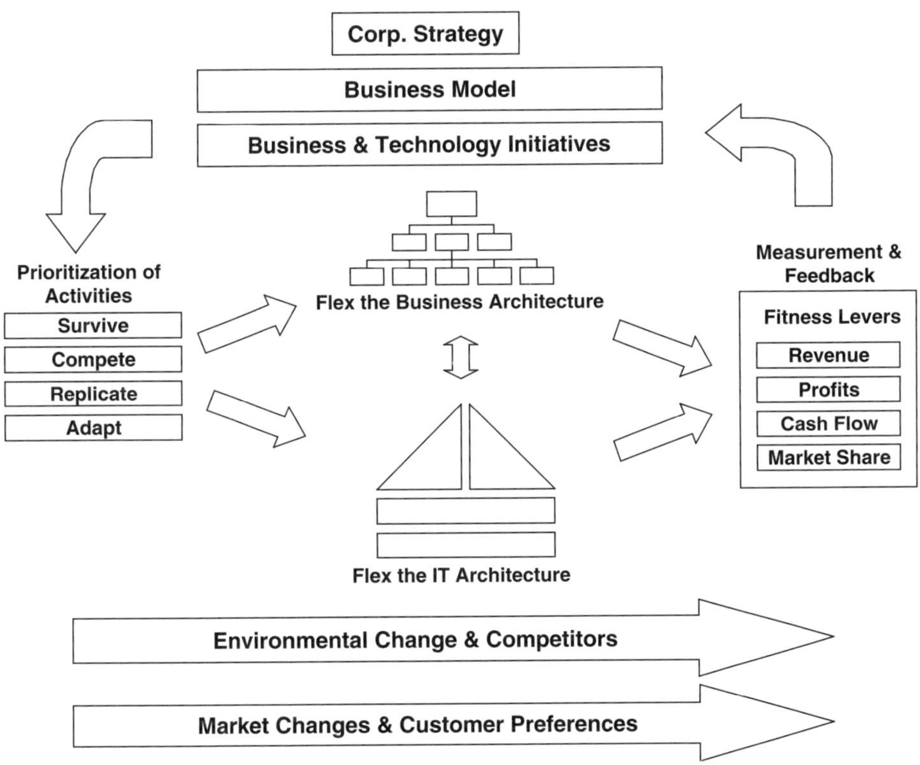

Exhibit 7.1 Business Evolution Model

replicate, and adapt. These four evolutionary processes of a firm determine both its short-term core needs and its longer-term needs.

As described earlier, surviving and competing are short-term requirements of a firm for it to subsist and make a living. A firm must undertake these activities to support its core business franchise and revenue streams. These actions are the lifeblood of a firm and must be performed at least well enough to ensure the ongoing survival of the firm as a business entity. This means supporting the fitness levers of any business, which are revenue, profits, cash flow, and market share. Lack of fitness in these categories means that a firm will eventually perish, much like a living organism will perish without being able to secure food for its day-to-day subsistence requirements.

The long-term needs of a corporation are replication and adaptation. These activities of the firm position the corporation for the future. Replication activities, as discussed, allow a firm to transition itself across generations of technological change and leadership changes. This is similar to reproduction in a living organism. Adaptation is the long-term process of surviving, competing, and replicating carried out across several generations of change.

Company initiatives must be filtered against these four criteria to determine whether and when they should be pursued relative to the firm's immediate and long-term goals. As Exhibit 7.2 shows, the four evolutionary activities of a firm focus on either short-term "make a living" activities or longer-term "pass DNA on to the next generation" activities. These activities act as an internal selection mechanism to ensure fit of corporate initiatives with survival needs of a firm as well as the future-focused needs of the firm.

In Exhibit 7.3, we show how the four evolutionary activities of a firm relate to its short- and long-term objectives. This is critical because in assessing what business and technology initiatives to take on, a firm must clearly understand where its emphasis must be and the urgency of the execution. Survive and compete are near-term objectives of a firm. The sets of activities relating to these categories are oriented toward the here and now of a firm, its ability to continue its core operations and serve its core customers. Business and technology initiatives in these categories are focused on taking care of today's needs: serving core customers, generating revenue from core lines of business, generating profit from core ongoing operations, and sustaining market share with core business processes. The core business operations of a firm allow it to survive long enough to replicate its success with future products and services, for future customers, and in future markets. In other words, the core operations of a firm have one purpose—to support a firm's ability to replicate its success in the future. This leads to the other activities of a firm: replicate and adapt.

Replicate and adapt are longer-term company objectives. Business and technology initiatives that fall into these categories are concerned with the future

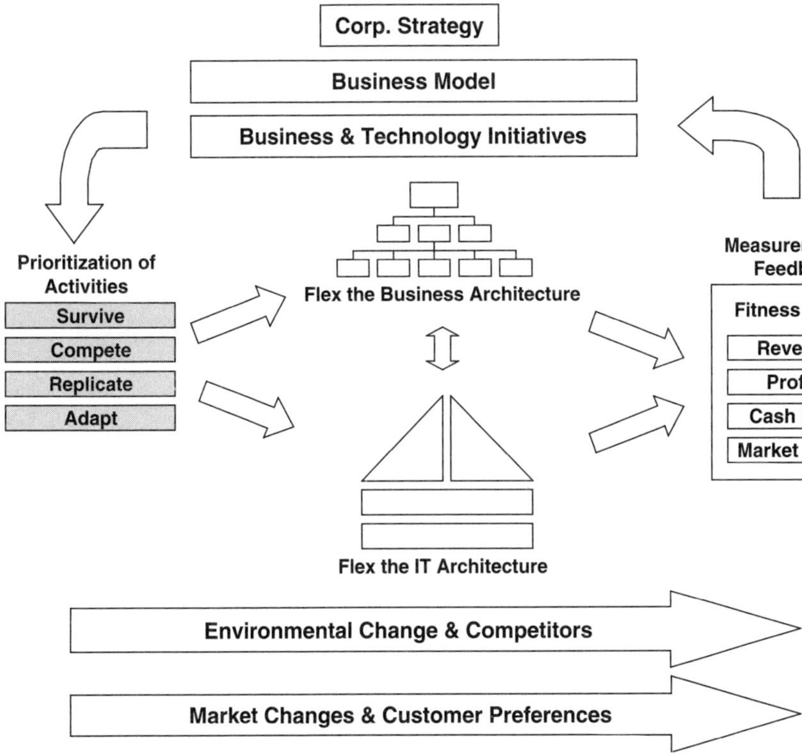

Exhibit 7.2 Evolutionary Activities of a Company

of the company—how it will transition its business model from its current core business to future products and services, future customers and markets, and future leadership regimes.

Replication activities are medium-term initiatives that bridge the corporation from a current business model to a future business model. These processes

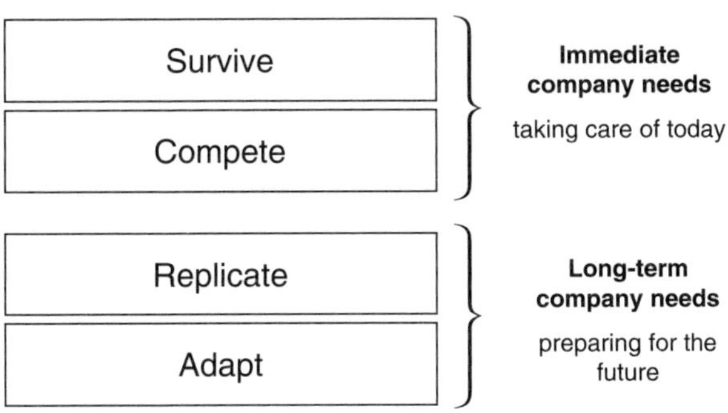

Exhibit 7.3 Internal Selection Criteria

and capabilities facilitate the transition across a technology shift or a management shift. These activities are required for a firm to reinvent itself in a period of corporate malaise, for example, where its fitness metrics are suffering, revenue is falling, profits are sagging, market share is eroding, and cash flow is weak. Replication activities, unlike survive and compete activities, are more periodic and are only required when a firm finds itself in a transition period, where fitness may be suffering or where the business model is poorly adapted to its environment. A firm may also choose replication activities to preempt a technology shift or a strategic shift by a competitor.

Adaptive activities are those that position a firm for its long-term evolutionary progress. These activities can include the processes that maintain strategic variability for the firm in terms of research and development, organic innovation processes, and strategic marketing and research. Adaptive activities are more ongoing, similar to survive and compete, but are focused on a time horizon 5 to 10 years out from the present. Adaptive activities ensure the tracking of environmental and market trends, as well as the attainment of critical corporate DNA—skills, core competencies, technology, innovation, and research and development (R&D) efforts—that will allow the firm to engage in replication activities when they are needed for survival.

The ability of a company to withstand change or, more aptly, to absorb change without dislocating its basic business functions depends on its readiness for and ability to change. Business initiatives that are similar to the central business functions of a corporation will be more easily adopted by the firm than completely new infusions of processes, capabilities, and behaviors. This is similar to an organ being rejected after a transplant procedure. It is a foreign organ that does not match the physiology of the receiving body. Initiatives that conflict with the central business functions of a firm will be more difficult to absorb and integrate into the fiber of the company.

Ultimately, the internal selection filter of a firm that accepts or rejects change is its corporate DNA. Recall that in Chapter 3 corporate DNA was defined as a unique configuration of core competencies and core business processes, supported by corporate knowledge and organizational learning processes, and encoded and enforced by the corporate culture of the firm. The internal selection of corporate initiatives will vary by a firm's relative fit to its business environment and its competitors. The poorer a company's fitness, the more readily change can be incorporated into its structure to respond to change. This, naturally, does not mean that a company can implement the appropriate changes to respond to environmental pressures that threaten its survival, or that it will take an appropriate series of actions to change itself in response to threats from competitors or the environment. The capacity for change, as well as the ability to change given the desire to, is not a given in any organization.

CAPACITY FOR CHANGE: CORPORATE MUTATION RATES

An organization has a finite capacity to absorb changes to its structure and processes and still function. Biologically, organisms have an internal mutation rate that is ascertainable through time. The human mutation rate as a species is about one in one million per generation for individual genes.[3] Researchers have learned, however, that not all genes are equally likely to mutate. Each locus on a chromosome has its own characteristic mutation rate, and some parts of chromosomes have "hot spots," or higher than average turnover of genes. This is a locally higher mutation rate than other parts of chromosomes.[4] The mutation rate is the empirical rate at which genetic changes are introduced randomly into the species through evolutionary timeframes. The mutation rate of a species is the maximum possible rate of evolutionary change in the absence of natural selection, which suppresses or dampens the amount of change that actually makes it into the gene pool. Remember how mutation occurs in a species: through the replication and recombination processes of DNA and RNA, this photocopying machine makes "mistakes," which are then captured in the DNA of individuals through reproductive processes. If these genetic changes confer a physical advantage to the individual or individuals of the species, those individuals will realize more reproductive success than other members of the species. The physical characteristics that conferred the reproductive success on the individual arose through the processes of development that were embodied and "programmed" in the DNA makeup of that individual. Some mutations do not result in advantage, and in fact many do not at all, at least not that are discernable by the limited lens of human observation. Nonetheless, mutations do occur and are recorded in the DNA history of the species and may or may not result in phenotypical traits that do allow survival or superior competitiveness of the individuals of the species over time.

Mutation for corporations or any human-based organizations is a slightly different concept from genetic mutation. The reason that culture has become the primary adaptive tool for humans is its efficiency and its speed. Cultural evolution allows changes within generations as discussed previously, as opposed to genetic evolution at the individual and species level, which occurs across generations. The question that should arise is: "What is the corporate equivalent of genetic mutation for a company, or its mutation rate?"

For corporations, the mutation rate of the firm is its *internal* ability to generate change and its tolerance for incorporating those changes into its day-to-day activities. This is the internal *innovation limit* of a firm, and it represents a lower limit of change in a stable environment. When the business model is well adapted to its ambient environment, the corporate change rate approaches the hypothetical internal mutation rate of the firm, the innovation rate, which is the hypothetical lower limit of change that would occur naturally in a corporation over time. This is the rate of innovation in processes, products, and core capabilities that occurs on a continuous improvement basis daily in the corporation.

When a business model is poorly adapted to its business environment, however, the corporate change rate must accelerate for survival purposes. The upper limit of change that can be tolerated by an organization is the *disruption limit.* Change at a rate higher than the disruption rate causes the business to fail in its execution of basic business functions, causing its ultimate demise. The upper limit of change that a business can tolerate and still remain a viable business entity is determined by the internal makeup of the corporation. The hypothetical upper limit of organizational change is established by the corporate culture, the organizational structure, and the core processes of the firm, as well as by the processes and capabilities for managing change. Depending on the industry and the corporation, the distance between the upper and lower limits of change will vary. Some firms are simply better at introducing and managing change than others by necessity. These firms more likely compete in fast-clockspeed industries, where new product development and product innovation are on much shorter cycles than in other industries.

Compare the clockspeeds of semiconductor manufacturing, or the closely related electronics assembly industry, versus the automobile industry, which is much slower. Exhibit 7.4 shows the hypothetical upper and lower limits of change that are possible in a given corporation. When a corporation is faced with a need to change faster than its internal innovation rate, several initiatives will be launched to attempt to improve the company's fitness relative to its business environment. This accelerated rate of change, depending on what the nature

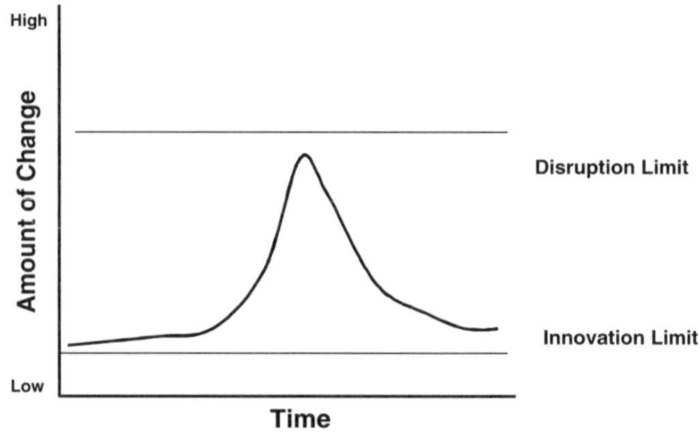

Exhibit 7.4 Corporate Change Tolerance

of the changes are and where they occur, will have a maximum limit before the basic business functions are disrupted and the business begins to fail. Implementing change beyond this theoretical limit may result in negative effects that impact customers, revenue and profits, cash flow, and market share.

Exhibit 7.4 also shows a possible change scenario where a firm is initially well adapted to its business environment, with its change rates above but near its minimum internal change rate, its innovation rate. As a company's business model becomes less well adapted to its business environment, the rates of change accelerate as management attempts to address the situation. If management does not incorporate changes, the organization will fail.

In responding to the business environment and changes in markets, new competitive threats, and other forces, a company must change. The spike in change rates shows how a firm will launch new business and technology initiatives in response to being poorly adapted to the current business landscape. After the amount of internal changes peaks, ideally somewhere below the upper change limit, or the disruption rate, the rate of corporate change will slow and stabilize at or near the innovation rate again.

It is important to note that these hypothetical limits are changeable. That means that a firm, through its corporate culture and business processes, can incorporate more or less change in a given time frame than its competitors. This agility means advantage in most cases. The internal innovation rate for a firm may be inherently higher than that of its competitors because of higher R&D budgets, a culture of experimentation and innovation, and grassroots idea harvesting processes that result in new ideas for processes, products, and other continuous improvement opportunities. By the same token, companies in higher-clockspeed industries will have a higher upper limit of change absorption because of a culture that is used to high change rates.

A few examples of corporate change are instructive. A company I used to work for was infamous for its reorganizations in its North American sales and marketing organization every fall. The predictability of these changes was such that in September, the entire company would grind to a halt while the reorganization was being planned and rolled out. This equated to a three- to four-month loss of productivity because of the work stoppage while waiting for the restructuring and then the ramp-up time it took for the new organization to be worked out and tuned. This firm clearly had a culture that was used to change, but the impact of the anticipation of the changes was negative, and the changes, as a result, were also negative.

Conversely, a current example is an experiment in the making. Hewlett-Packard (HP) is in the midst of a massive corporate restructuring under Carleton S. (Carly) Fiorina. This restructuring effort is breaking apart the 60-year-old decentralized model of HP and creating three product development groups—

one for printers, one for computers, and one for digital appliances. In addition to these product development groups, Fiorina is splitting sales and marketing into three organizations as well, for consumers, corporate customers, and consulting services. This reorganization was initiated in early 2000 and has not produced the results that Fiorina had hoped for. In fact, HP has forecast slow to no growth for the next two quarters as it struggles through these organizational changes. Clearly, at least in the short term, HP is experiencing difficulty as a result of the massive restructuring it is undergoing. A question to consider, given the amount of change being introduced to the organization, is at what point does the amount of change exceed the limits of the organization to absorb it and internalize it? How much change is needed to attain the product and market leadership HP once had, and will it ever be able to reach that position again? Given that some elements of the HP organization have been in place for decades, up to 60 years according to some, one could surmise that the culture of HP is not comfortable with great magnitudes of change. The HP story will be one to watch as it struggles to reinvent itself.

Once a firm has introduced a series of changes that are required to attain a new competitive position in its market, it must make these changes part of the behavioral fabric of the organization. This means making the new behaviors habits. A firm's corporate culture must be able to codify the changes into its corporate DNA. The adoption of these changes is analogous to the incorporation of mutations into the gene pool of a species. The internal selection filter in Exhibit 7.3 is a primary sorting mechanism for the rate of change that is tolerable by a firm's internal makeup. The firm's corporate culture determines a firm's ability to cope with change; however, a corporation's internal capacity for change and its ability to change are far deeper capabilities. These are affected by corporate culture, as well as by the internal structure, core processes and capabilities, and information management practices of the firm. We previously established that corporate culture binds the firm's vision, strategy, and objectives to its business model, structure, and core capabilities. The corporate culture guides the behavior of the firm in executing the functions of making a living—surviving and competing, as well as replicating and adapting.

The role of corporate culture cannot be overemphasized in a corporation's ability to change. The following change vectors affect how well a business entity can adapt to the environmental and competitive threats (see Exhibit 7.5):

- *Need to change.* The need-to-change vector is determined by corporate culture and a firm's behavioral system. This provides the incentive and urgency for employees and the organization to change, as well as the tolerance for higher-than-normal change rates. This is the corporate cosmology or worldview, and it prescribes the set of interlocking behaviors

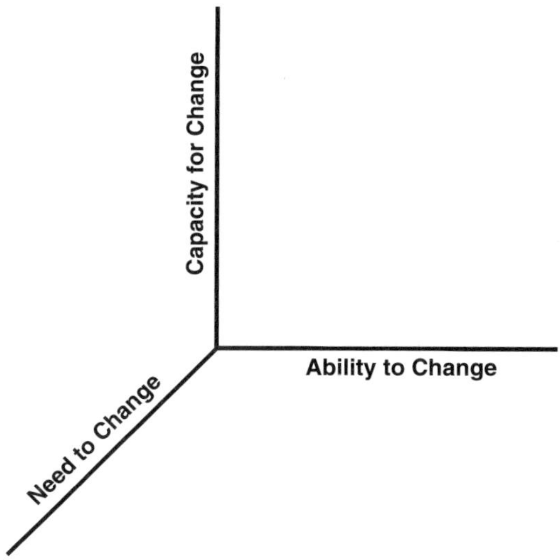

Exhibit 7.5 Corporate Change Vectors

and shared beliefs and values within the firm that guide decisions and regulate corporate citizenship. The desire to change establishes the potential cultural and behavioral limit for changing the firm's corporate culture, beliefs, and values.

On a 1 to 10 scale, rank your organization on its need-to-change vector and justify your ranking based on the corporate culture, behavioral systems and norms, and other organizational elements. (Scale: 1 = low; 10 = high.) Ask yourself, "Given our ranking, how can we implement the necessary corporate changes to enhance our short- and long-term survival goals?"

- *Capacity for change.* The capacity for change describes a company's internal ability to absorb change into its structure, processes, and core capabilities, as well as establishing the upper limit for how much change can be introduced into the firm. The capacity for change is determined by the flexibility of the business architecture and the IT architecture of the firm. More rigid business and IT architectures will be less able to quickly change in response to environmental and competitive threats. The capacity for change is also influenced by the need to change, which establishes the behavioral limits on the amount of change that can be introduced and successfully absorbed by an organization. Together, these forces determine how much change can be implemented in an organization.

  On a 1 to 10 scale, rank your organization on its total capacity for change, and justify your ranking based on the corporate structure, the business processes, the organizational structure, and the IT structure, IT processes, and the IT organization. (Scale: 1 = low; 10 = high.) Ask yourself, "Given this self-ranking, how can we implement the corporate initiatives required for short- and long-term survival purposes?" What changes in the business and technology architectures will be mandatory to succeed with these business and technology initiatives?

- *Ability to change.* The ability to change refers to the firm's overall ability to accommodate change in its corporate culture given the need and desire to change. A strong ability to change means that a firm could potentially absorb the upper limit of its capacity to change if the need to were sufficient. The overall ability to change is determined by the business architecture and the IT architecture of the firm, as well as being heavily influenced by the corporate culture of the firm. These two components of a firm's makeup—its information structure and processes, along with its business structure and processes—are mission critical to a firm's ability to modify itself in response to the business environment.

  On a 1 to 10 scale, rank your organization on its total ability to introduce and implement business change successfully. (Scale: 1 = low; 10 = high.) Justify your self-ranking based on your business architecture, your IT architecture, and your corporate culture and behavioral norms. Ask yourself, "How can we successfully implement a program of corporate change given our total ability to change?" What cultural, business, and IT architecture changes are required to begin a program of business evolution?

A company's relative adaptive fit to its business environment will largely determine how much change is needed to bring its core processes and capabilities into environmental alignment. The core survival and competitiveness needs of the firm are mission critical to sustaining the firm as a viable business entity as measured by the fitness levers of revenue, cash flow, profits, and market share. A company must also be able to survive in order to position itself for the future. Like living organisms, corporations have to survive and compete well enough to be able to reproduce or, in our usage of the analogy, replicate. Corporate initiatives will always be cast against the internal selection filter of surviving, competing, replicating, and adapting, but there is an inherent tension between the short-term core business functions of a firm and the longer-term replication and adaptive functions of the firm. This tension can be resolved by building a corporate culture based on change and by building the necessary corporate "muscle" that can be flexed in response to environmental and competitive threats, or change. The corporate muscle that is most instrumental in responding to environmental and competitive pressures is twofold: flexing the business architecture and flexing the IT architecture.

FLEXING CORPORATE MUSCLE: BUSINESS ARCHITECTURE AND IT ARCHITECTURE

The issue facing a firm is "How to balance the possible universe of corporate initiatives with limited organizational bandwidth and its inherent capacity to absorb change and still function as a business entity?" This challenge confronts every corporation and essentially becomes a prioritization issue. The following questions might be considered:

- How many business initiatives can the firm execute successfully at one time?
- How do business initiatives reinforce one another for maximal chances of success? If business initiatives do not adhere to a larger corporate vision, strategy, and business model, how can they succeed?
- How much change can be introduced and absorbed into a firm's organizational structure, behavioral system, and corporate culture over a particular time period? How can the organizational infrastructure be "flexed" to facilitate the firm's ability to absorb change and build it into the fabric of the firm?
- How can these initiatives, many of which are technology-based, be executed quickly for maximal business impact while achieving the long-term corporate objectives?
- What IT processes and capabilities enable a firm to accomplish all of these things?

The key to these questions is flexing the business architecture and the IT architecture of the firm.

FLEXING THE BUSINESS ARCHITECTURE

Once the priorities of the corporation have passed through the internal selection filter based on the short-term core business needs (survive and compete) and the future-focused evolutionary needs (replicate and adapt), they can be incorporated into the firm's structure and processes. The capacity for change depends heavily on the business architecture of the firm. The business architecture of a firm consists of the following elements:

- *Company organization and structure,* which includes business unit definition, organizational structures, and personnel and human resources.
- *Value chain,* which includes the unique configuration of company processes and core competencies that result in value to customers.

- *Core business processes and strategic assets* of the firm, which provide the core revenue and profits of the firm.
- *Organizational learning processes,* such as knowledge repositories, product data management repositories, and customer databases.
- *Corporate fitness metrics,* which provide the measurement benchmark against which the firm must compare its performance and make adjustments to the structure, value chain, core processes, learning processes, and even the metrics themselves.

Exhibit 7.6 shows where flexing the business architecture fits into the Business Evolutionary Model.

Flexing the business architecture is simply the premeditated introduction of business and technological change into the core business activities of a firm. Flexing the business architecture allows a firm to successfully initiate both business and technology initiatives that ultimately help the firm survive, compete, replicate, and adapt. Both types of initiatives require flexing the business architecture. Flexing the business architecture refers to the ability of a firm to adapt its structure and processes to incorporate change. The capacity for change

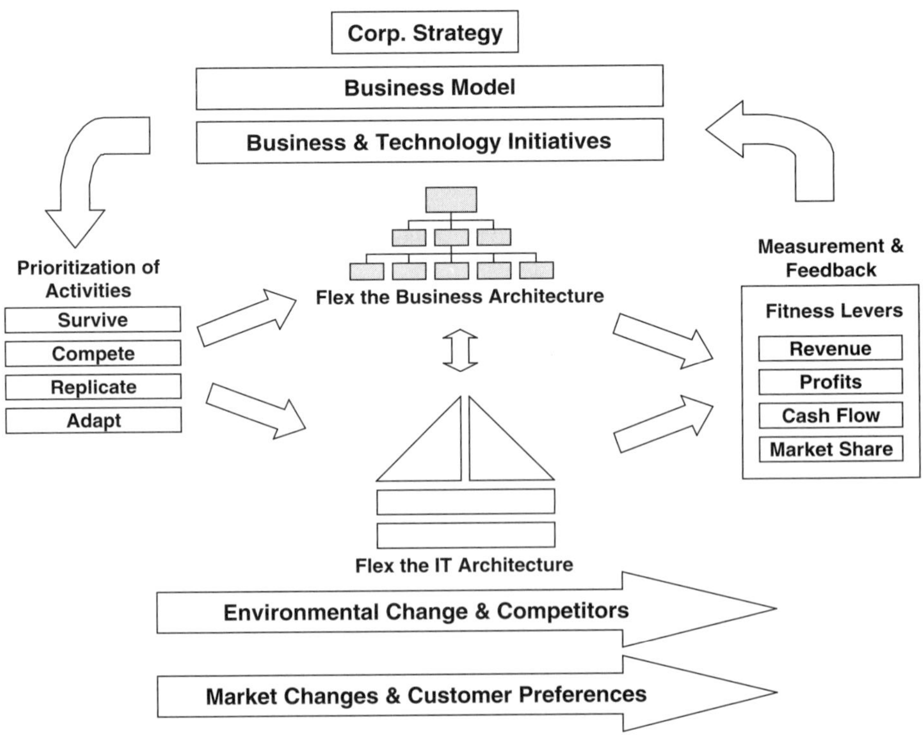

Exhibit 7.6 Flexing the Business Architecture

in an organization is its maximum ability to incorporate change into its business functions without disrupting those core business functions. Change management as a consulting discipline, for example, is concerned with this topic. Flexing the business architecture means that company processes and organizational structure can be adapted to incorporate change more easily than a rigid, inflexible business architecture. Like muscle, flexing business architecture implies the ability to demonstrate the strength and capability of the business architecture by incorporating change as needed to support the core business survival and competitive needs of the firm, as well as positioning the firm for the future through replication and adaptive processes.

Flexing the business architecture can be difficult for some companies because the structure and core processes of a firm can be a source of drag on change initiatives. This is not because the processes are necessarily bad, but because they have been learned and ingrained as reinforcing behaviors that unify business functions and employees around a shared purpose of the firm. The Hewlett-Packard example is a case in point. It is difficult to change six decades of organizational habits with a year-long restructuring exercise. This type of massive change takes time, and in the case of HP, the jury is still out on whether the organization has the ability to absorb the amount of change that Fiorina is implementing and still remain a viable, vibrant corporate entity.

Flexing the business architecture means that a company has invested in the organizational ability to absorb change in its structure, processes, and core capabilities. This takes work and practice. It is similar to an athlete working out in a gym or performing weight training. When the strength and conditioning are required for competing in a live sporting event, the practice pays off. Companies must also work out to strengthen the corporate muscles that allow flexing the business architecture. This means conducting various "exercises" to improve the company's performance in live competition, which, in a corporation's case, is every day. In order to flex the business architecture, a firm must have the athletic ability to make changes to its structure, processes, core capabilities, and learning functions.

FLEXING THE IT ARCHITECTURE

In conjunction with flexing the business architecture, a firm must simultaneously flex its IT architecture to accommodate the business and technology initiatives required for survival. Flexing the IT architecture will occur for both business initiatives and technology initiatives, just as for flexing the business architecture. Both require flexing to incorporate change into the company's fabric. Flexing the IT architecture simply means investing in specific elements of the IT architecture to accomplish the organizational goals of survival, competing, replicating, and adapting. This strategic governance of the IT architecture and application portfolio, as shown in Chapter 6, is threaded into every element of the company's business model.

Exhibit 7.7 shows where flexing the IT architecture fits into the Business Evolution Model.

Flexing the IT architecture and portfolio is a primary mechanism by which a firm in today's economy evolves and competes in its environment. The following activities are required to flex the IT architecture to incorporate necessary changes into a corporation:

- *IT organization and structure,* which includes the organizational structure of the IT organization, along with the personnel and human resources needs
- *Information value chain,* which includes its unique configuration of IT processes and core competencies that result in value to the business according to the new definitions of information value as a strategic asset

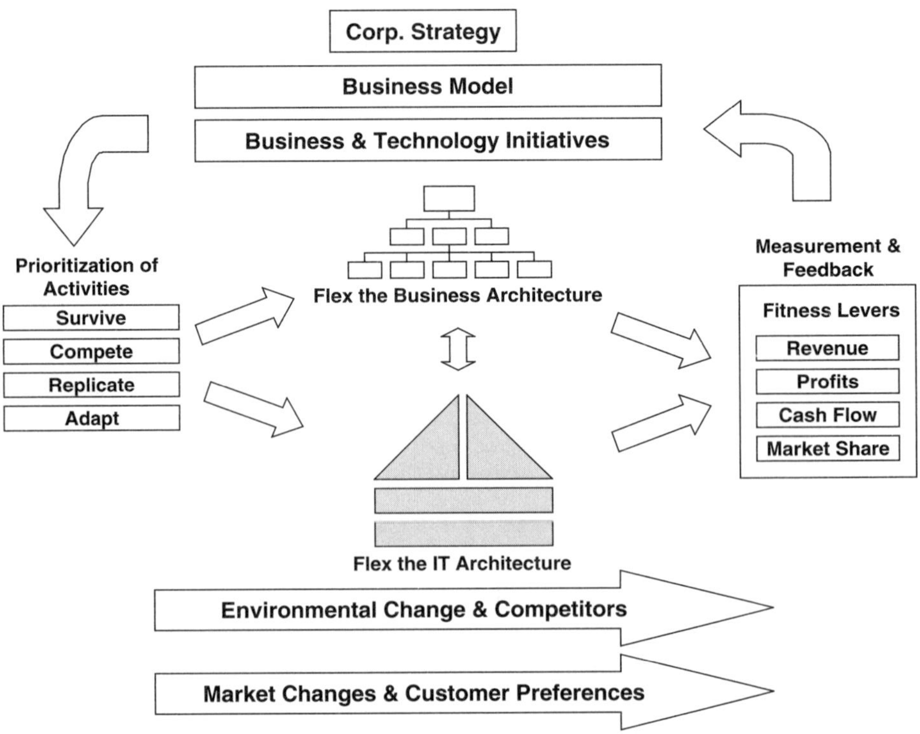

Exhibit 7.7 Flexing the IT Architecture

- *Core IT processes and strategic information assets* of the firm, which provide both support for the core revenue and profits of the firm, as well as helping generate new value streams from information-based processes and information-driven initiatives, including the following IT architecture elements:
  - — Infrastructure systems and technologies
  - — Transactional systems and technologies
  - — Informational systems and technologies
  - — Strategic systems and technologies
- *Organizational and technology learning processes,* such as knowledge repositories, product data management repositories, and customer databases
- *Information value metrics,* which provide the measurement benchmark against which the firm must compare its performance and make adjustments to the structure, value chain, core processes, learning processes, and even the metrics themselves

Flexing the IT architecture requires an understanding of the technology requirements of business and technology initiatives once they have passed the internal selection criteria of survive, compete, replicate, and adapt. These criteria have implications for the IT architecture. Recall the IT architecture model developed in Chapter 6, which broke IT investments down into infrastructure, transactional, informational, and strategic initiatives. All four IT categories support the survival and competing needs of a firm, which are the short-term core business functions of a corporation; however, all four IT categories also support the replication and adaptive needs of a firm, which are the longer-term business functions. As discussed in Chapter 6, spending on infrastructure can have a strong bearing on the future adaptive stance of a corporation. This is because infrastructure spending provides more agility to firms that invest more heavily in infrastructure, which means they can launch and roll out business applications more quickly than firms that do not invest in infrastructure. By the same token, investing in strategic technology can also provide future-oriented competitive advantage to a firm. Spending on these categories of IT functionality can equate to the replication and adaptive functions of a firm.

Similarly, spending on transactional technology and informational technology can equate to operating efficiencies of the core business franchise, which can be equated to the survival and competitive functions of a firm. Transactional technology can have a direct impact on core business process execution, which leads to cost reductions and operational efficiency. In addition, informational technology investments are also required by the core business processes of a firm in order to assess performance and monitor ongoing operations.

DOUBLE FLEXING: BUSINESS AND IT ARCHITECTURE INTERPLAY

Flexing the business architecture and flexing the IT architecture are conjoined activities. Enough has been said about the lack of alignment of IT with the business. In the business modeling framework, we showed how the insertion of information management planning in all aspects of a business model will prevent the lack of alignment between IT and the business. But this requires the premeditated and explicit incorporation of information-based strategy objectives into the business modeling process, something that has always been talked about but in reality has fallen short in execution. Beyond the development of the business model, which is done initially and then tuned as the business executes the model, there is a continuous interplay of the business architecture and the IT architecture. Exhibit 7.8 depicts the double flexing action of the business and IT architectures in response to the internal selection and prioritization criteria.

In some cases, a particular initiative engendered by the business model may be more heavily business than technology, or vice versa, but nonetheless there

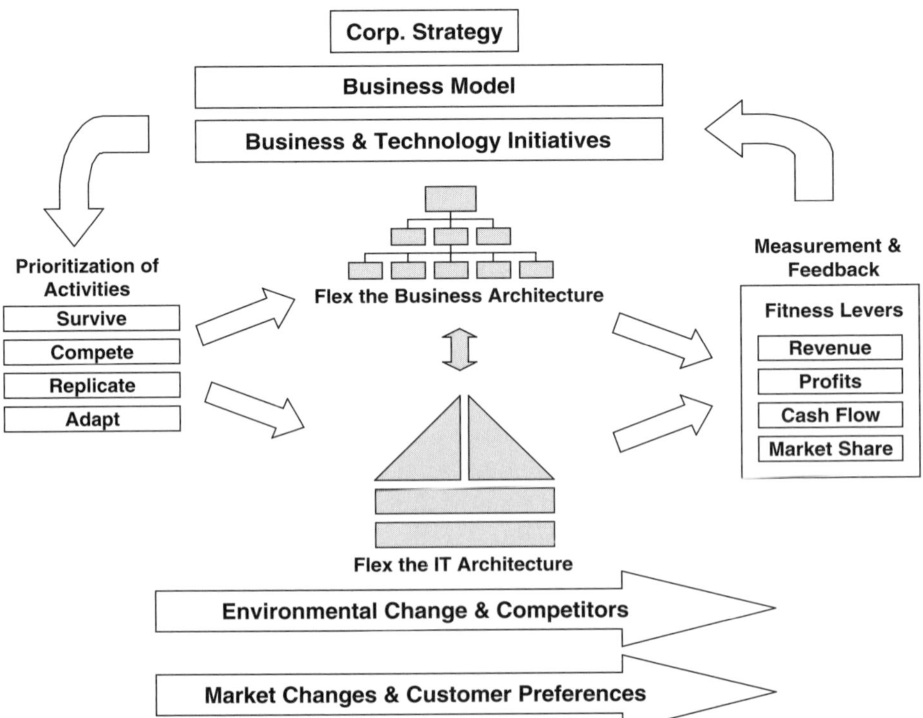

Exhibit 7.8 Business and IT Architecture Interplay

will still be a dual flexing of both the business and IT architectures as appropriate for the successful execution of the particular business initiative. The dual flexing of the business and IT architectures provides a real-time synchronization of both architectures, which helps ensure that the information-based components of a business or technology initiative are explicitly embedded, as well as making sure the business-based elements of a technology initiative are included.

FITNESS LEVERS: METRICS AND FEEDBACK

The final pieces of this iterative business evolution model are metrics and feedback. Any business must be healthy in order to survive and remain a viable business entity. Like living organisms, which must be able to obtain food for energy as well as other life support ingredients—the things that a life-form requires in order to subsist and survive—a firm must also harvest energy in order to make a living. There are many ways to assess the health of a firm. Some include customer satisfaction, employee morale, R&D conversion and the new product pipeline, and the more common financial indicators of revenue, profit, cash flow, and shareholder value. Market share and growth rates might also be considered. Of all corporate performance metrics, market share and profitability are the two most common indicators of competitive strategies.[5] For the purposes of this discussion, though, we simplify business fitness metrics down to a few core survival metrics. The four primary metrics of business fitness for a corporation are:

- *Revenue.* Revenue is a critical fitness metric because it shows that a firm has something valued by markets and customers, and creates cash flow.
- *Profit.* Shows that a firm can make money by selling products and services to customers.
- *Cash flow.* Shows that a firm can generate cash from its ongoing operations to finance its internal activities.
- *Market share.* Shows that a firm can compete consistently on a medium- to long-term basis, and provides a temporary buffer from competitive threats and market changes.

Exhibit 7.9 shows the placement of the fitness metrics in our Business Evolution Model. Interestingly, these metrics are mentioned by Michael Dell in his book as requirements for balanced success, which he defines as "growth of market share (or revenue), profitability, and liquidity (or cash flow)."[6]

These metrics must absolutely be healthy in order for a firm to remain viable, both in the short and the long term. Our model is based on relative fitness in all four metrics for survival purposes. For example, as the e-business first wave demonstrated, many corporations that went out of business in the last

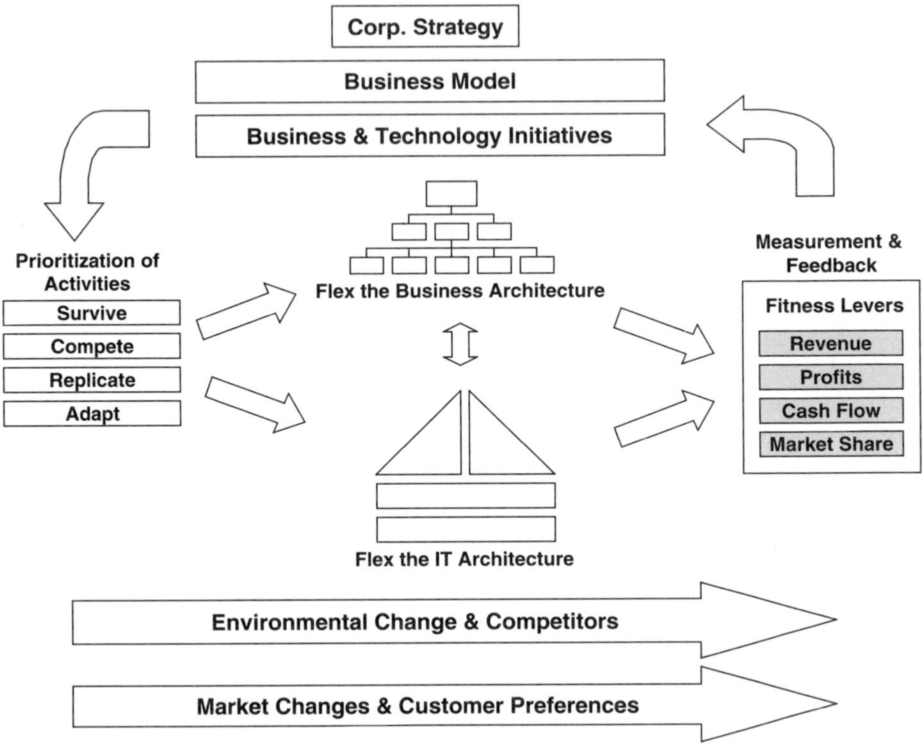

Exhibit 7.9 Fitness Metrics of Business Evolution

18 months were not viable according to these four fitness metrics. They may have had sky-high stock valuations for a while, as well as advertising revenue and click-through rates through their web sites, but these were not long-term, sustainable business metrics. They were not grounded in revenue-generating activities based on providing real value to real customers. If a company cannot generate revenue from real, paying customers, it will fail. Venture capitalists will not support an investment that will not pay off eventually. If the revenue is not sufficient to generate the necessary cash flow to support the ongoing processes and activities of the firm, it will fail.

Cash flow is a sign of corporate health because it shows that revenue is healthy and that debts are being paid. If cash inflow is less than cash outflow, the firm is not fit—it is not making profit. Profit shows that a firm can provide products and services to paying customers, generate revenue and cash flow to pay for variable expenses such as raw materials and labor, and make money doing so. The firm's expenses in providing the product or service are less than the revenue generated, which results in operating profit. Making money is the ultimate fitness lever of a firm, and as we hear all the time, cash is king. Retained earnings in the form of cash allow a firm to invest in R&D activities and other initiatives that lead to longer-term sustained success.

Finally, market share is an important fitness indicator for a firm. Market share shows that a firm can repeatedly execute its business model for a given market with a given strategy and execution model. Market share shows that some formula for competitive advantage has worked because customers are buying what the firm has to sell. As many researchers warn, however, market stability and strategic opacity help firms with dominant market share retain that share, while market share in immature industries where competitive forces are rapidly evolving may be more fleeting.

The importance of these business fitness metrics is that they indicate a firm's relative fitness to its business environment, or, more accurately, the fitness of its business model to the business environment. Suffering in one or more of these fitness levers means that a firm may have to adjust its strategy and business model, and the potential business and technology initiatives that are required to carry out a given strategy and business model. In our business evolution model, this step assesses a firm's performance against these fitness metrics and provides feedback to the strategy and the business model. Out of this feedback step may come a new set of business and technology initiatives that are deemed necessary to achieve corporate objectives. Then the entire business evolutionary model is executed again to drive better adaptive fit to the business environment based on the firm's strategy, business model, and the palette of business and technology initiatives it executes to compete and survive in the short term and to replicate and adapt over the long haul.

A summary of the complete Business Evolution Model follows:

1. Define (or revise) the corporate strategy.
2. Develop (or revise) an information-based business model.
3. Identify critical business and technology initiatives.
4. Prioritize initiatives by business evolutionary goals.
   - *Survive.* Short term, core business survival
   - *Compete.* Short term, core business survival
   - *Replicate.* Medium term, future business positioning
   - *Adapt.* Long term, multiple future positioning
5. Flex the business architecture to implement change.
6. Flex the IT architecture to implement change.
7. Assess performance against fitness metrics.
8. Adjust the business model and do it all over again.

A company's business evolution depends on continuous cycles of survival and competition, along with replication and long-term adaptation. This cycle of adaptive change becomes part of the business execution requirement for corporations. Information-based competition is a critical component of business modeling in today's business landscape and must be an integral element of business strategy as well as business model execution.

Exhibit 7.10 is a sample worksheet for prioritizing business and technology initiatives that are required by a given strategy and business model. Before implementing business and technology change within a corporation, the needs of the firm as a whole must be balanced against the needs of the short-term core business as well as against the needs of the future business. The exact needs of the future business will not be entirely known. Nonetheless, investments in future business capabilities must be made while taking care of the near-term core business survival and ensuring competitiveness. The exact implementation of change programs in a firm will inevitably be spread across all four evolutionary processes to varying degrees, based on how fit the firm is relative to its business environment. Higher adaptive fit may mean less effort spent on survival initiatives, while more effort may be spent prepositioning the firm for multiple future business opportunities, or adapting. These choices must be made before introducing business change.

Business and Technology Initiatives	**Evolutionary Objective**	**Business Architecture Implications**	**IT Architecture Implications**	**Metric Affected**
TBD	Survive	Current Core Processes and Capabilities	Efficiency and Cost Control	Revenue, Cash Flow, Profit
TBD	Compete	Current Core Processes and Capabilities	Effectiveness and Winning	Revenue, Cash Flow, Market Share
TBD	Replicate	Future Core Processes and Capabilities	Knowledge Retention and Learning	Future Revenue, Cash Flow, Profit, and Market Share
TBD	Adapt	Future Core Processes and Capabilities and Variation Portfolio Mgt.	Agility and Flexibility	Future Revenue, Cash Flow, Profit, and Market Share

Exhibit 7.10 Prioritizing Initiatives in Business Evolution

A sample questionnaire to facilitate the dialogue in devising a firm's Business Evolution Model is offered in Exhibit 7.11. These are not the only questions that should be considered, but they are a handy starting point for corporate strategists to begin the process.

1. What is the corporate strategy?
2. Does the corporate strategy require modification based on environmental or competitive changes?
3. What are the firm's big ideas and goals?
   - Lead the Next Wave with innovative applications of technology.
   - Follow other firms with me-too initiatives.
   - Exist on par with peer competitors.
   - Seek lessons from other industries for competitive advantage.
4. What is the firm's business model? Does it need to be modified?
   - Does the core strategy still apply? Does it require modification?
   - Have the strategic resources changed? Must they be changed?
   - Does the customer interface require modification?
   - Should the value network be changed? Has it changed?
   - For all of these, how can information-based competition facilitate the firm's competitive posture?
   - How can information-based business modeling techniques increase business fitness?
5. Next, what fitness levers will be affected by the particular business strategy?
   - Revenue growth
   - Market share growth
   - Increased profit
   - Cash flow
6. What business initiatives will facilitate meeting corporate objectives?
   - What structural changes are needed?
   - What organizational factors must be changed?
   - What core capabilities must be added or strengthened?
   - What skills and human resource issues must be upgraded?
7. What technology initiatives will facilitate meeting objectives?
   - What infrastructure initiatives?
   - What transactional technology initiatives?
   - What informational technology initiatives?
   - What strategic initiatives?
8. What is the firm's overall ability to implement the necessary changes to become more fit and better adapted to its competitive and environmental landscape?

Exhibit 7.11 "How-To" Questionnaire for the Business Evolutionary Model

9. Perform the Change Self-Assessment and determine the firm's overall ability to implement change.
   - Need to Change (1–10 scale)
   - Capacity for Change (1–10 scale)
   - Ability to Change (1–10 scale)
10. What initiatives can be successful given the results of the Change Self-Assessment?
11. What survival initiatives will be required?
   - How viable is the core business franchise?
   - Is the core business franchise clear, or are there multiple revenue streams?
   - Is revenue growth stagnant, increasing, or falling?
   - How loyal are the core franchise customers?
   - How stable is the core franchise market share?
   - Are core business profits stable or shrinking?
   - What is the cash flow position of the core business operations?
   - Can the core business be used to sustain the firm through a replication cycle?
12. What competitive initiatives will be necessary?
   - Compete for market share and customers
   - Compete on product and service breadth, quality, and delivery
   - Compete on reach and distribution
   - Compete on technology
   - Compete on sales and marketing
13. What replication initiatives will be needed to transition the business across generations of change?
   - Is a technology transition in progress or pending?
   - Is a new generation of leadership pending or in progress?
   - Is the competitive environment mature with stagnant growth and little opportunity for innovation?
   - Does the firm need to reinvent itself? If so, along what dimensions: leadership, products and innovation, organizational structure, markets and customers?
14. What adaptive initiatives will be needed to implement lasting, long-term change for the benefit of the firm?
15. What business architecture elements can be flexed to successfully implement the necessary changes?
   - What organizational changes may be required?
   - What corporate structure modifications are necessary?
   - How can the value chain be changed or improved?
   - How can core processes be changed or improved?
   - What skills and core competencies are needed?

Exhibit 7.11 *(continued)*

16. What IT architecture elements can be flexed to ensure successful harvesting of the intended benefits?
    - Infrastructure investments and agility strategies
    - Transactional investments and efficiency and cost-reduction strategies
    - Informational investments and market, customer, and environmental intelligence strategies
    - Strategic technology investments and competitive actions and tactics
    - IT research and development investments and replication strategies, variation strategies
    - IT intellectual property and variation, replication, and value creation strategies
    - IT revenue generation and value creation
17. How do these all connect to drive a coherent action plan for the modern organization?
    - Role of IT
    - Goals of IT
    - Sources of value from information
    - What new value can be created from IT?

Exhibit 7.11 *(continued)*

EXAMPLES OF BUSINESS EVOLUTION IN ACTION

The best way to demonstrate the power of the evolutionary model is to use some current examples. We examine a current example of business evolution to illustrate the power of the Business Evolution Model. Hewlett-Packard is in the midst of radical change as Carleton S. (Carly) Fiorina attempts to remake the company into an innovation powerhouse for Internet services and cutting-edge hardware and software products and technologies. The information for this analysis has been gathered from public sources and only applies the decisions being made at HP retroactively into the Business Evolution Model. HP is an excellent current example because we will soon know whether Fiorina is successful with the change programs she has introduced.

HEWLETT-PACKARD'S JOURNEY

When Carly Fiorina was chosen to lead Hewlett-Packard, she faced many daunting challenges. First was the HP legacy of innovation of new technologies over its 64-year history. The list is impressive, as demonstrated in Exhibit 7.12, which highlights selected HP innovations in both technology and management practices over the last 60-plus years.[7]

Fiorina's job was to take HP's legacy of innovation and management leadership and reinvent it into a new HP, one that will be poised to deliver sorely needed technology and services to leading corporations and consumers in the Internet Age. Fiorina has taken radical steps to remake HP, from the standpoints of strategy, structure, culture, compensation, product development, marketing,

Management/Structure/People	Technology/Innovation
1940s Management by walking around (MBWA) Open-door policy	
1950s HP objectives written—the HP Way Division structure with separate P&L accountability Stock-purchase plans for employees	High-speed frequency counter
1960s HP labs established Flexible work hours Decentralization, grouping of related product lines under group general managers	HP 9100, the first scientific desktop calculator
1970s	HP 35, the world's first handheld scientific calculator
1980s Four "sector" organizations are formed to oversee increasing number of product groups HP reorganizes, placing all technical computing activities in the same sector	HP 9000, the first desktop mainframe HP enters the printer business: • ThinkJet printer • LaserJet printer, HP's most successful product ever HP DeskJet printer, HP's first mass-market printer

Exhibit 7.12 HP's History of Innovation

Management/Structure/People	Technology/Innovation
1990s	
Telecommuting policies are formalized to provide better job satisfaction for at-home workers	An 11-ounce PC introduced by HP HP Pavillion PC takes HP into the home computing market in 1994 JetSend, a wireless communications standard for computer peripherals, is introduced HP expands the printer business with the HP OfficeJet 700 series, a multifunction color product
2000s	
Carly Fiorina's front-back restructuring	e-services E-Speak, an Internet software platform for using the Net, is spawned in HP labs

Exhibit 7.12 *(continued)*

and sales; however, as a recent *Business Week* story pointed out, this reorganization is not your typical reorganization. This massive overhaul encompasses a magnitude never attempted at a company the size or complexity of HP.[8] But in Fiorina's mind, the complete remake of HP was justified based on its slow growth rate of recent years and lack of blockbuster innovations out of HP Labs. In fact, the last major product hit was the inkjet printer in 1984, and the growth rates of that product had slowed to 4 percent before Fiorina took over.

We demonstrate the power of the Business Evolution Model by reverse engineering the strategy, business model, and corporate and technology initiatives that are being implemented at HP. This analysis is done at a high level, based on public information, to illustrate some of the issues a company will face during times of high change.

WORKING THE MODEL

Corporate Strategy

According to a recent *Business Week* article,[9] HP depends on maturing markets such as personal computers (PCs) and printers, which contributed 69 percent of HP's revenue and 75 percent of its earnings in 2000; however, those businesses are expected to slow to single-digit growth, and profitability is expected to shrink as well. HP's market share of home printers was 60 percent in 2000, and it was tied with Compaq in market share of PCs, at roughly 12 percent. Dell passed both HP and Compaq in the first quarter of 2001, taking 13 percent of market share to Compaq's 12 percent. Slowing growth in HP's core printer business will also impact revenue for printer supplies, which includes consumable items such as ink and replacement printer cartridges. Fiorina's strategy for HP based on the market dynamics we have observed would essentially boil down to the following kinds of statements:

> Transform HP from a maker of low-margin consumer products such as PCs and printers into a leading Internet company focused on high-end corporate servers, storage products, e-business software, and services. The goal: 20 percent growth by 2002. Some strategic themes that logically emerge from this corporate strategy summary might include the following:
>
> - Continue printer dominance by creating new printing and imaging products.
> - Increase sales of high-margin corporate servers and storage products.
> - Develop and sell Internet software and related services in conjunction with its core computer and printer products.
> - Dramatically enhance professional services offerings through a merger or acquisition, for example, HP acquisition of PriceWaterhouseCoopers.
> - Increase innovation of new products by revamping R&D capabilities of HP Labs.

Business Model Summary

Using the information-based business modeling framework, we can similarly reverse engineer some of the business model changes that were implemented at HP in order to effect the broad changes required by Fiorina's restructuring program. The following business initiatives capture highlights of HP's business model based on public sources.

Business Initiatives

- Reinvigorate the sales organization by providing incentives for higher-margin products, as well as enforcing more discipline in meeting sales targets.
- Revitalize HP Labs by providing incentives for big-bang innovations versus R&D extensions of existing technology.
- Restructure the corporation by implementing a front-back organizational model.
- Add professional services as a product and service line, similar to IBM's Global Services, to provide high-margin consulting and implementation services.
- Develop new markets and new products through cross-company initiatives focused where product organizations intersect and overlap.

Change Vector Analysis

Need to Change In implementing the massive restructuring at HP, Fiorina had to choose between dramatic change and a possible slow death because HP's innovation engine was slowing and its core products were showing signs of slowing growth, both in printers and in computers. Fiorina chose to implement massive changes in three phases. The Business Evolution Model suggests that in order to successfully launch business and technology initiatives, a firm has to understand its need to change based on its corporate culture and its behavioral system. These factors have a direct bearing on how much change can be introduced to an organization, how much will be tolerated, and ultimately how much will be successful. In the HP case, Fiorina is challenging some 64-year-old behaviors and a corporate culture that is embodied in the HP Way, the decentralized divisional structure for product groups that has been around for decades. While there surely was a need to "shake things up," the question an executive will always face is "How much change can my company tolerate?" That is for history to decide in HP's case, although from the initial indications, perhaps too much change was intruded into the HP system too soon. *Need to Change Ranking: 5*

Capacity for Change HP's total capacity to change is being pushed to its upper limits by Fiorina's sweeping restructuring. The primary elements impacting a corporation's total capacity for change include the organizational structure, core processes and value chain, and core capabilities required for process execution. In addition to these business architecture issues, a firm must consider its IT architecture as well, such as the IT organization and structure, the information processes and value chain, and the IT core competencies required to implement business change based on information-architected processes. Together, these broad areas of corporate activity make implementing change a looming prospect for any firm. In HP's case, its restructuring is focused on processes that have been in place for decades, which adds the corporate culture and behavioral dimensions to this change equation. Folding the 83 autonomous product divisions into a four-unit structure—two product units focused on printers and computers, and two sales and marketing units focused on corporations and consumers—has proven to be a major hurdle. In addition, revamping HP Labs by adjusting incentives away from incremental enhancements to existing technology and instead rewarding new innovations will, it is hoped, result in blockbuster products and the creation of new markets. As mentioned previously, HP has not had a major new product since the inkjet printer in 1984. With HP's new front-end–back-end structure, sales and marketing processes and behaviors will have to change, along with the way that market and customer information is gathered from corporate and consumer customers by the front-end units and passed to the back-end product units for incorporation into new product designs, ongoing enhancements, and the addition of new features and functions. Given the scope of the organizational and process changes being imposed on HP by Fiorina's restructuring, assuming the core capabilities for execution exist already, HP will be challenged for the foreseeable future. *Capacity for Change Ranking: 3*

Ability to Change: HP's total ability to change, based on the previous discussions, will be challenged by Fiorina's restructuring plan. The combination of the corporate culture—60-plus years of the HP Way, which will linger because it was such a successful corporate methodology and behavioral model—will prove difficult to modify for HP. Combining the cultural and behavioral hurdles with the organizational structure, business processes, and core capabilities developed within the old HP structure will be a monumental challenge, especially in the time frame that Fiorina has allocated to implement her program of massive change at HP. Based on the earnings pressure from being a high-profile public company, as well as the expectations heaped on HP and Fiorina by the business press, the real question is whether HP will have time to incorporate and fully internalize the changes that have been implemented and that are planned. Combining HP's need-to-change factors with its capacity-for-change factors, HP's total ability to change will amount to a 4 on a 1 to 10 scale. This is a subjective analysis, but it points to some of the potential roadblocks to implementing any program of change in a corporation. *Ability to Change Ranking: 4*

Evolutionary Goals A brief summary of HP's high-level corporate goals will suffice here, but they are placed in evolutionary terms for our analysis. They are as follows:

- *Survive.* Shore up the maturing printer and PC businesses. Reduce costs and slow margin deterioration until new products and services become viable. Nurture core customers and ensure their participation in reinventing the firm.
- *Compete.* Revitalize the sales force with the front-back structure and focus on corporations and consumers. Provide incentives for higher-margin products such as servers and storage products, and reduce incentives for lower-margin products. Reduce costs to drive better earnings and margin performance. Launch innovative new products ahead of competitors to capture market share and attain better margins.
- *Replicate.* Reinvent the innovative engine of HP. Reorganize into a front-back structure for product groups and sales/marketing. Consolidate 83

independent product groups into two back-end product groups and two front-end sales and marketing groups to focus on short-term execution while pursuing new markets. Position HP for the next stage of the technology revolution in all facets—leadership, organization, business processes, innovation, products, and services.

- *Adapt.* Position HP for the next technology transitions. Transition the HP Way into the Internet Age, where speed and capability will help HP excel at technology, software, and consulting services, in effect combining the best of IBM's services strength with Sun Microsystems' product and technology excellence. Preposition HP for the future business environment by rebuilding the agility and innovation that once defined the HP Way.

Flex the Business Architecture For HP, Fiorina's restructuring was a huge gamble based on the amount of change that was introduced into the organization. The amount of business architecture change caused by Fiorina's restructuring is tremendous and clearly is pushing the limits of HP's ability to incorporate those changes into its business model without breaking it. The financials seem to indicate this quandary. HP is hyperflexing its business architecture based on its history of change and its ability to change. This poses a danger because as a firm approaches its upper limit of change, the business model can become stressed. In HP's case, it is instituting business changes—deep structural, organizational, and process changes—that may harm the business model in the short to medium term as the organization struggles to incorporate the new changes and attune HP to them. In this case, HP has not been accustomed to this amount of change, which is why it scored lower on the capacity-for-change ranking and on its overall ability to change. HP does not have the corporate muscle to implement the types of changes it is attempting simply because, as an organization, it has not exercised its corporate muscle this way before.

Flex the IT Architecture The Business Evolution Model requires flexing of the IT architecture in conjunction with the business architecture. The magnitude of the changes at HP clearly necessitated changes in information systems to accommodate them. In the case of Fiorina's restructuring, for example, a new financial system was implemented to support the more centralized front-back structures. This system will let management work off the same set of real-time financials, unlike the former stovepipe financial systems that supported the individual product organizations; however, one wrinkle was that Fiorina rushed the reorganization into place before HP's information systems were modified to reflect the changes. Although the financial systems clearly had to be modified to reflect the business changes at HP, we can also guess that other related systems changes were required to support the massive restructuring effort. These would have included human resources (HR), customer relationship management systems (CRM), sales tracking and sales force automation systems, and many more in addition to the financial systems required to roll up costs and track profits and losses. Consolidating the 83 autonomous product groups into the two back-end product groups and the two front-end sales and marketing groups must also have required significant systems support for product design and engineering functions. Surely there were others that we can only guess. In HP's case, the IT architecture was not capable of absorbing the changes required to support the parallel business architecture changes. Therefore, the result would be failed business and technology initiatives, as well as long and potentially costly implementation cycles.

Feedback: The Fitness Metrics

Finally, in order to work the Business Evolution Model, the results have to be compared to the business fitness metrics of revenue, profit, cash flow, and market share. Because we are talking about business evolution, the quarterly results that the stock market demands are clearly not measures of long-term competitive advantage, nor are they measures of business model success. The success of corporations in business evolutionary time frames must be measured across generations of corporate leadership, generations of technological change, and generations of environmental change. In HP's case, Fiorina has been in charge for only two years. So although the leadership baton has been passed to Fiorina from Lou Platt, the programs of change that are being implemented by Fiorina are just unfolding, and the results will not be truly accurate for some time. While Wall Street is becoming impatient, business evolution measures success over longer time frames, and that is precisely why stock price is not considered a primary fitness lever.

Lessons Learned from HP's Evolution

The HP story is still unfolding before our eyes, which is exciting because we can track how the changes that Carly Fiorina is implementing take or do not take within HP. In the case of the fitness metrics, it is too soon to tell what the impact will be because Fiorina's change program is still taking hold at HP; however, there are a few observations from our working the Business Evolution Model that stand out:

- Clearly, understanding an organization's need to change, capacity for change, and its overall ability to change is vital to successfully undergoing any renewal initiative. Carly Fiorina's massive restructuring may have hyperflexed both the business architecture and the IT architecture because of the magnitude and the pace of the changes.

- Flexing the business and IT architectures separately will create a strategic discontinuity. In HP's case, the business architecture was flexed before the IT systems were ready to support it, which caused the much-publicized financial reporting fiasco. To recover, the financials had to be gathered manually from each division. This is a small example of what may inevitably occur if the business architecture is flexed without considering the IT architecture.

CONCLUSION

The Hewlett-Packard example is not exhaustive but shows at least in a current sense how a corporation can use the business evolutionary model to adapt itself to changes in the business environment through a calculated program of change. We demonstrated how a new corporate strategy will lead to a new business model, which, if performed according to information-based business modeling, will lead to a business model that can be executed based on information.

Out of the corporate strategy and business model will fall several business and technology initiatives that must be prioritized by the evolutionary goals and needs of the corporation—survive, compete, replicate, and adapt. As explained, these initiatives have different objectives and different impacts on the business and IT architectures, which must be flexed to support them. Understanding a corporation's total capacity for change will have a heavy impact on any organization's ability to introduce change of any kind, whether the initiatives are business/functional changes or IT changes. Flexing the business and IT architectures must occur in parallel to avoid possible discontinuities between the business and organizational elements of an information-based business model and the information elements of the business model.

All business changes must ultimately affect the business fitness metrics of revenue, profit, cash flow, and market share. These lead to a company's ability to sustain itself as a viable entity. These feedback mechanisms are the bottom-line financial fitness levers that are mandatory for a corporation to survive long enough to be *able* to transition to its next future, whatever that future may be.

The business evolutionary model is a cyclical process of adapting the corporate strategy and business model to the business environment. It is a continuous learning process for a company to adapt itself to its ambient business landscape. The firms that have the basic business agility to quickly and easily implement business and technology changes to support their evolutionary goals and objectives will be the survivors of the Next Wave. In Hewlett-Packard's case, we have an example of evolution in real time, and over the coming months and years the outcome of Carly Fiorina's massive change program will be revealed. One thing is sure: natural selection works in business, and that will be the ultimate judge of HP's survival.

NOTES

1. Richard R. Nelson, "Why Do Firms Differ, and Why Does It Matter?" *Fundamental Issues in Strategy* (Boston, MA: Harvard Business School Press, 1995), p. 259.
2. Ibid.
3. Steve Jones, *Darwin's Ghost* (New York: Random House, 1999, 2000), p. 113.
4. Ibid.
5. George S. Day, "Maintaining the Competitive Edge: Creating and Sustaining Advantages in Dynamic Competitive Environments," in *Wharton on Dynamic Competitive Strategy,* George S. Day and David J. Reibstein, eds. with Robert Gunther (New York: John Wiley & Sons, 1997), p. 60.
6. Michael Dell with Catherine Fredman, *Direct from Dell* (New York: HarperBusiness, 1999), p. 201.
7. From Hewlett-Packard's web site, www.hp.com.
8. Peter Burrows, "The Radical," *Business Week* (February 19, 2001), p. 72.
9. Ibid., p. 74.

8

BUSINESS EVOLUTION THEORY AND PRACTICE

People are the quintessential element in all technology . . . Once we recognize the inescapable human nexus of all technology our attitude toward the reliability problem is fundamentally changed.

—Garrett Hardin,
Skeptic, July–August 1976

With the Business Evolution Model developed in Chapter 7 in place, we can now examine how businesses can employ these concepts in their ongoing operations. This chapter develops some examples of business evolution from various sources to show how this framework provides a way to view corporate change as a natural function of the development cycle of a firm. One thing that should be clear is that corporate strategies change. They change in response to environmental and competitive pressures from the business landscape. Business models are adjusted in response to these changes and business pressures, and the specific operational activities and choices of a business model are implemented to attain the performance goals defined by the corporate strategy. As business models are adjusted over time, the various business and technology initiatives that are undertaken by a firm on top of its day-to-day operations are limited. They must have relevance to the firm in one or more of the evolutionary categories of survive, compete, replicate, and adapt. These internal selection mechanisms of a firm determine the relevance of business and technology initiatives and whether they will lead to a positive impact on the fitness metrics of a firm: revenue, profit, cash flow, and market share. The cycle of activity follows the Business Evolution Model developed in Chapter 7.

Exhibit 8.1 summarizes the Business Evolution Model, highlighting the core elements of the model. For this discussion, we focus on examples of how various

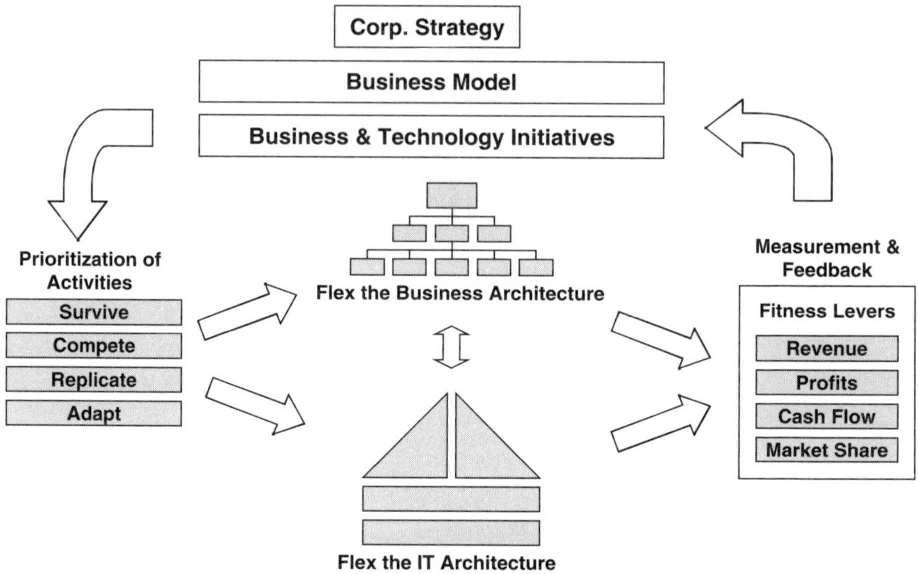

Exhibit 8.1 Business Evolution Model

business and technology initiatives relate to the evolutionary activities of survive, compete, replicate, and adapt, and how the business and information technology (IT) architectures must be flexed to accommodate these initiatives. Ultimately, these initiatives must positively affect the fitness metrics of revenue, profit, cash flow, and market share.

A logical question regarding this model, given the finite bandwidth any organization has to implement new business and technology initiatives, is: How often does this cycle occur? Are all of these evolutionary activities concurrent, or are some emphasized over others based on the corporation's performance and relative adaptive fit to its environment?

Exhibit 8.2 shows the time frames and periodicity of the evolutionary activities for a corporation.

Evolutionary activities in the survive and compete categories are immediate, day-to-day survival needs of a firm. These initiatives are targeted toward core business survival, and therefore are an ongoing set of activities that provide the core life support of a corporation: revenue, profit, cash flow, and market share. Survival initiatives are solely focused on today's core business franchise and how it generates the revenue, profits, and cash flow required for ongoing corporate activities and basic business viability. Survival initiatives are concerned with the here and now of a firm, today's basic business survival. Compete initiatives are similar to survive initiatives in their frequency and focus.

Evolutionary Activity	Frequency	Focus	Desired Result
Survive	Day-to-Day/Ongoing	Take care of today	Core survival of the firm—generate revenue and profit
Compete	Day-to-Day/Ongoing	Take care of today	Core survival of the firm—protect and grow market share
Replicate	Periodic/Intermittent	Transition to the future	*Reposition* the firm for a new generation of technology or leadership
Adapt	Ongoing	Prepare for multiple futures	*Preposition* the firm for an unknown future

Exhibit 8.2 Frequency and Focus of Evolutionary Activities

Compete initiatives are also day-to-day and focused on taking care of today's business needs. Compete initiatives are focused on protecting core market share, or the core revenue pipeline of the firm. Compete initiatives can involve multiple dimensions: competing on products, sales, marketing, distribution, price, and others. Regardless of which dimension or dimensions the initiatives target, they must help the firm protect the core business model and revenue.

Replicate and adapt initiatives are longer-term activities. Unlike survive and compete, these activities are oriented toward preparing the firm for the future. Replication activities seek to transition a corporation across generations of change, such as technology transitions, leadership transitions, and industry transitions. Replication activities are periodic in nature. Although the ability of a firm to perform replication activities may be groomed in times of industry and environmental stability, replication itself is intermittent. Replication takes energy because it involves change—changes in leadership, changes in business processes and core capabilities, and changes in technology for products and services as well as for internal use, such as IT. Replication activities help a corporation transition from one business environment to another. They help the firm cross the generation gap from one leadership regime to another, from one technology generation to another, or from one business model to another. Replication activities transition a firm to the future. They help reposition the firm for competing in the next generation of the business model, based on new leadership and new technology.

Adaptive activities are also future-oriented like replication activities, but they are longer-term focused. Adaptive activities are ongoing in nature and provide to the organization a planning horizon of 5 to 10 years ahead. Adaptive activities help an organization prepare for the next future, which may be completely unknown but can be anticipated by adding variability and business portfolio breadth, as well as developing new skills and core competencies that may contribute to competitive advantage. Adaptive activities preposition the firm for an unknown and uncertain future by adding strategic variability of businesses and core capabilities.

Exhibit 8.2 also shows how the business and technology initiatives that are launched from the business modeling process will fall into the four evolutionary activities of survive, compete, replicate, and adapt. Because the survive and compete initiatives are more the day-to-day processes and activities of a firm's core business model, they will naturally take up most of an organization's bandwidth for implementing change because these are more closely related to activities that are already taking place. Replication activities can be difficult because they involve higher rates of change being introduced into an organization. This is why replication is more of a periodic activity. It requires a significant investment of organizational energy and effort to implement replication initiatives. The HP example (see Chapter 7) shows how much energy it takes to remake a corporation, especially one the size and scope of Hewlett-Packard. But even at the business unit level, implementing large-scale change programs can be disruptive. As discussed, there is a theoretical upper limit to the amount of change that can be introduced into an organization before the changes begin to negatively impact the functions of the system.

A summary of the focus and differences among survive, compete, replicate, and adapt initiatives is detailed as follows. These concepts will be further embellished in examples of each type of initiative later in the chapter.

- *Survive.* How a company manages its operations and executes core business processes. Survive initiatives relate to core business processes, streamlining ongoing operations, and fine-tuning business execution. Survive initiatives tend to focus on how efficiently and consistently core company processes can be executed to service customers. Given this focus, survive initiatives may often seek operating efficiencies and cost reductions, as well as reduce cycle time for process execution, reliability, and other process metrics that ultimately result in healthy fitness metrics.
- *Compete.* How a firm competes against its direct enemies on customer-perceived value, such as price, products, technology superiority, sales and marketing, supply chain, distribution channels, or other dimensions that significantly determine a firm's success in a given industry. Compete initiatives significantly impact competitiveness in any of these dimensions.

Compete initiatives are focused on winning customers and market share in head-to-head competition with rival firms by attacking a competitor or defending market share on dimensions of customer-perceived value.

- *Replicate.* How a firm transitions its business model across a generation of change in technology, leadership, ownership, or overall business change; involves initiatives that contribute to the repositioning of a firm for a substantially "known" future. Replication initiatives focus on investing in reinvention activities, or efforts to reposition a company for its next future, a new business environment or a new technology paradigm.
- *Adapt.* How a firm positions itself for multiple futures, largely unknown and longer term; involves initiatives that add variability and business portfolio breadth to a company, which enhances its ability to adapt in multiple directions in response to unforeseen changes in the business environment.

BUSINESS EVOLUTION STRATEGIES: SURVIVE AND COMPETE

Survive and compete are the two evolutionary processes of a firm that are primarily focused on short-term viability. This means generating revenue and profit from core business processes. It means developing and delivering products and services valued by core customers. It means protecting the basic ability of the corporation to subsist as a viable business entity. Surviving and competing are the primary "make a living" activities of the firm that provide business fitness for the firm. The essence of surviving and competing is taking care of the core business as it exists today by preserving the ability to make a living as a corporation. The survive and compete activities of a firm are the day-to-day ongoing core activities that sustain the corporation and allow it to remain viable. Exhibit 8.3 highlights survive and compete initiatives in the Business Evolution Model.

PROTECT THE CORE BUSINESS SURVIVAL SYSTEM

This is the corporation's life support system, or the basic processes that allow the firm to remain a viable business entity, to pay its employees and its suppliers, and to support development of new products and services. These core activities and processes generate revenue for the firm. The fundamental goal of these core processes is to generate revenue with products and services that are currently available. This is not a strategy for tomorrow's products and services; it is a strategy for today's products and services.

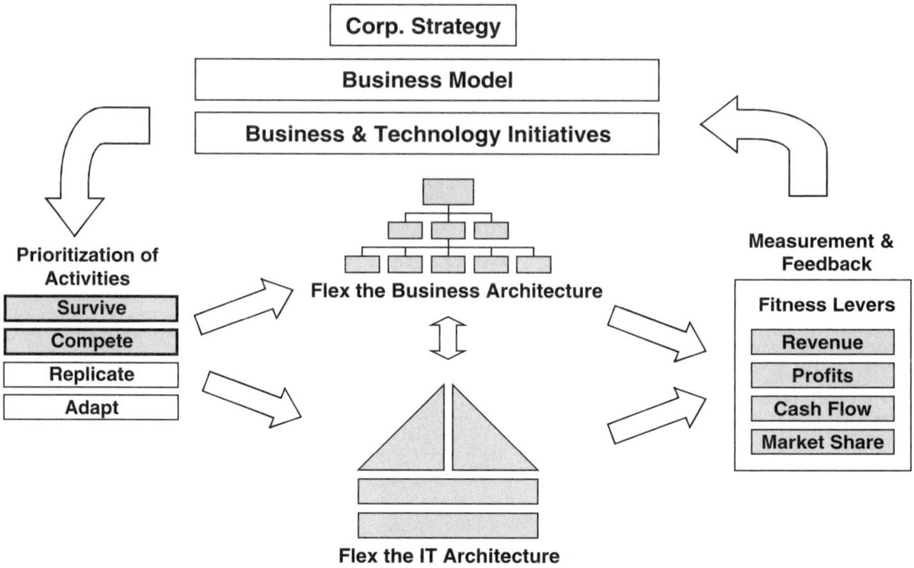

Exhibit 8.3 Business Evolution Examples: Survive and Compete

WHAT IS CORE?

What is the core business of a firm? How does a firm identify its core business franchise? The key to this analysis is focusing the analysis at the business unit level of a corporation. This is because a firm may have one primary business unit, with its own unique business model, or it may be a multiple business unit structure operating multiple, distinct business models. Protecting the core survival system of a corporation might begin with the following questions:

- What value can the firm deliver to the marketplace with its current assemblage of knowledge, assets, personnel, and products and services?
- What is the core set of products and services that contribute to sustaining the firm today?
- What are the firm's capabilities to continue producing and delivering the products and services of the core franchise today?
- How long will these core products and services continue to produce revenue and profits for the firm? What window of opportunity exists for maintaining the core operations?
- Are the basic processes required to deliver these products and services threatened by factors within the firm?
- Are they threatened by environmental changes?

- Are these processes under attack from competitors?
- Is your market share from these core products and services stable, eroding, or growing?

These questions are not exhaustive, but they should begin the identification and analysis of the bread-and-butter operations of a corporation so that they can be protected, nurtured, optimized, and, eventually, replaced with new value contributors, new products, and new services. In the immediate term, these core products and services, and the processes that make and deliver them, must be maintained. This is the lifeblood of the corporate organism, the air it breathes, the energy it consumes. Without these things—air, food, and water—the organism fails. Without revenue from paying customers and profits from continuing operations, the corporate entity will begin to fail.

MAKE CORE PROCESS AS EFFICIENT AS POSSIBLE: CONSERVATION OF ENERGY

The key here is to drive waste and inefficiency out of the core value-creating processes used to deliver current products and services. While delivering the core products and services to the marketplace, the firm must use technology and process improvement initiatives to make these core operations as efficient as possible along several dimensions. Possible dimensions to examine for process improvements include:

- Cycle time for manufacturing production or service delivery, or other time-based metrics that are perceived as valuable by customers
- Product and process cost relative to competitors, and in absolute terms for improved margin attainment
- Product and process quality, and overall process repeatability
- Customer service metrics such as call center wait time, customer service response time, order placement time, and others
- Product delivery time
- Web site speed and content

The specific attributes will vary from firm to firm, but the intent here is to focus on the core operations of the firm and make them profitable and efficient in and of themselves. Because this is a short- to medium-term strategy, the objective is to make the best out of the current situation by driving maximal revenue and profit from the currently available products and services, while protecting existing market share. These activities make money for the firm today and protect its ability to develop the products and services for competing tomorrow. In the biological organism example, these activities sustain the firm long enough for its reproductive success. In other words, the organism's goal is to survive long enough to reproduce. A corporation attempts to do the same thing—survive—and its version of reproductive success is to survive across generations of change. The core revenue model of the corporation must be insulated from price and margin erosion from increased competitors, so any excess costs embedded in transaction processing, in customer service, and in distribution and handling must be examined for improved efficiency and low cost structure. This does not mean competing on a low-cost basis. The intent here is to make the core products and services as simple and easy to sustain as possible, while exploring and supporting the ability of the firm to examine new products, services, and processes for delivering value for the future. In the meantime, the basic business functions of today must be highly optimized, and the customers of today must be nurtured.

SECURE MARKET SHARE AND PROTECT "FRANCHISE CUSTOMERS"

Performing the aforementioned actions must all lead to securing the firm's market share through defensive actions and excellent customer service. In other words, take care of the customers who contributed to your current levels of success (if the firm has been successful), while seeking market share gains through flanking maneuvers and precise targeted product and service programs. Market share translates into a war chest of cash for the long haul, so maintaining market share will help ensure a firm's ability to compete long term in its chosen markets. Market share retention is critical for sustaining the cash flow and revenue of the firm to support ongoing operations. Potential activities include:

- Shore up potential defections from the core customer base and implement loyalty programs to defend accumulated market share.
- Ensure that core market share is profitable market share by culling out unprofitable customers.
- Nurture the "franchise customers," or the blue chip loyal customers who are considered partners for the future.
- Implement marketing and sales programs that help sustain market share while "profitably" taking share away from direct competitors.
- Use flanking strategies to grow market share while avoiding costly, head-to-head competition.
- Add incremental services to products to continue to innovate around the core products and services of the firm without necessarily undergoing a full product development cycle.

These actions are all focused on maintaining the current market share while opportunistically taking share from competitors without eroding profit margins. Opportunistically taking market share means avoiding head-to-head battles that may cause price wars and other margin-eroding outcomes. Flanking maneuvers should be used as the primary means of competing, unless the firm has a dominant share of its chosen market.

Notice the relationship to the fitness levers described earlier in the book: revenue, market share, and profits. These must be accomplished in order to ensure survival of the business idea that originally created the company.

INSURANCE EXAMPLE: SURVIVE AND COMPETE

Consider insurance companies. The core business model for a typical insurance company revolves around selling insurance products to businesses and consumers. Many nuances of the insurance industry will not be covered here, but it is a complex and highly regulated business environment. A typical commercial property and casualty insurance carrier might sell a variety of products such as workers' compensation, general liability, commercial automobile for fleets of vehicles, commercial multiperil (bundled coverages), and business owners policies (similar to commercial multiperil but targeted for small business owners). Selling these insurance policies results in collection of premium, which is the revenue derived from selling the insurance policies.

This core business model is known as underwriting, which requires gathering customer data, evaluating the risk of insuring that particular customer for particular insurance needs, and determining a price that provides adequate coverage for the customer and protects the insurance company from severe losses from potential future claims. Making money on the core business model is known as an underwriting profit. After collecting the premium dollars from the buyer (insured) of the insurance policy, the insurance carrier then places the money in a variety of investment tools of varying risks and returns. In many cases, these investments are where insurance companies make up for losses in their core operations. The bull stock market of the late 1990s into the 2000s allowed many carriers to operate their core operations at a loss while offsetting those losses with investment income. This is a case where the core revenue model, profitably selling insurance products and minimizing losses on claims, was allowed to operate less than optimally because the investment income more than offset the core business results.

What initiatives might an insurance carrier consider to facilitate its survival and competitive posture? Let us work the business evolution model and derive a solution. First, a little more background is in order. The insurance industry is generally considered technologically challenged by virtue of its lack of investment in information systems. This stems from the culture of financial control because insurance is a part of the financial services industry. As observed earlier, the financial control legacy of IT has largely contributed to its underinvestment by corporations around the world, regardless of industry. The insurance industry clearly exemplifies this pattern of IT spending, or, rather, lack of IT investment. The irony is that computer systems for insurance companies are their primary production systems. These are their primary business assets that generate their core business revenue (premiums from insurance policies), profits, cash flow, and market share. Multiple sources cite the insurance industry's poor IT capabilities.[1] The following paragraph from Goldman Sachs' annual insurance industry study illustrates the state of IT for insurance companies:

> Historically, technology spending has not been a priority for insurance carriers. Most companies use technology, but adoption has generally been slow and internally focused with little standardization and integration of architectures. Cost often determines development, not usefulness or need. For example, many Y2K repairs were "Band-Aid" solutions for old technology, not new technology platforms to support Internet growth or create operating efficiencies.[2]

I affectionately refer to this pattern of information systems underinvestment as the "Rip Van Winkle effect." It is as if insurance companies "fell asleep" by not investing in their IT architectures, infrastructures, and application portfolios for the last 20 years, and they have suddenly "awakened" and are realizing that to catch up, they will have to invest millions on their infrastructure, application portfolios, consulting fees, and internal skills development to get up to par. The insurance industry is conservative by nature and maintains a 1970s view of IT, which was focused on efficiency and automation. This cost-control view of IT resulted in tremendous investments in outdated legacy information systems that cannot support the needs of today's business environment. This Rip Van Winkle approach to IT, where a firm ignores its technology architecture, infrastructure, and application portfolio for 20 years and then suddenly "wakes up," will not work in the new millennium.

As a result of the dramatic rise of the Internet, suddenly new virtual insurance companies are appearing with direct sales models that bypass the traditional agent/broker distribution channels. This approach has challenged the cost structure for insurance products because the commissions normally paid to agents are no longer needed, and these savings can be passed onto the customers. These are new and more nimble competitors. In addition, recent regulatory changes such as the repeal of the Glass-Steagal Act now allow banks and other financial institutions to enter the insurance industry. Because banks and brokerage firms already manage individual and corporate financial transactions on a daily or weekly basis, they are well positioned to add insurance products to their portfolio of other financial services.

In addition to more competitors entering the insurance industry, the competitive environment has intensified as corporations are aggressively pursuing growth strategies by underpricing insurance policies. As price competition increases, premiums charged to customers fall, while the expenses to service insurance policies, manage claims, and handle losses remain constant or rise. The combined ratio (CR) is a primary indicator of insurance profitability. The CR is the ratio of an insurance company's costs, such as loss expenses, claims and underwriting expenses, and general and administrative costs, divided by the premium dollars charged to customers. A combined ratio of $1.00 indicates that, theoretically, an insurance company is breaking even by spending $1.00 on expenses for every $1.00 of premium taken in. An expense ratio of $1.083 indicates that for every dollar of premium gathered from customers, a company is spending $1.083 on expenses. Incidentally, this is the industry average from a 1999 Dowling Partners study of the top 54 commercial insurance companies.[3] In recent years, insurance companies were able to operate with a higher CR because they could offset underwriting losses with investment income. With the bear market of 2001, this operating strategy is not viable. Insurance companies must operate profitably based on their core business operations, which are their underwriting activities. Clearly, the insurance industry is beginning to be challenged by these forces of change.

Survive and compete initiatives that will help insurance companies improve their core underwriting business while fending off the competition might include:

- Reduce expenses, which will improve the combined ratio and profits.
- Increase premiums charged to customers, in effect increasing prices for insurance policies.
- Exit unprofitable lines of business or states where competitive intensity is too high.
- Implement technology to automate core business operations and drive costs down.
- Upgrade the IT architecture to allow web-based business models, provide better customer service, and reduce maintenance expenses of legacy systems.
- Explore a direct sales business model that eliminates agents and brokers from the distribution channel and therefore reduces commission expenses paid.
- Add new lines of business or expand into new states or regions that are more attractive for writing insurance based on the competitive and regulatory landscape.

Out of this range of possible business and technology initiatives, insurance carriers have multiple options. One choice picking up momentum in the marketplace is the implementation of web-based underwriting front-end systems. As a survive and compete initiative, this choice has many merits.

Web-based underwriting front-end systems first and foremost are focused on the core business activity of an insurance company—underwriting. These are relatively new solutions for the insurance industry and deliver value in several ways. First, they are modern, web-based technology architectures that can be added to an insurance company's existing legacy architecture, with necessary integration, and rapidly migrate business functionality to the Internet. In other words, the insurance carrier does not have to completely replace all of its back office computer systems to quickly implement a web-based business model. This is an attractive alternative to replacing the entire back office suite of computer systems.

Second, these solutions can automate the underwriting process for commodity insurance products, such as small and medium-sized workers' compensation policies. Underwriting is the process of selecting and estimating an insurance risk for purposes of issuing coverage under an insurance policy. Underwriting is usually a labor-intensive process that requires manually filling out paper forms, faxing, mailing and hand transport, and multiple handoffs among agents, administrative staff, underwriting assistants, underwriters, and underwriting management, which ultimately may result in a quote to a customer. Once the quote is accepted, more paperwork ensues until a paper policy is generated and mailed to the customer. In many cases, a large percentage of these policies are standard policies that can use template underwriting procedures, which means that underwriters do not have to manually underwrite them. This saves labor and improves underwriter productivity, especially for small and midsized policies, which can cost on average \$1,200 to \$1,500 per policy for small workers' compensation policies, for example, up to \$25,000 to \$30,000 for a medium-sized workers' compensation policy.

Studies have shown that a large percentage of small policies, up to 80 percent depending on the types of insurance policies an insurance company chooses to offer and to whom (based on the types of risks an insurance company chooses to underwrite), can be completely automated using computer systems, from the initial insurance application (submission) through the actual underwriting process, which assesses the risk, performs the rating process (calculations based on actuarial data and proprietary algorithms), and ultimately determines the price of the policy for that particular case. This process results in a quote to a customer. In the case of medium-sized policies, up to 50 percent of these can be completely automated using an automated underwriting application.

Third, web-based underwriting front-end systems, by virtue of automation, capture and enforce standard underwriting rules and procedures for every insurance policy every time, which eliminates the variation that arises from manual underwriting and variable application and enforcement of an insurance company's policies for accepting or rejecting an insurance policy. Assuming that the rating guidelines and underwriting rules are stringent enough, an insurance company will be able to develop a better-quality book of business, which translates into fewer claims being filed and paid, or reduced losses. The obvious benefit here is more profitability for the insurance company.

The value proposition from web-based underwriting front-end systems essentially boils down to the following financial benefits:

- Cut costs by automating underwriting for small and midsized insurance policies and by streamlining underwriting staff.
- Grow the business without adding incremental underwriting staff by increasing underwriting productivity, increasing quote volume and throughput, and reducing quote cycle time from hours to minutes.
- Reduce losses and improve the quality of the portfolio of insurance policies (book of business) by standardizing underwriting procedures, which after one renewal cycle (annually) would begin to show results.
- Provide the insurance carrier with the option to renegotiate commission fees paid to agents because, on a per-quote basis, agent labor has been reduced and therefore more quotes can be processed by agents using automated submissions and quoting.

Using the business evolution framework, we have already established that web-based underwriting computer systems are clearly survive and compete initiatives because they are targeted at an insurance company's core business operations—underwriting—and they clearly have bearing on core revenue and profitability by potentially reducing costs, increasing premium volume (revenue) while controlling costs, and reducing losses over the long run by standardizing underwriting procedures.

Flexing the business architecture for the web-based underwriting front-end system involves changing the core processes and workflows of submitting an insurance application (submission), quoting and issuing an insurance policy. Flexing the business architecture in this case requires the following organizational, process, and related changes to be successful:

- *Company organization and structure.* Automating the underwriting process may involve staff reorganizations, staff reductions, and redefining the rules, roles, and responsibilities of underwriters; new job designs and procedures will be required.

- *Value chain.* The underwriting process is toward the front of the insurance value chain, and to a large extent it determines the profitability for an insurance carrier as well as the number of claims filed and losses incurred by insurance companies. Web-based underwriting will streamline the front end of the insurance value chain, taking costs and cycle time out of the process, and allowing higher productivity by participants in the value chain, including agents/brokers, underwriters, and related staff. Exhibit 8.4 shows the insurance value chain generically and then functionally where underwriting occurs in the process.
- *Core business processes and strategic assets.* Underwriting is a core business process in the primary value chain of an insurance company. Improving the process of underwriting, a critical process in the insurance value chain, will help drive better performance for the core revenue and profits of the firm. The strategic assets in this case refer to two elements of the business architecture: the underwriting personnel, and the proprietary processes and algorithms that are required for underwriting. As mentioned earlier, personnel changes will be required, including possible cross-training and education of underwriters, as well as documenting underwriting rules and algorithms for addition to the software systems. Other related processes may be affected as well, depending on the particular insurance company's value chain and process designs.
- *Organizational learning processes.* Changing the underwriting processes using a web-based underwriting front-end system will change the way that new insurance policies are quoted and issued. With the attendant changes in roles and responsibilities, processes will require new documentation and, as cycles of learning are accumulated, process enhancements will be required. This will only be possible with organizational learning processes in place.

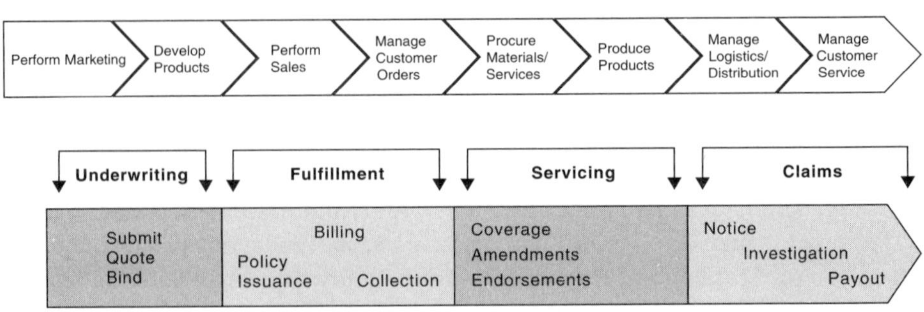

Exhibit 8.4 Insurance Value Chain

- *Corporate fitness metrics.* The fitness metrics that are potentially affected by a web-based underwriting front-end system are listed previously, but the obvious ones relate to revenue, profits, and cash flow. In many cases, insurance companies are not growing market share but rather are being more selective in the business they accept. This means sacrificing market share for "good" customers with less likelihood of claims, lower losses from claims paid, and better profitability.

Flexing the IT architecture for this type of initiative is potentially a simpler exercise than flexing the business architecture because many insurance companies do not have flexibility built into their IT architectures. Most are saddled with outdated IT platforms and legacy applications that are rigid, proprietary, and cannot be modified to meet today's business needs. Even so, for insurance companies, flexing the IT architecture may not be easy because of the outdated technology platforms that are typical of many insurers. Legacy IT architectures, infrastructure, and application portfolios dominate the insurance landscape, so the ability to flex these outdated and inherently rigid IT architectures is limited. In order to implement the variety of web initiatives required of today's business environment, insurance companies will have to replace large portions of their legacy IT architecture and application portfolio. To many insurers, this is a huge investment they would rather avoid, even though it is a worthy investment by today's business standards. In addition, the wholesale replacement of core business systems, most of which are mission-critical to day-to-day operations, is fraught with risk. To overcome these typical issues and objections, software vendors have developed flexible service-based business models versus the typical licensing models.

Web-based underwriting front-end systems are typically offered by the vendors as hosted services, where the software configuration, implementation, and ongoing operation are provided by the vendor on a rental basis, typically a fixed monthly fee or based on a percentage of transactions. This outsourcing model of computer services is convenient for many insurance companies because it means they do not have to upgrade their infrastructure and applications all at once in order to begin conducting business over the web. In the traditional licensing model, an insurance company would purchase the software licenses, buy and implement the necessary infrastructure, hardware and software, network components and media, as well as upgrade the user desktops to use the software. This is what made many enterprises software applications so cost prohibitive, and also helps explain the reluctance to replace them. The hosted model for providing web-based underwriting front-end systems eliminates the need, at least for this particular initiative, to flex the existing IT architecture. The hosted approach is an add-on system that integrates to existing policy issuance and related back-office systems, rather than replacing them. It adds web-based capabilities with workflow functionality and an underwriting rating engine that allows the complete automation of the underwriting process, without having to add new IT infrastructure, yet provides a best-of-breed web-based solution for today's business environment.

Finally, referring to the fitness metrics of the Business Evolution Model, implementing the web-based underwriting front-end system can affect an insurance company's business fitness in some positive ways. As mentioned earlier, the value proposition of these solutions is based on whether an insurer desires cost reductions, growth in premium volume (revenue), or reduced claims and losses by standardizing underwriting practices and rules. Exhibit 8.5 shows how a web-based underwriting front-end system initiative fits into the Business Evolution Model.

This example from the insurance industry is not comprehensive and did not demonstrate the full power of the Business Evolution Model because the original business model was not devised from an information-based perspective. What we have done is simply work from a set of potential business initiatives, through the selection process based on the evolutionary priorities of survive, compete, replicate, and adapt, then we flexed the business and IT architectures, resulting in the improvement in the business fitness metrics of increased revenue

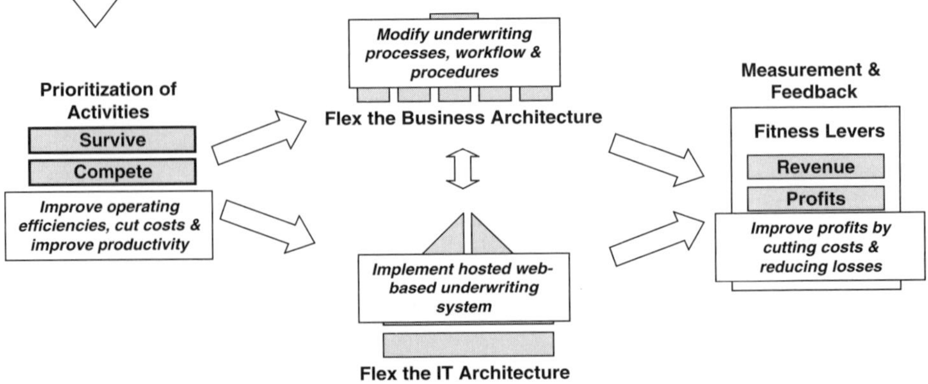

Exhibit 8.5 Business Evolution Insurance Example

and profitability. Had we begun with information-based business modeling, we could clearly demonstrate the power of the model.

COMPETITIVE STRATEGIES

Compete initiatives, similar to survive initiatives, are targeted at core operations, but in a slightly different fashion. Compete initiatives impart competitive advantage for the firm in one or more facets of its business and significantly determine its position relative to its direct competitors. While survive initiatives can apply across many or all facets of a firm's core business operations and business processes, compete initiatives are focused on particular company activities that can determine success against a direct competitor in a determinable time frame. Compete initiatives seek differentiation along a particular dimension of a company's capabilities, whereas survive initiatives seek efficiencies, which may provide enough improvement to be considered compete initiatives. Examples of compete initiatives might include competing on pricing strategies, product features, product line breadth, supply chain management, sales and marketing tactics, distribution channels, or other definable and somewhat focused initiatives. Ultimately, however, compete initiatives have one clear outcome: winning and keeping more customers, and therefore market share, than a firm's primary direct competitors. Competing in this sense requires enough total performance along all company processes and competitive dimensions to win more than the enemy—a firm's competitors.

Compete initiatives are generally more focused than survive initiatives. Compete initiatives are directed at enhancing a firm's posture against its direct competitors, which ultimately must mean serving customers better in tangible, customer-perceived ways. Compete initiatives are focused initiatives seeking a definable improvement in specific elements of a corporation's competitive stance against its head-to-head competitors. They are attacking or defending a business based on a particular dimension of customer-perceived value. Examples of compete initiatives are listed below:

- Modify sales and marketing strategy and tactics to attack a new market segment or improve sales of higher-margin products and services. HP is still adjusting to the massive restructuring of its product development organizations, as well as sales and marketing operations. Creating the front-back structure with two sales/marketing groups—one for consumers and one for corporate customers, as well as adding professional services, has been a complex organizational challenge. The objective for HP's CEO Carly Fiorina is to make HP an Internet products and services powerhouse with leading-edge, high-margin servers and storage products combined with consulting capabilities and related services.

- Implement a customer relationship management (CRM) solution to automate front-office sales and marketing functions, manage sales contacts and customer data, and perform automated marketing programs. CRM is an extremely popular initiative today, driven by market leaders such as Seibel Systems, Oracle CRM, SalesLogix, and several other vendors in the category.
- Improve the product development process to reduce time to market for new products and consolidate product families to use more common components and reduce the total number of components. This initiative is being examined by Motorola in response to loss of market share, revenue, and profits in its mobile phone division. Motorola realizes that it must be able to launch new products on time with new features and functions sought by the cellular carriers as part of specific marketing launches. This places the burden on product development and engineering processes, as well as manufacturing flexibility. Nokia, the world's leading cell phone designer and manufacturer, has world-class product development capabilities and tremendous manufacturing capacity that it controls, which have helped to make it the dominant player in cell phones in a mere 10 years' time.
- Implement a supply chain management strategy to improve supply chain execution, supplier management, and procurement practices to reduce direct and indirect material costs and drive total inventory costs down. This is similar to what Dell Computer does with its supply chain execution, which has made Dell the low-cost provider of computers in the world. In 2001, Dell launched a withering price war against its competitors to take away market share and force the weak suppliers to exit the business. This is a clear case of turning low-cost operational excellence into a competitive weapon.
- Outsource manufacturing operations for noncore products to reduce costs and focus resources on strategic products. Cisco placed heavy emphasis on outsourcing manufacturing while controlling engineering and design, along with marketing and sales of its high-technology communications and network gear. This has helped Cisco achieve higher margins on sales because of a lower cost structure and less capital investment in plants, property, and equipment. In response, many communications infrastructure companies have tried to become Cisco-like by shifting to outsourced manufacturing models, primarily to shave costs and reduce headcount. This strategy has been accompanied by selling off manufacturing plants and operations to contract manufacturers.

- Overhaul the product line with new features and functions to attack a particular competitor in a particular market segment.
- Implement a competitive intelligence program to better monitor market conditions and competitor products and sales tactics.

From the sample list, it is clear that compete initiatives are mostly focused on achieving particular results based on specific sets of actions. The supply chain management initiative is a broad-scope initiative that actually comprises several smaller initiatives. Compete initiatives still follow the basic Business Evolution Model that the survive initiatives do, beginning first by prioritizing them, assessing the organization's ability to tolerate change, flexing the business and IT architectures, and then measuring the desired results against the fitness metrics. Exhibit 8.6 shows a manufacturing example of one of the compete initiatives, improving the product development process.

In working the Business Evolution Model with a compete initiative, the steps and analyses are identical to the survive example. In the example, the business initiative is to improve the product development process to reduce time to market for new products as well as consolidate the number of product families in the firm's product portfolio. This initiative would be a logical response to lost market share and being late to market with critical products, as well as from

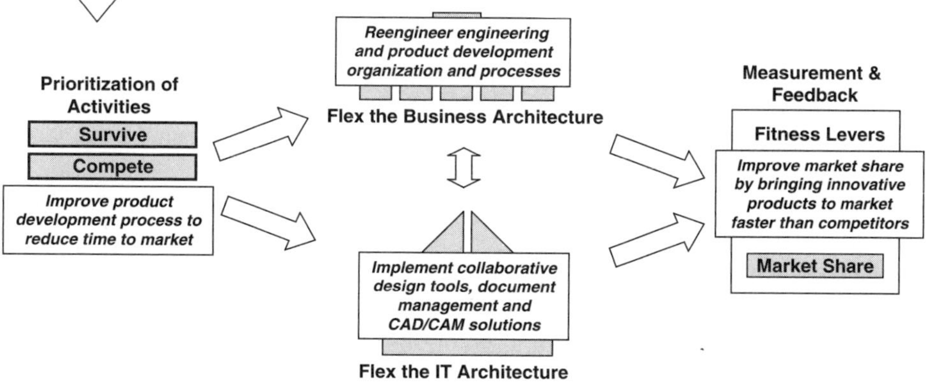

Exhibit 8.6 Complete Manufacturing Example

higher costs relating to product complexity and lack of common component strategies. Remember, compete initiatives are attacking and defending initiatives.

This is similar to what Motorola is attempting to accomplish in its personal communications sector, the division that makes cell phones and pagers, accounting for 29 percent of Motorola's $37.6 billion in revenue in 2000.[4] Motorola was notoriously late in shifting from analog technology to digital technology, which cost it dearly versus Nokia, which attacked the market with a slew of new digital designs and captured a dominant market share position. In addition to that strategic technology shift, Motorola has also been late to market with specific product programs for its carriers, failing to incorporate carrier-specific enhancements to their cell phones, such as trendy multicolored face-plates, safety messages on displays, and carrier-specific colors. To remedy being late to market with critical new cellular phone designs, Motorola is revamping new product development to reduce time to market by 50 percent. To reduce high unit costs and eliminate product complexity, Motorola is reducing the number of phone types by 84 percent, from 128 to 20, and simplifying phone designs to reduce the number of components from about 600 parts to 150 parts.[5]

Continuing with the Business Evolution Model, improving the product development process will involve modifying the structure and flow of critical processes in flexing the business architecture. The R&D and engineering organizations will have to be examined and potentially restructured by product families, product platforms, or some other market-focused criteria. Processes will have to be deconstructed and redesigned to take slack and wait time out of new product development process. Gate review processes and synchronous design techniques may allow certain activities to proceed in parallel before they fall into a sequential flow downstream. The handoff to manufacturing operations must also be clean. Manufacturing processes must also be designed or modified in lockstep with new product designs. Many parallel activities are required during new product development that are not solely product related, such as designing, modifying, and validating the manufacturing process, establishing critical supply chain and procurement relationships for component supply from outside vendors, as well as internal suppliers in Motorola's case, where they are more vertically integrated than other competitors, providing many semiconductor components to their product divisions.

Flexing the IT architecture for Motorola will also be required for success with this new product development initiative. While the specific technology programs have not been revealed by Motorola in public documents, we can infer the types of information technologies that will be required to successfully speed up new product development. Several IT solutions play into this initiative: computer-aided design (CAD) and computer-aided manufacturing (CAM), simulation tools, product data management (PDM) solutions, enterprise document management solutions, workflow management systems, and even today's modern collaborative design tools that leverage Internet technologies to provide access to all aspects of a product architecture synchronously can shorten time to market and eliminate the traditional "over the wall" mentality that is typical of the handoff from design to manufacturing. These products all potentially play a role in shortening new product development time by allowing sharing of critical design data by downstream organizations and processes that need it in order to design manufacturing processes, develop manufacturing assembly instructions, and produce product documentation and service manuals that ship with the product.

Without knowing specifically what Motorola is implementing to flex its IT architecture, clearly technology plays an important role in new product development. New product development embodies a workflow-intensive series of processes, and many new IT solutions are clearly focused on addressing the collaboration requirements of engineering and design functions, while fulfilling the information-sharing needs of downstream users of design data as well. Automating the workflow of the product development process can also enforce gate reviews, signoffs of key process deliverables, and checkpoints, which can shave significant slack and wait time from an existing business process.

The fitness metrics addressed by this example relate to revenue and profits. The ability to launch new products to market faster than the competition allows a firm to leapfrog its existing product technology as well as features and functions. This provides a first-to-market advantage, which ultimately drives higher revenue though sales of new products. Motorola has missed several opportunities with carriers by being late with carrier-specific product programs or by its inability to quickly customize existing products with new colors and features. This has also cost Motorola dearly in market share and revenue. On the cost side of the fitness equation, eliminating redundant models of products and reducing the number of components from 600 to 150 will significantly drive product costs down. Fewer product families will facilitate streamlining the new product development process, but it will also allow greater cost reductions in inventories, in engineering and design personnel, and in unit costs through component reduction and greater part sharing among models.

This example of a compete initiative demonstrates how a company can respond to a given competitor or competitive situation with a business or technology initiative focused on achieving success in a particular area of its operations. Compete initiatives can also be broad initiatives that consist of several smaller, focused initiatives. Exhibit 8.7 shows a generic manufacturing value chain and how compete initiatives might fit into enhancing a company's competitive position in a specific manner.

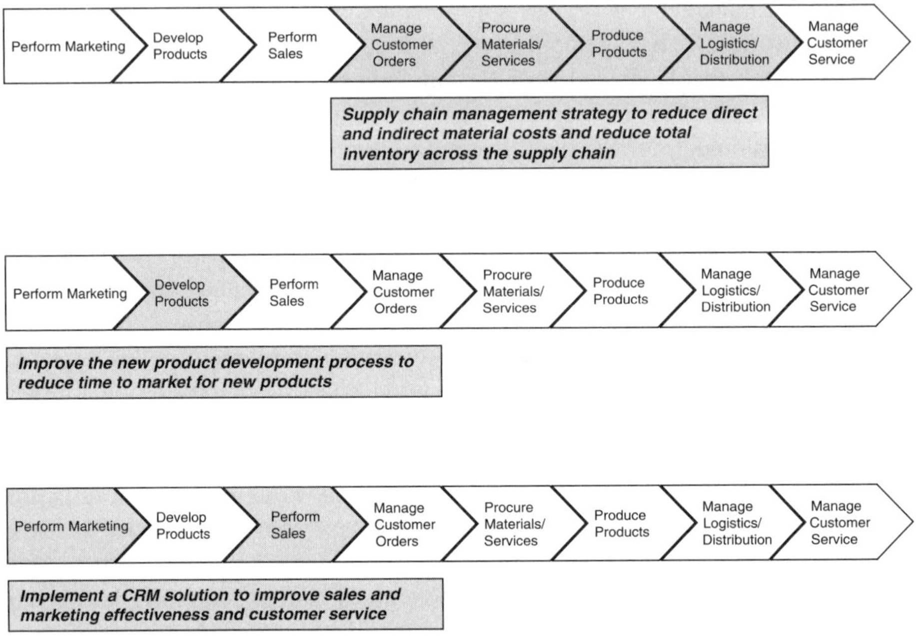

Exhibit 8.7 Manufacturing Compete Initiatives

SURVIVE AND COMPETE CONCLUSION

Survive and compete initiatives are focused on the core business franchise or franchises of a corporation. They are aimed at taking care of today's business, making it as efficient and profitable as possible given the current business conditions and environmental trajectory. Survive initiatives are based on making the core business as operationally efficient as possible by continuous improvement means, such as reducing costs, streamlining business processes, reducing cycle times, and simplifying business transactions. They are about sustaining the performance of the core business model by fine-tuning and honing its effectiveness and reliability. Survive initiatives can fall anywhere along a corporation's value chain and can be considered broad activities that may affect several business processes or the entire value chain. Compete initiatives are more focused. Compete initiatives are directed at attacking a competitor or defending market share from a direct competitor along a particular dimension of customer-perceived value. Compete initiatives are specific actions taken to improve market share and grow revenue and profits. These types of initiatives are what a company must do to sustain itself as a viable business entity, by driving its core business model to be the best it can be.

BUSINESS EVOLUTION STRATEGIES: REPLICATE AND ADAPT

We now shift our discussion to future-oriented evolutionary activities of a firm: replication and adaptation. Exhibit 8.8 shows their fit in the Business Evolution Model. As discussed, these activities are focused on the medium- to long-term survival of the firm.

Replicate initiatives are concerned with how a firm transitions its business model across a generation of change in technology, leadership, ownership, or overall business. Replication requires initiatives that contribute to the repositioning of a firm for a substantially "known" future. Replicate initiatives focus on reinvention activities or efforts to reposition a company for its next future, a new business environment, or a new technology paradigm.

Adapt initiatives are longer term. Adapt initiatives focus on how a firm positions itself for multiple futures, largely unknown and longer term. They involve initiatives that add variability and business portfolio breadth to a company, which enhances its ability to adapt in multiple directions in response to unforeseen changes in the business environment.

Replication and adaptation initiatives require the same process as survival and competitive initiatives: analysis of change capabilities, then the dual flexing of the business architecture and the IT architecture, followed by comparison to fitness metrics for feedback, and then completing the cycle again. The fitness

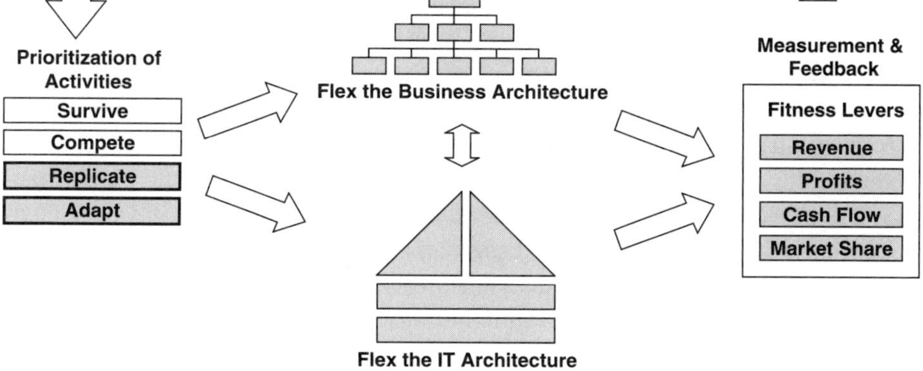

Exhibit 8.8 Business Evolution Examples: Replicate and Adapt

metrics are identical for replication and adaptive initiatives: revenue, profit, cash flow, and market share.

The concept of business fitness here must be expanded. We established earlier that for survive and compete activities of a firm, which relate to how it "makes a living" day to day with its core business activities, business fitness boils down to the four fitness criteria in our model; however, much like the Darwinian concept of fitness, we have to modify our business fitness concept slightly. Recall that Darwinian fitness is essentially surviving long enough to pass one's genes on to the next generation. This is reproductive success and defines Darwinian fitness. Business Darwinian fitness is similar. It means surviving and competing well enough to allow a business model to transition across a generation of business change, technology change, or leadership change. If a firm cannot successfully navigate a course across a generation of change, then it was not fit in the sense of Business Darwinism. While a firm may be profitable within a technology generation, and under a particular leadership reign, or during a particular set of business environment conditions, the real measure of a company's success is whether it can transition its business model across a generation of change. That is the challenge of replication and adaptation.

BUSINESS REPLICATION: CROSSING THE GENERATION GAP

The true test of a corporation is its long-term survival across generations of leadership, as well as across major changes in technology and the business environment. Consider firms such as General Electric and Nokia, which began in one set of industries only to end up dominating multiple others or a completely different industry. How are firms able to cross the generation gaps of technology, leadership, ownership, and business change? What skills and capabilities are required to enable a firm to successfully compete in a different business with a different business model?

Replication initiatives are repositioning efforts. Replication initiatives seek to reposition a firm for a new future, which may or may not be known but is an available strategic option for the firm based on analysis. Replication efforts are based on a real or perceived lack of business fitness in a firm's core business franchise(s), which again is based on the business fitness metrics in our model: revenue, profit, cash flow, and market share. Deteriorating results in these metrics may trigger a replication initiative by the existing leadership team, which may involve examining the corporate strategy, business model, organizational structure, core processes and capabilities, and several other factors. A replication initiative can be triggered as a result of several factors, but ultimately the relative fitness and financial performance of the current business model determines whether a corporate renewal is required. Replication can be initiated by a board of directors, which may result in a change of leadership or even installing an entirely new management team. Ultimately, the replication initiative is undertaken because of flagging performance against the business fitness metrics, which may have resulted from issues with the corporate strategy, the business model, the core business performance by virtue of poor processes, lack of capabilities, organizational issues, or others. Whatever the root causes of the poor business fitness are, the end result is a business model that is poorly adapted to the business environment, to the competition, to the needs of the marketplace, to a fundamentally different technology paradigm, or to a combination of all of these problems. A change is required to allow the business entity to evolve itself to an anticipated future state based on a new corporate strategy and a new business model.

Replication initiatives are focused on transitioning a corporation's business model across a generation of change, which may occur in the following forms:

- *Technology.* A change in the fundamental technology paradigm for an industry may require wholesale changes in the business model, product and service strategies, targeting of new customers and markets, and other ripple effects. Examples include the shift from analog cellular phone technology to digital technology, or the rise of the Internet and the massive changes wrought by this technology revolution.
- *Leadership.* A change in leadership may lead to widespread changes in strategy and the business model, as well as the way a company is organized and managed. Examples include the appointment of Carly Fiorina as CEO of Hewlett-Packard, which resulted in the massive restructuring HP is currently undergoing, as well as the appointment of two GE veterans as CEO of Home Depot and 3M, respectively. These leadership changes were followed by the implementation of a new style of leadership, as well as a system of management that is clearly the "GE Way" of running a corporation. Crossing the leadership generation gap can be as dramatic a change as crossing a technology generation gap, an ownership gap, a technology gap, or any others. For example, the Jack Welch period of GE can be described by a few dominant themes, such as:
  — Be number one or number two in your industry
  — Six Sigma
  Similarly, the Lou Gerstner era of IBM will be characterized by IBM's massive growth in services, licensing its technology to other companies, and embracing open technologies such as XML, Linux, Apache, and the Java programming and development environment invented by Sun Microsystems. Both executives presided over their respective firms

during a particular technology era, which witnessed the same technological changes affect their companies differently. They were within one technology age—the mainframe to PC to client-server to Internet age. These shifts in technology have had varying impacts on these two corporations. IBM gave away the PC and made billionaires of many executives; however, IBM rebounded with services, the Internet, and e-business. Now IBM is competing on open systems and architectures such as Linux, Apache, Java, and XML. This is a different competitive model from the proprietary technology war chest IBM had traditionally competed with.

- *Ownership.* A change in ownership through the divestiture of a division or an outright acquisition by another firm results in replicationlike changes to a corporation as well. How the firm transitions its business model from the original concept to the new concept is also a replication initiative. Consider the processes that Cisco has refined for performing acquisitions and integrating them into its operations quickly and efficiently. The success of an acquisition depends on how quickly the acquired firm can be integrated into the financial and operational processes, systems, and philosophies of the buyer. Cisco has been on the forefront of using its stock price to fuel acquisitions to gain access to new strategic technologies for networking and communications.
- *Business change.* In addition to these largely identifiable changes, there can also be a series of changes in the business environment that in the aggregate leads to a need for replication initiatives. The insurance industry is such an example. The passage of the Gramm-Leach-Bliley Act, which repealed the Glass-Steagal Act, allows financial institutions such as banks and brokerage houses to begin selling insurance. This regulatory change, combined with the conservative nature of the industry, and then compounded by the lack of IT investment by insurance companies, means there is tremendous need for replication initiatives.

Replication as a process is significantly different from survive and compete for one primary reason: transitioning a corporation across a generation of change requires changes in corporate strategy, a new business model, a new organizational structure, and new core business processes and core capabilities—all of the elements of a business model. It may require a completely new business architecture and a new IT architecture to support the business model. Depending on the nature of the changes a corporation faces in its replication efforts, the types of strategy, business model, and associated business and technology initiatives will vary.

Replication initiatives also may not concern themselves with the core business franchise of the corporation, but rather will define a *new* core business franchise for the firm. Business replication will almost always move a company in new directions, incrementally by extending core capabilities it already has—as in the Intel case amplified as follows—or it may completely remake the firm into a new business, as exemplified by Nokia's transformation from a manufacturing conglomerate into a high-technology superstar. The differentiation of survive and compete versus replicate and adapt rests with their respective emphases on either enhancing or preserving the core business franchise as it exists today versus moving the company away from the core business franchise. That means either adding new businesses to replace the core, either immediately or eventually, or augmenting the core with a diversification approach to buy time to explore other options. Replicate and adapt approaches seek to move the company to its next future or futures, and they may or may not carry forward the legacy core business franchise strategies, business model, and business and technology architectures that accompany them. Exhibit 8.9 shows a schematic of business replication in the context of our Business Evolution Model. Replication is the process of migrating a corporation from its current business model to a new or revised business model. This repositioning of the firm takes place through the reexamination of corporate strategy and the business model, as well as assessing the degree of change required to support the new business model. This will require flexing the business and IT architectures in potentially new ways as a new business model concept is implemented.

An example of a replication effort is the wide-reaching restructuring of Hewlett-Packard by Carly Fiorina over the last three years. This is a classic

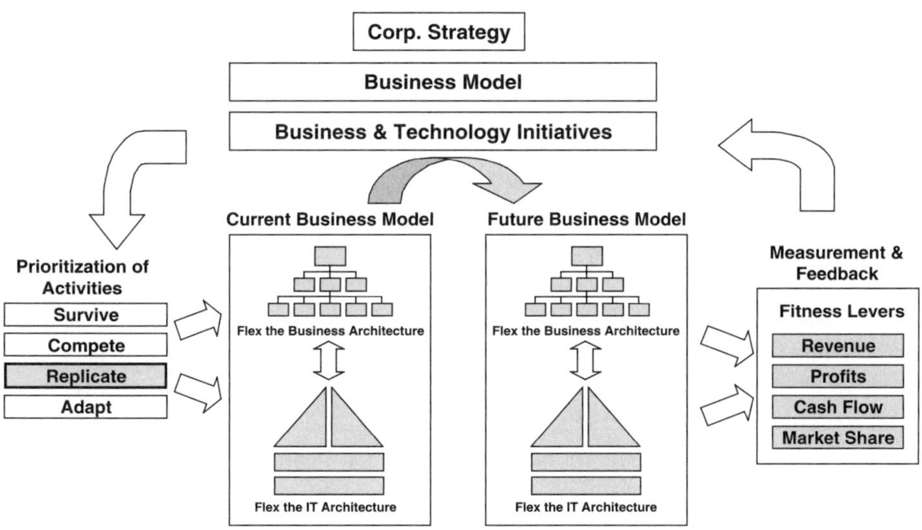

Exhibit 8.9 Business Replication: From Now to Next

case of a change in leadership, in this case bringing Fiorina into HP from the outside, that was intended to transform HP into the innovation juggernaut it once was. Recall from our discussion in Chapter 7 that in working our business evolutionary model, HP required changes in its corporate strategy and its business model, which engendered a series of initiatives in order to implement the strategy and business model. The business and technology initiatives were clearly focused on remaking HP. They required massive changes in HP's business architecture and its IT architecture, including the R&D organization, product development organizations, sales and marketing organizations, and the addition of a new core competency—professional services. That core competency was to be created through the acquisition of PriceWaterhouseCoopers' management consulting services organization. We highlighted one example of the IT architecture not being flexed in conjunction with the business architecture, which in the HP example was implementing the business architectural changes without the requisite financial systems being completed to measure the business performance. The jury is still out on the effectiveness of the replication activities at Hewlett-Packard, but time will tell if Fiorina can reinvigorate HP through her massive restructuring efforts.

INTEL: CROSSING THE SEMICONDUCTOR TECHNOLOGY GENERATION GAP

There are many examples of business replication in recent business history. Intel is an example of a firm that successfully transitioned itself across one technology to another. In Intel's case, the generation gap was the technology shift from dynamic random-access memory (DRAM) chips to microprocessor chips. Intel invented DRAM chips in 1970, followed in 1971 by the microprocessor. Gordon Moore became CEO of Intel in 1975, which led to the ill-fated foray into digital wristwatches, which after three years produced a disastrous $15 million in losses. Intel exited the wristwatch business. It was the leader in DRAM chips until Japanese chipmakers began to attack its dominant market share position. By the time IBM introduced the first PC in 1981, Intel was losing so much money on DRAMs that its future was in jeopardy. The wristwatch debacle combined with the vicious attack on its core DRAM business by Japanese chipmakers had Intel on the ropes. Moore, faced with this dire situation, decided to exit the money-losing DRAM business and gambled Intel's future on microprocessors. The rest is history. The meteoric rise of the PC, based on Intel's microprocessors, made Intel the world's biggest and most profitable chipmaker.

But what did Intel do to exit the DRAM business and focus its business model solely on microprocessors? What changes to its business model, business and IT architectures, and metrics were required to successfully engineer this replication initiative? One could argue that Intel's replication initiative was not that dramatic of a shift, that focusing its efforts on microprocessors, which Intel invented, was simply a concentration of resources on an emerging product line that it already had. The core business processes, core capabilities, and technology innovation were already present in Intel's corporate DNA to allow it to be successful with microprocessors much the way it had previously been the market leader in DRAMs. In Intel's case, the business model required tuning to focus its organizational structure, core processes and capabilities, and resources on one set of products rather than dilute its R&D, engineering, product development, manufacturing, and marketing and sales efforts on money-losing products such as wristwatches and the more mature DRAM products.[6]

Other more fascinating examples of replication initiatives better reflect the phenomenon of a corporation transitioning its business model across a definitive period of change. Nokia represents an example of true business replication.

THE NOKIA STORY: BUSINESS AT THE EDGE OF CHAOS

Nokia was able to successfully recast its strategy against the knowledge that the cell phone industry was about to make the wholesale changeover to digital technology from analog technology. With this knowledge in hand, Nokia prepared itself for the transition from an industrial company to a technology company by taking advantage of its core competencies in communications technology. Nokia's fascinating transition from a nineteenth-century paper mill to a twenty-first-century wireless powerhouse is an excellent example of business replication. The following section is summarized from the article "Nokia Bets It All on a Wireless Future,"[7] "A Finnish Fable,"[8] and "The Nokia Revolution."[9]

Nokia was founded in 1865 as a pulp mill along the banks of the Nokia River in Finland. By the end of World War II, Nokia had evolved into a manufacturing conglomerate, manufacturing and selling diverse products such as toilet paper, diapers, rubber boots, and even electricity. Now Nokia is the world's leading mobile-telephone company with more than 35.3 percent market share, which is almost three times number-two Motorola's 13.2 percent market share. Nokia transformed itself from a manufacturing conglomerate into a technology firm by adding new skills to existing ones and by focusing itself on a single core market: digital cellular phones. Nokia already had some of the corporate DNA necessary to make the transition to high technology. In the late 1970s, Nokia began investing profits from its core manufacturing businesses into acquisitions of technology and electronics businesses (e.g., computers and televisions). In addition, Nokia was already a major supplier of radio telephones, which were a necessary communications device in sparsely populated Scandinavia. Based on this core competency in communications technology, Nokia was a logical choice as the supplier of phones for Ericsson in the 1980s to support its early cellular network based on Bell Labs' technology.

By 1991, Nokia was in trouble. The Finnish economy was in dire straits because of the collapse of the Soviet Union. This seriously wounded Nokia and forced it to sell off company assets to raise cash for survival. Meanwhile, demand for mobile phones was quickly ramping up, but Nokia could not meet the rising demand with its mobile-phone business unit. In fact, the unit was nearly sold because of the capacity issues. Jorma Ollila, Nokia's chairman, was in charge of the mobile-phone unit at the time and was able to sort out the production bottlenecks and bring the new Global System for Mobile Communication (GSM) mobile-phone technology to market. In 1992 Ollila became CEO and decided on a radical new strategy: Nokia would become a mobile-phone pure-play and sell off all other nonmobile phone assets. Nokia's core business would henceforth be technology, not paper products, and not even computer or television technologies. This decision came as Nokia launched its 2100 series GSM cell phone, which was an incredible success. The 1994 sales goal was 500,000 units. Nokia manufactured and sold 20 million. The rest is history. Nokia successfully transitioned itself from a manufacturing conglomerate, to computers and televisions, and from radio telephones to cellular handsets. Nokia's stunning transformation was perfectly timed with the right product and the right technology.

The changes required to complete this transformation were many. Selling off the legacy assets that were part of Nokia's past success was an emotional watershed event for the corporation. Shifting the corporation from slower-clockspeed products to fast-clockspeed technologies, with increasing software and information content, clearly was a necessity. Nokia had to restructure the organization and the business processes, and develop the core capabilities required to execute its business model based on a mobile-phone pure-play. Working the Business Evolution Model, it is clear that Nokia made wholesale changes in virtually every facet of the model. A brief review demonstrates the challenges that Nokia faced in transitioning itself across the technology generation gap in 1991:

- *Corporate strategy.* Focused the corporation on a cell phone pure-play to capitalize on the exploding demand for digital cell phones. This provided superior revenue growth and profits to Nokia better than any of its legacy manufacturing business units could have provided.

- *Business model.* In order to execute the cell phone pure-play corporate strategy, several processes and capabilities were mandatory. Some examples of what Nokia did to support its replication efforts include:
  — Invest heavily in R&D capabilities to ensure cutting-edge technology research and product designs in the fast-clockspeed industry of wireless in anticipation of the wireless web and other emerging trends.
  — Implement world-class design and product engineering processes and skills to bring new cell phone designs to market faster than the competition.
  — Enhance manufacturing capacity and scale, allowing rapid product launches and production ramp to support required volumes.
  — Implement supply chain management and logistics processes to drive costs of manufacturing down while providing best-in-class market demand responsiveness and product distribution.
  — Perform best-in-class product marketing and company branding to help sustain market presence and margins, transforming the cellular phone industry to a consumer electronics business versus the engineering approach to cell phones taken by Motorola, Ericsson, and other competitors.

This is not a comprehensive list, but it provides a snapshot of some of the decisions that would have been made at the time of Nokia's decision to focus solely on cell phones and to jettison its other manufacturing businesses. The business model that Nokia eventually settled on required the appropriate changes to its business architecture and its IT architecture to support its replication efforts. From the partial list, we can surmise some of the business and technology initiatives that helped Nokia transition its business model from a multiproduct, multidivision manufacturing conglomerate to a singular focus on wireless devices. The requisite flexing of the business and IT architectures would have been required in order to complete the implementation of Nokia's new corporate strategy and business model. Some examples of the necessary flexing might include:

- *Flex the business architecture.* Nokia had to modify its corporate structure, business processes, and skills to support a cell phone pure-play business model. These would have affected all areas of the corporation, including R&D, engineering and product development, supply chain management, manufacturing and distribution, and marketing and sales. In Nokia's case, many of these skills were already in house to an extent because of its core competencies in radio telephones and its early entry into wireless devices with Ericsson's cellular network. Certainly this helped Nokia to "develop" the corporate DNA to support its transformation to a cell phone pure-play.

- *Flex the IT architecture.* Nokia certainly had to implement technology programs in order to support its transformation efforts. The IT initiatives must have mapped closely to the business architecture initiatives in order to be successful. Examples should have been product design and engineering tools, supply chain management tools, enterprise resources planning tools, manufacturing execution systems, and a host of others.

Exhibit 8.10 shows the Nokia example of working the Business Evolution Model through a case of business replication. The corporate strategy and business model descriptions are based on how Nokia elected to focus on digital cell phones in 1991. This example is a perfect demonstration of business replication, where a corporation was faced with a decision about what future to pursue, and based on analysis and sheer courage, Nokia chose the cell phone pure-play strategy. The necessary changes to its corporate strategy, business model, business and technology architectures, and performance against the business fitness metrics are all well documented.

Nokia went from near bankruptcy to being a $27 billion company based on its stock price. It has nearly three times the market share of number-two

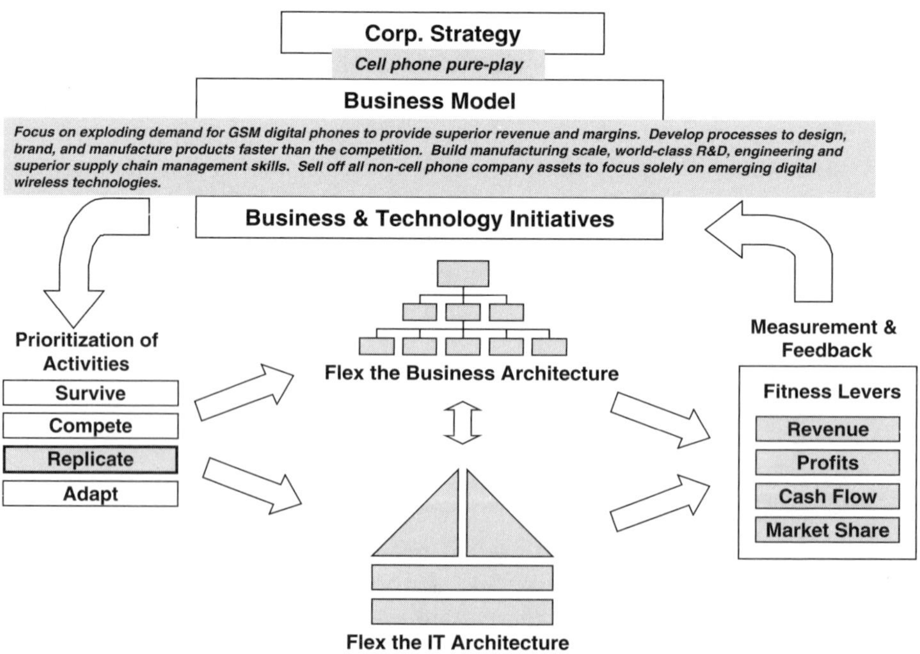

Exhibit 8.10 Nokia: Business Evolution Example of Replication

Motorola at more than 35 percent, is debt-free with $2.5 billion in cash in the bank, and is the world's fifth most valuable brand, ahead of such companies as Sony, Nike, and Mercedes-Benz.[10] Nokia enjoys operating margins of 20 percent compared to 5 percent for number-two Motorola and 30 percent for distant third Ericsson. By all of the fitness metrics used throughout the business evolutionary model, Nokia is healthy. Nokia is truly a wonderful example of crossing a business generation gap, which in its case was the marvelous transformation from a manufacturing conglomerate to a high-tech superstar.

BUSINESS ADAPTATION IN CORPORATE EVOLUTION: ANTICIPATING THE UNKNOWN

The final evolutionary process for corporations is to adapt. Adaptive activities, similar to replication, are part of a company's ability to reposition itself, but in this case it is repositioning the firm for multiple potentially unknown futures. Adapt is a longer-term business strategy that seeks to position the firm for long-term survival by adding new corporate DNA, the business equivalent of adding genetic variation through mutation and internal innovation. It also occurs through noninternal processes. This can take the form of mergers and acquisitions, as well as through strategic alliances, consortia, and industry associations.

We stated earlier that adapt activities *preposition* a corporation for multiple futures. This occurs through the process of adding new core capabilities and skills in advance of the environmental need that makes them necessary for survival. In other words, adapt is the ability to preadapt a business model to the unknown. In order to make adapt initiatives reality, however, they will necessarily invoke a replication initiative, which is the process of transitioning the firm from one business model to its next business model. This can only be done once a corporation's "next" future is clear enough so that the necessary changes to the corporate strategy and the business model can be executed.

Adaptive activities are ongoing processes that are focused on futures 5 to 10 years ahead of the current business model. These differ from replication initiatives, which are invoked only when the company is faced with a competitive challenge, where its business model suddenly is not well adapted to its business environment. Adaptive activities preposition the firm, whereas replication activities reposition the firm from one business era to another. Adapt as a business evolutionary strategy requires a continual process of assessing the performance of the current business model against the current and short-term business environment, and watching emerging trends in customers, evolving markets, regulatory changes, the direct competition in current businesses, and emerging competition. Clearly, adaptive activities include the sensing processes of a firm that monitor the business environment with an eye toward guiding investments in skills and core capabilities that will enhance a firm's competitive stance given several potential scenarios.

Recall our discussion of change tolerance. There we defined two hypothetical levels of change that will affect any organization's evolutionary capabilities: an *innovation limit* of change, which represents the minimal level of change that will occur from within a firm via its organic company processes, and a *disruption limit* of change, which is the hypothetical upper limit of change that can be tolerated by a business system before it begins to break down and fail. Adapt activities affect the spread of the upper and lower change levels of a firm by creating the ability to introduce change in the organization by internal means, or innovation processes, or by external means, which might take place through acquisitions, mergers, strategic alliances, industry consortia, and other related diversification actions. Exhibit 8.11 shows how adapt activities fit into the Business Evolution Model.

Adaptive activities preposition a firm for multiple unknown futures by adding variability to a company—new business units, new skills and knowledge, and new processes and capabilities. As Exhibit 8.11 shows, adaptive activities may result in distinct business units or potential business units, each with its own unique business and IT architectures. There will be multiple opportunities to promote one or more of these business unit opportunities as the core business

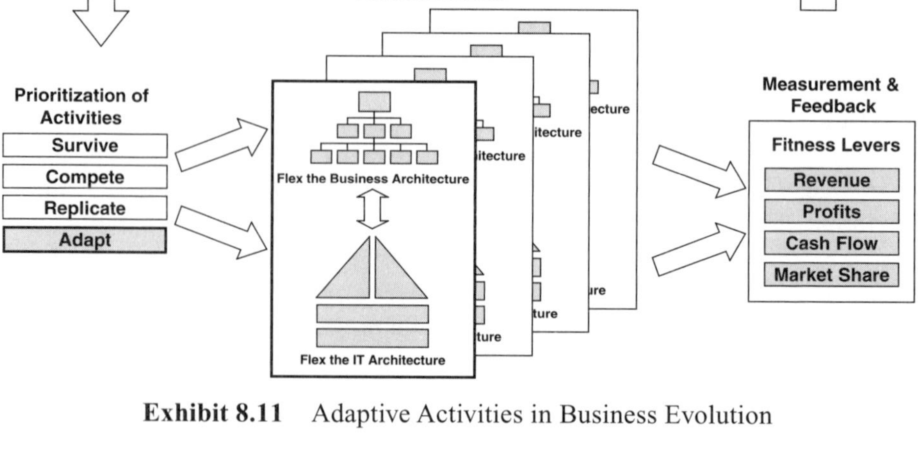

Exhibit 8.11 Adaptive Activities in Business Evolution

model or as part of a company's portfolio of businesses. There are many ways a corporation can prepare itself for multiple, unknown futures. A list of potential adaptive initiatives for companies to augment their corporate DNA follows:

- *Mergers and acquisitions (M&A).* Adding portfolio breadth through acquisitions, as well as gaining access to new technology at a faster rate than internal R&D processes, can develop the technology in-house. Cisco and Tyco International have excelled at acquiring other companies and integrating them into their business models to augment their portfolio breadth. In Cisco's case, its M&A skills allowed it to quickly gain access to technology and commercialize it faster than it could internally. In Tyco's case, M&A represents a growth and diversification strategy more than an R&D hedge.
- *Internal innovation processes.* Through internal corporate processes, encourage and harvest new ideas and innovation as part of the corporate culture and innovative engine of a firm. 3M and Hewlett-Packard (the old HP) represent firms that have outstanding internal processes for R&D and internal innovation. Carly Fiorina's restructuring of Hewlett-Packard's R&D Labs represents an attempt to regain the innovative edge that HP once had.
- *Increase or restructure research and development (R&D).* Nokia and Microsoft have plowed billions of dollars into research and development activities as ways to continue their innovation and new product development processes. Nokia, for example, has the largest R&D budget of any cell phone manufacturer, and every third employee works for the R&D organization.[11]
- *Initiate strategic alliances and joint ventures.* These represent ways a company can experiment with new technologies without having to foot the entire R&D bill alone. Strategic alliances, joint ventures, and joint technology agreements are shared investments in developing and marketing products that are common between firms, or where a firm partners with another firm to gain access to its technology or products.
- *Participate in industry consortia.* Consortium activities represent ways a firm can participate in R&D efforts on a shared basis by collaborating with competitor firms as well as other partners to develop standards and technologies that can be leveraged by all participants.
- *Establish collaborative R&D programs.* Collaborative R&D efforts with universities, government agencies, and even other corporations are ways to share the rising costs of R&D for basic research, as opposed to directed R&D, which is shorter term and focused on commercializing innovations. Increasingly, collaboration is becoming an important technique for

product development with partners and allies, as well as for sharing often expensive R&D costs for basic scientific research.

- *Implement a competitive intelligence process.* We have stated that adaptive initiatives are also environmental monitoring functions, which provide early glimpses about what the future holds for a corporation in the way of business opportunities, market developments, and emerging competitors from other industries.
- *Implement knowledge management processes.* Corporations are increasingly realizing the value of the process and product knowledge that resides in their mobile information assets—namely their employees. Documenting and sharing lessons learned from customer interaction, from successes and failures, documenting processes and procedures—these are all valuable knowledge resources for any firm for training purposes. Carrying forward the body of knowledge of a company's history is a valuable information asset that can be leveraged in many ways on behalf of employees and customers alike.

These are all examples of adaptive initiatives within the context of the Business Evolution Model. In order to implement these types of initiatives, the same flexing of the business and IT architecture is required, as well as assessing the potential future impact on the fitness metrics of a firm.

Enhancing the R&D capabilities for a firm, for example, might involve reorganizing the structure of the R&D organization as well as enhancing the internal innovation and idea-harvesting processes of a company. Flexing of the business architecture would require a new organizational structure to drive R&D processes and measurable returns within appropriate time frames. Whether the R&D organization is centralized with a central corporate laboratory, decentralized with business unit research facilities, or hybrid with a central R&D lab with business unit research labs performing applied R&D for that particular business unit, the structure will require new organizations, research processes and capabilities, and knowledge and skills to drive the returns desired. Commercialization of R&D results is yet another critical skill that many companies have not mastered. There are many examples of companies whose R&D capabilities resulted in benefit for others over themselves, such as Xerox's Palo Alto Research Center (PARC), General Motors' Tech Center facility, and even IBM's research. If collaborative R&D is one of the initiatives, the organizational ability to closely partner with suppliers and even competitors is essential. How should such a business architecture be implemented to allow the freedom of research and yet maintain the corporate oversight and ownership of the results? Skunkworks research also requires different flexing of the business architecture to implement, especially if the research agenda is exclusive.

Flexing the IT architecture is also critical for adaptive initiatives. Collaborative R&D requires shared networks and IT resources, as well as other software tools and solutions to support the real-time sharing of information and data from joint R&D efforts. In many cases, these will be separate IT systems carved out of a company's normal IT architecture to maintain the independence and autonomy of potentially highly sensitive research. Consider how flexing the IT architecture is required for implementing a knowledge management solution for a company. A knowledge repository requires not only the business processes and discipline to post relevant information to the knowledge management system, but also the technology capabilities to filter relevant content, publish it for sharing across a diverse user base, and maintain that content. Many of these solutions are built on enterprise document management engines, which are complex, horizontal applications with the normal document and content management functionality combined with workflow management engines. These information solutions require significant flexing of the IT architecture to implement and manage within the context of the overall adaptive initiative.

Finally, consider the business and IT architecture flexing required for mergers and acquisitions. In order to acquire and integrate a target firm, a significant amount of effort is required to integrate the financial reporting, the existing IT systems, and its business processes and intellectual property into the acquiring firm. From both a business and IT architecture perspective, flexing of both is critical for successfully integrating an acquired company into an existing corporation. The same is also true for spinning off a division of a company, except in reverse. The spinoff has to have its IT systems established as an independent entity, which means adding both the necessary business processes and the IT systems in order to prepare a division for a spinoff or even an acquisition.

Finally, the fitness metrics must be considered. Success in the case of adaptive initiatives is not measured by the metrics of today's business model—the financial performance from our fitness metrics. It is instead measured in future success, by providing to the corporation a set of viable futures from which it can select as directions of focus for the future business model. The role of adaptive efforts is to ensure a viable future through R&D, through joint ventures and alliances, and through acquiring the skills and core capabilities to compete.

All of these methods are ways to augment a firm's corporate DNA, to alter its genetic makeup, which over multiple iterations of business evolution will result in better adaptive fit of a corporation's business model to its business landscape. Each of these techniques for adding genetic variability to a corporation's gene pool can result in long-term adaptive fit to an unknown business landscape. Given our discussion about internal innovation processes and capabilities versus mergers and acquisitions as ways to add to the corporate DNA of a firm, a few examples will illustrate these points.

Cisco is widely viewed as a world leader in acquiring other companies and quickly integrating them into its operations. Cisco has acquired more than 70 companies since 1993, largely based on its lofty stock valuation.[12] This acquisition strategy was primarily to gain access to the latest networking innovations in the fast-paced digital networking arena. Once the acquisition was completed, Cisco's sales and marketing machine would then begin purveying the acquired technology to corporate customers and to telephone companies. This resulted in tremendous growth for Cisco over the last several years, with revenue of nearly $19 billion for its fiscal year 2000, which represented a four times multiple of its revenue four years earlier; however, because of the stock market plunge that plagued the high-technology sector in 2000 and 2001, Cisco will have to resort to other means to drive its innovation processes, which means developing the internal R&D processes and capabilities to drive an organic growth model, perhaps augmented by M&A, but not solely based on M&A activity.

Collins and Porras distinguish two processes by which firms outperform their direct competitors, one based on big hairy audacious goals (BHAG) and another based on evolutionary progress, or purposeful evolution.[13] While the BHAG approach involves clear and unambiguous goals for the corporation, evolutionary progress involves the incremental process of adding variation through genetic mutation, and then letting the business environment select what will eventually be a winning business model or formula for success. In Collins and Porras' words, "evolutionary progress usually begins with small incremental steps or mutations, often in the form of quickly seizing unexpected opportunities that eventually grow into major—and often unanticipated—strategic shifts."[14] Collins and Porras also note, correctly, that while evolution in nature is an unplanned process, for corporations, and especially the visionary corporations they allude to in *Built to Last,* it is a purposeful and planned addition of variation to the corporation's genetic makeup that allows it to pursue multiple strategies over time as the business future unfolds before it. They call the corporate version of evolution and natural selection *purposeful evolution* because human organizations can make conscious decisions about how to evolve themselves, using culture and technology as their evolutionary weapons within generations of corporate leadership and within generations of technological landscapes.

Referring back to our Business Evolution Model, it is clear that Adapt activities are ongoing processes of watching the business landscape and developing or acquiring new skills and capabilities that will help ensure that the corporation will have a future and, it is hoped, multiple futures to pursue at any given point. Adapt activities are ongoing processes much like the M&A process used by Tyco International to screen potential acquisition targets—more than 1,000 per year—and then executing a cycle of first-pass business fit, due diligence, negotiation, and implementation, or integration into Tyco's overall business model and management philospophy.[15] But once the next future is clearer for a corporation based on its adaptive activities, the processes of transitioning its business model to fit a particular set of environmental conditions becomes a replication activity.

Similar to living organisms, variation is continually being added to the gene pool through mutation processes, even when the species is well adapted to its business environment; however, the differential selection of the successful genes of a species depends on the reproductive success of those that are physically able to survive and compete long enough to reproduce. For corporations, this means being able to survive and compete long enough to replicate their success across generations of business change. The adaptive activities represent the mutation processes, or the variation-adding processes, that help ensure diversity of options to accommodate multiple unknown potential futures.

CONCLUSION

Exhibit 8.12 shows how the fundamental evolutionary processes fit into the larger context of business change and reinforces what has been discussed throughout this chapter. Survive and compete initiatives are focused on the core business model of a corporation and help ensure that a company can execute its basic business processes long enough and well enough to allow it to remain viable.

Business replication is focused on transitioning a firm from its current business model concept to a new business model concept. These changes are triggered by poor adaptive fit of the current business model to the business environment and are often driven by changes in technology, company leadership, ownership, or overall cumulative business changes. All of these situations can result in renewal initiatives similar to Fiorina's reinvention efforts at Hewlett-Packard. Finally, adaptive activities are those that add variability to a firm's corporate DNA, which help preposition a firm for multiple futures and multiple future business models. These initiatives maintain corporation genetic variation, which leads to more strategic options for the firm, or what Kenichi Ohmae refers to as strategic degrees of freedom.[16] More variability in the genetic sense leads to more strategic degrees of freedom, or more ways that the corporation can evolve based on what the future holds in store. These are plans for multiple unknown futures. The cycle of business evolution proposed in the Business Evolution Model seeks better adaptive fit of the current business model, as well as future adaptive fit for the next and future business models. This is only possible, though, by building the information capabilities into the

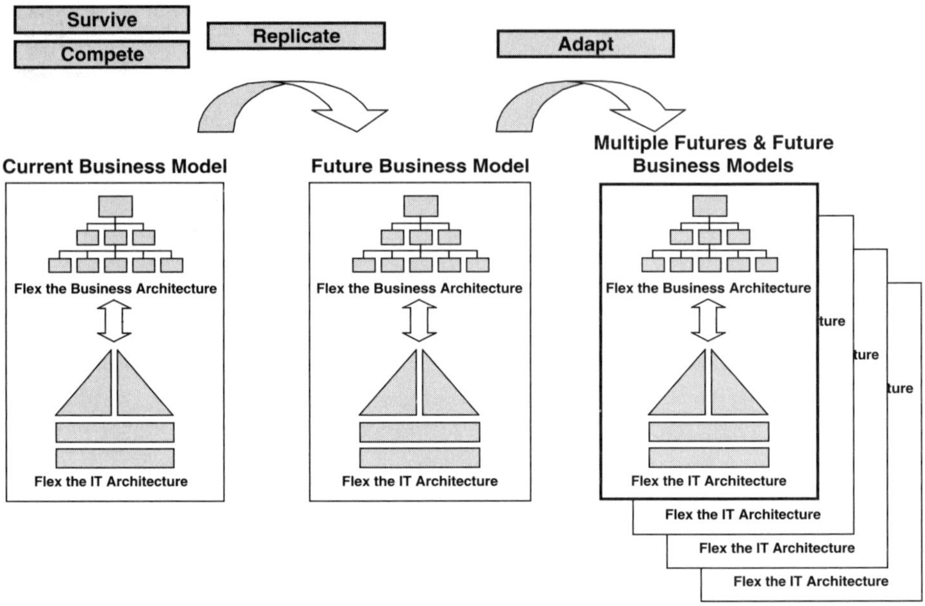

Exhibit 8.12 Business Evolution in Action

business model and then flexing the business architecture and the IT architecture to implement that business model. This approach will ensure that corporations are able to take advantage of increasingly critical information-based competitive strategies while flexibly adapting their organizations to the types of changes needed to survive, compete, replicate, and adapt over the long haul.

NOTES

1. See Goldman Sachs Global Equity Research, *Insurance, United States,* November 27, 2000, and Conning Insurance Research & Publications, *Workers Compensation: Resolving a Self-Inflicted Crisis,* 2000, p. 16.
2. Goldman Sachs Global Equity Research, *Insurance, United States,* p. 2.
3. Dowling & Partners Securities, LLC, *IBNR Insurance Weekly,* vol. VI, no. 34, August 22, 1999.
4. Andrea Petersen, "Motorola Struggles with Cellphone Line Amid Industry Slump," *Wall Street Journal* (May 18, 2001), pp. A1, A8.
5. Roger O. Crockett, "Chris Galvin Shakes Things Up Again," *Business Week* (May 29, 2001), pp. 38–39; *see also* Petersen, "Motorola Struggles with Cellphone Line Amid Industry Slump," *The Wall Street Journal* (May 18, 2001), pp. A1, A8.

6. Otis Port, "Farewell, Mr. Moore—and Thanks," Commentary in *Business Week* (April 30, 2001), p. 42.
7. James Hattori, "Nokia Bets It All on a Wireless Future," CNN.com.
8. "A Finnish Fable," from *The Economist* print edition, October 12, 2000.
9. Dan Steinbock, *The Nokia Revolution* (New York: AMACOM, 2001).
10. Stephen Baker, John Shinal, and Irene M. Kunii, "Is Nokia's Star Dimming?" *Business Week* (January 22, 2001), p. 68.
11. Dan Steinbock, *The Nokia Revolution,* p. 198.
12. Peter Elstrom, "Sorry, CISCO. The Old Answers Won't Work," Commentary in *Business Week* (April 30, 2001), p. 39.
13. James C. Collins and Jerry I. Porras, *Built to Last* (New York: HarperBusiness, 1994), p. 145.
14. Ibid.
15. William C. Symonds, "The Most Aggressive CEO," *Business Week* (May 28, 2001), p. 72.
16. Kenichi Ohmae, *The Mind of the Strategist* (New York: McGraw-Hill, 1982), p. 40.

9

INFORMATION DARWINISM IN THE FUTURE

We work day after day, not to finish things, but to make the future better . . . because we will spend the rest of our lives there.

—Charles F. Kettering

Our journey through human and corporate evolution, and specifically the rise of information technology in the modern business enterprise, documents one perspective on how technology has shaped the human experience. Technology drives change. Technology occurs incrementally, as well as in great, disruptive bursts of innovation and rapid adoption of new ideas in the business environment and in everyday life. From the printing press innovation complex to the Internet, technology has unleashed the seeds of massive business and social change time and time again, and the human experience has flourished as a result of these technological innovations. We experienced firsthand the impact of technology on business and society with the Internet, and we also witnessed business evolution in progress.

The dot-com demise of 2000 and 2001 demonstrated the criticality of business fitness in business evolution. Companies that do not perform according to the fitness metrics of revenue, profit, cash flow, and market share will not survive, and they surely will not be able to replicate or transition themselves across a generation of change. We now know that the business version of natural selection is as absolute as nature's version of natural selection.

Chapter 1 laid the groundwork for a new paradigm of information management. The Principle of Information Darwinism was developed, suggesting that corporations and business leaders must invest in information technology (IT) more aggressively in order to ensure business survival. The executives and companies that do will not only survive, they will thrive. Those that do not will be deselected. A new value discipline of Information Mastery was also forwarded as a critical core capability of any modern organization. Clearly, Information Mastery is more than a core capability. Information Mastery is a way of conducting business based on superior use of information in a broader and more strategic sense. The role, organization, processes, and metrics of information are different under the value discipline of Information Mastery.

Chapter 2 was a review of major technology trends over the course of history, beginning with the printing press and ending with the Internet. That abbreviated technology review showed how technology has had a dramatic impact on human history and how what I have termed an "innovation complex" can coalesce and drive a sustained, disruptive wave of massive business and societal change. The Internet was one of these events, much as the printing press was. They were similar in their impact on human civilization in that they broke an information bottleneck and unleashed access to information to the masses. Information, we maintain, is clearly power.

In Chapter 3, we developed the evolutionary framework for businesses, equating them to living organisms and hypothesizing that businesses must survive, compete, replicate, and, over (it is hoped) generations of business change, adapt. We posited four business fitness metrics—revenue, profit, cash flow, and market share—as the things most critical for corporations to be "fit" and able to transition across generations of business change. We equated the trajectory of human evolution with the increased use of information to drive corporate evolution. If culture replaced physical evolution in humans, then information is the cultural equivalent for firms. All activities that manage information and knowledge of a firm are those that will augment and, in some cases, replace competing on physical assets alone.

Chapter 4 traced the development of information technologies and the information delivery function as a formal discipline. From the early computer applications in GE's Louisville facility to the rise of the PC, client-server computing, and the Internet, we showed how these changes in IT have strained the organizations that were devised to "manage" them. That historical review suggests that today's corporations are still managing information delivery with an Industrial Age management paradigm. We finished Chapter 4 knowing that the IT results from the last 10 years or so are logical outcomes from managing information delivery from an Industrial Age perspective.

In Chapter 5, the notion of IT architecture was explored. Reviewing several leading IT strategists' views and approaches to IT management, IT architecture management, and portfolio management, we settled on the approach of Weill and Broadbent, which breaks IT into four categories of spending—infrastructure, transactional, informational, and strategic technologies. We then introduced a business evolution framework and integrated these IT categories into that evolutionary framework to show how the IT architecture can be "flexed" in response to the needs of the business to incorporate change and facilitate business evolution.

Chapter 6 presented a discussion of corporate strategy and business modeling. We reviewed Gary Hamel's compelling business modeling methodology from his book *Leading the Revolution*[1] and adapted it to our discussions of information management. The result was a concept called *information-based business modeling,* which builds information management concepts into the fabric of corporate strategy and the resulting business model. Information-based business modeling, we discovered, eliminates the classic alignment problem we have continually wrestled with in the Industrial Age.

Chapter 7 extended our discussions of IT architecture and information-based business modeling into a larger context: a model of business evolution. We devised a macro-model of business change based on corporate strategy, an information-based business model, and the ability to successfully implement business initiatives by flexing the business architecture and the IT architecture. We showed how evolutionary activities of a firm—survive, compete, replicate, and adapt—have different objectives and requirements for implementation, but they all involve flexing the business and IT architecture for success.

Chapter 8 embellished the business evolution framework with examples. We "worked" our Business Evolution Model to demonstrate how the four evolutionary processes of a corporation—survive, compete, replicate, and adapt—are accomplished by a firm. We described how survive and compete are core business model activities with their respective goals for success. We described corporate replication and how it repositions a firm for its next future, essentially transitioning the firm across a generation of business change, using our Business Evolution Model. Finally, we showed how adaptive activities of a firm preposition it for multiple futures by adding the corporate variability and agility to respond to multiple unknown outcomes.

Business evolution is not unlike evolution in nature, and the parallels we have developed to help businesses use information to facilitate better fitness resemble those of humans as a species. We have developed a Business Evolution Model and an information-based business modeling approach to help companies adapt in their immediate environments, to help reposition them for their next futures, and to preposition themselves for the unknown, or multiple futures. But what actions must take place to help firms prepare for the Next Wave?

WAITING FOR THE FUTURE

Many futurists make grand proclamations of the future that they think will eventually unfold. Based on their analysis of current and emerging trends, they weave together visions of what will be in decades, centuries, and even millennia. For information technology, this would be an exercise in futility. Even modest attempts to foretell the future were way off base, even though these were not far-reaching predictions. Bill Gates predicting no need for more than 640 kilobytes of random access memory (RAM) comes to mind, or Ken Olsen of DEC wondering in 1977 why on earth personal computers would be used in the home. A more recent prediction was the emerging corporate mass market for thin-client devices, essentially dumb terminals as in the days of mainframe computing. The market for these devices never emerged, and PC prices fell so quickly (they are still falling thanks to a vicious price war launched by Dell Computer, which is forcing consolidation of the industry and causing all its competitors to lose money on their PC operations) that PCs remained the desktop device of choice for corporate users.

The point of these futurist stories is this: the seeds for much of the foreseeable future have already been sown, and our days on earth will be spent watching it unfold. There are infinite ways in which multiple futures may arise. To some extent, the human species has an impact on how the future will occur, but the ingredients are already in place, the potion has been mixed, and time will tell.

For our digital future, the same holds true. The foundation for the Next Wave has already been laid, and we will have to respond to whatever unfolds. The IT future will unfold in new ways, in unforeseen ways, and the best futurists can only guess about the eventual outcomes. But this much is clear—the IT future will be exciting to watch, and the leading firms of the Next Wave will be poised to ride this incredible wave of innovation and change, and they will be the Darwinian winners.

For example, the nature of today's corporate workforce is dramatically different from what it was 10 years ago. Today, the level of computer literacy is higher than it has ever been in the history of corporate computing. This has changed the way that corporate users can participate in IT initiatives. The IT dialogue of today's corporation is different because more people are now engaged. The Internet phenomenon, combined with the Year 2000 preparations by most firms, increased the knowledge and appreciation of IT and how far it extends into the day-to-day operations of corporations. Look at how well trained most workforces are these days based on the household penetration of the PC. Sixty-five percent of American households have PCs today, and the withering price war launched by Dell Computer is sure to help increase that penetration. As "being connected" matures as a phenomenon, whether it is by a PC, a personal digital assistant (PDA), or some other wireless device, corporations will be able to create, implement, and reap the benefits from various IT solutions faster than ever before. This is precisely because we are experiencing the highest level of computer literacy ever in human existence.

Companies of today have a tremendous opportunity awaiting them, *if they choose to use it.* The process of collecting IT inventories for the Year 2000 preparations showed to all employees how computing technology has reached virtually every department, every function of the firm, from human resources to plant floor machine control to security systems and fire alarms. This widespread understanding of the pervasiveness of IT in all corporate functions sowed the seeds for the Next Wave of corporate computing. More employees are users and are capable of understanding how information systems and technology can turbocharge aspects of their business processes and business performance.

Furthermore, the speed and widespread reach of Internet adoption have also contributed to the vastly increased knowledge of computing technology. The rise of the Internet and the penetration of PCs into American homes has created a new phenomenon: *the Home CIO.* Increasingly, users of home computing technology have a technology budget to manage much like corporations do, which includes voice and data communications, broadband and cable communications, wireless technologies, multiple PCs networked together in households, and even controlling home utilities, energy usage, appliances, and home security using computing technology. The Home CIO is a technology-literate individual, responsible for all the home computing functions required to save time, to pay bills, and to remain connected to friends, family, and business. But this same Home CIO goes to work with increased knowledge and understanding of technology applications, not only in his or her personal life but in the professional setting, too. People are capable of understanding the power of computing in today's business climate and are comfortable with automating business processes and using computer technology to perform ever more business functions.

These two forces—the Y2K planning and execution combined with the Internet explosion—are not the only factors for the IT future that is already occurring. They were merely necessary factors. The real reason for the imminent changes in the technology capabilities of firms is the next generation of leaders, those who are now in college or in business school, or are recent entrants into the workforce. They are more computer literate than any generation in history. They know only one way, the computing and technology way, driven by game consoles, by the ubiquity of personal computing in schools, in literature, on television, and in commercials. Technology is now romanticized where it once was mocked. Now it is chic to be nerdy, and those without Palm Pilots are considered dinosaurs. This new generation of IT- and technology-literate employees allows new productivity applications to be launched and rolled out companywide faster than was ever possible in the history of corporations. The new competitive advantage will be developing, launching, and rolling out new systems that help companies compete better and win more often.

A new role has also emerged in corporations of today: the *Distributed CIO Function (DCIO)*. The Home CIO concept has created an information-savvy population of computer users in corporations today. This phenomenon is just taking off, but one can clearly see how this increased knowledge base of IT distributed throughout every functional organization and discipline within a company has led to the nascent distributed CIO concept. The rise of departmental applications, combined with the increasing need for executives to know and understand their IT systems, will create the "distributed CIO," where the role of IT management is a shared responsibility across the business enterprise. This will make the task of managing IT a different one—one of collaboration based on shared appreciation of technology to drive the business model. There will no longer be antipathy for IT. Information technology's value will be widely known, and its success will be desired by increasingly business- and information-savvy leaders of the Next Wave. Information will not be managed from a perspective of control. Rather, information will be managed from an Internet perspective, where choices and freedom are the watchwords of the day. Now, this opinion does not suggest that corporate information security is not critical to a firm. It simply suggests that providing ready access to the information needed by increasingly knowledgeable "knowledge workers" will increase productivity, facilitate better decision making, and drive overall better corporate performance.

In the distributed CIO organization, everyone has a role and a responsibility for being an IT strategist, seeking new sources of information value and new ways to leverage information, to release it for use by the firm or by others. This is the "new IT dialogue" that is an imperative of the New Economy. The ability to launch and roll out new applications to incredibly tech-savvy employees is a competitive advantage that has not yet been exploited. The companies that are first-movers in achieving this information-based advantage will dictate the Next Wave of competitive advantage. They will define the new paradigm of building business models based on the new value discipline known as Information Mastery. These companies will derive superior business performance from their information-based business model because they will have learned what the information advantage is for modern corporations. The Industrial Age of IT will be over when the first-movers of the Next Wave define their Information Mastery agendas and begin demonstrating the power of competing on information.

NEXT GOLDEN AGE OF IT

Information technology is still a new discipline. Information technology has only been around for roughly 40 years or so. The science of managing IT has been developed from a financial control perspective, not one that allows it to flourish as a science in its own right. It grew up under financial oversight, and it must be released from this constraint. The Next Golden Age of IT is approaching rapidly. In order to be prepared for the Next Wave, companies have to be prepared in advance to take advantage of it, to weave information-harvesting processes and capabilities into the corporate fabric, into the corporate culture, into all activities and processes firmwide. This will require a different way of thinking about IT. It will require devising a new role for the information functions of the firm. It will require creatively structuring processes and metrics for information-based success. But there must be new processes for IT development and delivery. The metrics must be based on a new value equation, not a value equation that measures IT value by budgetary compliance and absence of downtime, but a value equation that measures IT's strategic contribution to the firm's financial performance, market share, customer satisfaction, efficiency, and other "real" metrics, not internal accounting measures of success. These things must be done to achieve Information Mastery as a value discipline. How can a firm begin to prepare itself for the Next Golden Age of IT? What actions are required to avoid digital deselection?

HOW TO AVOID BEING DIGITALLY DESELECTED

Corporations must begin their preparations for the Next Wave to avoid digital deselection, which means aggressively building an action plan for Information Mastery. Information Mastery requires ingraining digital strategies in all business processes and initiatives. A program to develop the value discipline of Information Mastery should begin with an assessment of how digitally competent the firm is. An IT value assessment should be conducted to determine first of all how a corporation measures the IT value contribution to the firm. This IT value assessment should identify how much of the total value the IT organization creates is based on Industrial Age metrics such as:

- Cost control and budgetary compliance
- Absence of downtime—system availability metrics
- Project timeliness
- Project budget compliance
- IT architecture stability and fending off change

Once the current IT value contribution is understood, the IT value equation for the discipline of Information Mastery can be developed. The IT value contribution from Information Mastery might be based on the following value metrics:

- Revenue creation
- Competitor preemption
- Customer intimacy and satisfaction
- Cost savings and operating efficiency
- Friction reduction internally and across the extended enterprise
- Facilitation of business change based on technology

This is simply a sampling of possible IT value that can be derived if and only if the business changes the value equation for IT. But there is a difference between the IT value statements in the first list versus the second list. This "IT value gap" must be closed in order for a firm to transition to Information Mastery. The IT value contribution under Information Mastery is more strategic and more customer-connected than the paradigm of the Industrial Age of IT management. The following sources of value can be achieved if a firm develops Information Mastery as a value discipline:

- *Business fitness value.* Market share, customer satisfaction, shareholder value
- *Financial fitness value.* Revenue, profit, and cash flow improvements
- *Organizational fitness value.* Information exchange, knowledge management, corporate culture development, organizational development, team building
- *Business process performance value.* Cycle time improvements, operational excellence, transactional efficiency
- *New product and service value.* Innovation processes, R&D capabilities, new product and service development, product launch capabilities
- *Customer value.* Better products, better service, customer satisfaction, repeat customers
- *Evolutionary value.* Survive and compete capabilities, replication and adaptive capabilities
- *Information value.* Valuation of intellectual property, valuation of information assets, knowing the true contribution of information to business performance

The IT value assessment will almost certainly divulge that IT investments are not mapped to real corporate value, but rather to internal, noncustomer, and nonmarket-focused measures of success. New measures of IT success must be derived that more accurately reflect the true value of information to a modern information-based enterprise. Measures of IT success should be based on the conversion of information into corporate value. Closing of the IT value gap is essential for Information Mastery to be achieved in a corporation.

CREATE YOUR OWN INFORMATION MASTERY AGENDA

Today's corporations must create their own version of Information Mastery in order to avoid being digitally deselected. This means devising the appropriate program of business change that reflects corporate strategy and an information-based business model. This means understanding where the firm is relative to its purpose and vision, as well as how the firm stacks up in absolute measures of fitness—revenue, profit, cash flow, and market share. Although a firm may often be based on visions and lofty business ideas, it must also be a viable business enterprise while living these business visions. The HP Way would not have survived without creating fitness along the four fitness levers described throughout this book as measures of basic business success. The dot-coms did not survive because they were not fit according to those metrics.

Information Mastery, then, does not follow a specific recipe for success. Information Mastery is based on a clear and present need for a firm to change the fundamental way it executes its business model, not the existing business model. An information-based business model that uses information to drive the business processes that make the firm successful. We have shown how an information-based business model can be constructed based on Gary Hamel's business model framework. This process of information-based business modeling will resolve the classic alignment problem plaguing IT practitioners for years and deliver vastly more value from the information capabilities of a firm because the information processes have been embedded in the business model they are meant to help execute. There is no way to drive a business today without using information-based processes to support execution and measurement of the processes of a firm.

Creating an Information Mastery agenda also requires knowing what business and technology initiatives are required based on the firm's fitness to its business environment. Recall that if a firm's business model is well adapted to its business environment and competitive landscape, then the processes of surviving and competing are working well for the core business franchises, and the firm is also performing activities that position it for the unknown forces of change and the indeterminate future that is a constant in nature and in business. The evolutionary processes of survive, compete, replicate, and adapt all have technology and business architecture implications, and therefore will require the best overall capabilities of a firm for execution. The business evolution framework developed in Chapter 8 demonstrates that technology change alone is not sufficient to ensure business evolution.

Information-based business modeling, in conjunction with the business evolutionary framework, establishes a powerful view of how business change must be initiated and for what purposes. With information-based business modeling, business and technology initiatives are almost one and the same. There are information elements of a business initiative, and there are clearly business elements of an IT initiative. They are two sides of the same business coin: information and the business are inseparable today, and will remain so. Companies must now embrace the information-based reality to be the new competitive leaders in their industries.

Exhibit 9.1 shows how Information Mastery fits into information-based business modeling. As the exhibit shows, Information Mastery as a value discipline requires the planning and execution of information-based business processes as a natural component of designing and tuning a business model. Information planning cannot be pursued separately from business planning, not even as a next step in the process. They must be concurrent activities in order to ensure that the proper information processes and capabilities are built into the fundamental business processes that, it is hoped, will produce the desired outcomes, namely fitness according to our Business Evolution Model. As discussed in Chapter 6, information elements must be built into the process of creating the business model. They cannot and must not be separate. This completely eliminates the classic alignment problem of IT and the business.

Exhibit 9.2 expands the view of Information Mastery to show the IT organization, the IT processes and value chain, and the IT architecture as elements of an information-based business model. Information Mastery, as a value discipline in and of itself, will result in a different IT organization from those derived from Industrial Age management principles. Our discussion of the Home CIO and the Distributed CIO shows that the information management processes and needs of an organization are being devised for a much more computer-

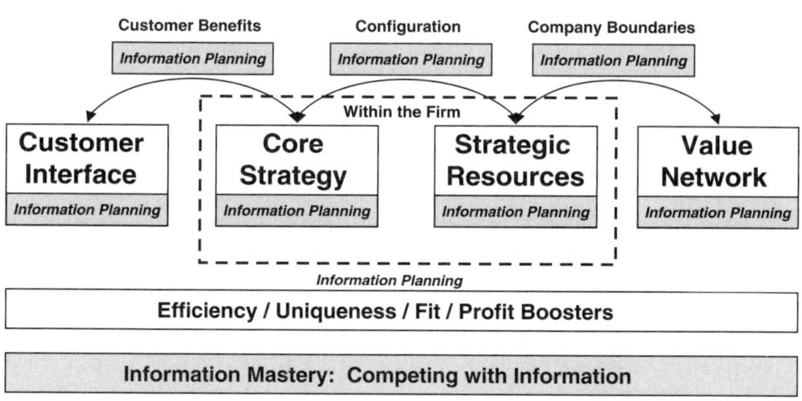

Exhibit 9.1 Information-Based Business Modeling

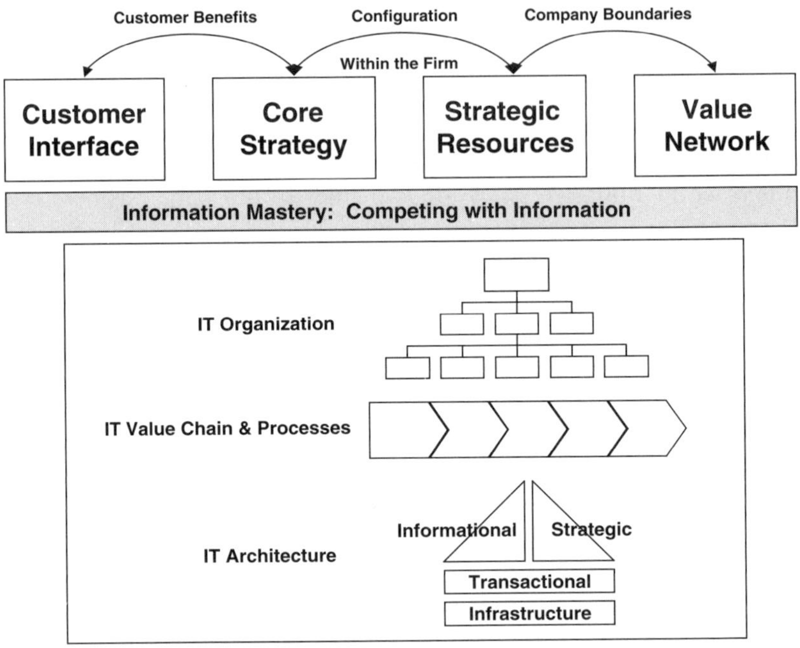

Exhibit 9.2 Information Mastery Essentials

literate audience than was available 10 years ago. These users will change the way that IT is planned, delivered, managed, and maintained for an organization. The IT organization and processes must therefore be fluid constructs that directly involve active users from the business as well as the leaders of various business and technology initiatives.

The IT organization of the Next Wave must be a structure that can flex with business and technology changes, supporting the business evolution needs of the corporation while providing increased agility and business flexibility to the firm. This is not the overcontrolling "information police" approach of the Industrial Age. This is not the cost-constrained IT structure that reports to the CFO of the firm. It is a much more strategically aligned, ubiquitous, and distributed core competency that allows the knowledge and experience of technology-savvy employees of the firm to flourish within an environment that values information and uses it more strategically to drive business execution. Achieving this type of an IT competency—the Information Mastery value discipline—will not be easy for most corporations; however, some immediate steps can be taken to begin the journey toward Information Mastery.

- Increase your corporation's brain-to-body ratio. Increase information capabilities of the firm by investing in key elements of the IT core competency, such as training, upgrading the IT infrastructure and IT portfolio, and making sure that information needs of the business are built into the business model.

- Increase IT spending, appropriately of course, in support of the new information-based business model. Increased IT spending must fall within the priorities of the firm's business evolutionary needs, which will be developed during the information-based business modeling process. The subsequent business and technology initiatives will drive the types of specific IT investments that are needed to support survival, competition, replication, and adaptation initiatives.
- Increase information conversion rates by defining new sources of information value, similar to those above, and developing information-based techniques for delivering that value. This means increasing the information content of company products, services, processes, and capabilities. This means defining the business from an information perspective as much as from a customer, process, product, and services perspective. This is critical because information contributes much more value to all of these than ever before.
- Make information part of the firm's evolutionary strategy for surviving, competing, replicating, and adapting. This is the value discipline of Information Mastery, which will become the way that firms evolve themselves to business change, both within generations of change as well as across generations of change.
- Understand the role of information management in your corporation's ability to evolve and adapt to change. Make Information Mastery a requirement for all senior executives by ensuring proper training and development processes for Information Mastery techniques for the Information Age, not the Industrial Age. An important point is this: These ideas are not taught in business schools.
- Understand the corporation's evolutionary needs based on the adaptive fit of the business model to the business environment. Remember that survive initiatives may have different business architecture and IT architecture requirements from compete initiatives. Replication activities, because they are invoked during times of transition across a generation of change, will clearly have different business architecture and IT architecture requirements from survive, compete, and adaptive initiatives. Repositioning a firm from one business model to another requires tremendous investments of energy and resources, and is therefore a more periodic activity than the other evolutionary processes. Adaptive initiatives are ongoing, prepositioning activities of a firm and are those capabilities that help a firm maintain agility and flexibility to contend with multiple futures and unknown business environmental changes.

STEPS TO INFORMATION MASTERY

Information Mastery is a sorely needed value discipline for the Next Wave. Developing your company's own Information Mastery agenda is necessary based on the particular makeup of the firm, from its corporate DNA and corporate culture to its basic organization and structure. The following list of actions will help a firm begin developing its own Information Mastery agenda:

- Devise a new, more strategic view of information for the firm.
- Create new organizational structures for IT development and delivery.
- Invent new roles for IT-literate management to lead the information and business functions of the firm.
- Define new roles for IT in business model execution.
- Develop new metrics for valuing information, such as information value to the firm and return on information and information technology.
- Devise new processes capable of using information tools and technologies to drive business execution.
- Develop or revise an information-based business model that information-enables business processes, products, and functions.
- Ingrain digital strategies in all business initiatives, business processes, business products, and customer-focused activities.
- Begin developing your Information Mastery agenda now to gain first-mover advantage with your information capabilities.

The corporate strategy and information-based business model must be modified to embed information into the firm's sinew, muscle, and bone. They must be fundamental elements of the firm's structure and capabilities. In other words, information competence cannot be a superficial veneer over the same business management foundation and processes that have always been used by the firm. Information Mastery demands that information-based capabilities are embedded in the fundamental business execution model of the firm and that all company processes are based on information and driven by information.

TREAT THE IT FUTURE AS AN OPPORTUNITY, NOT A THREAT

There are many reasons why an Industrial Age management paradigm would fear the IT future that is about to unfold. The Internet was a case in point. New companies blossomed from nowhere. New software platforms and new technologies appeared to challenge established software and technology providers. Suddenly, many new tools and solutions were needed to conduct business via the web. This shook the IT foundations for many firms. Many firms were and still are threatened by these changes, which are still under way as the dot-com implosion is digested and the suddenly slowing economy causes management to reexamine its business and its performance. But because change is constant and the pace of change is increasing, many companies are afraid of it. That makes them install processes based on maintaining control of their technology platforms, rather than building dynamic processes that can adapt and respond to change, and turn it into a competitive advantage for the firm. This also applies to how a corporation manages other elements of its business. Agility and adaptability can be assured only if processes and capabilities are implemented that allow for change, that embrace change, and that are able to anticipate change.

In order to treat the IT future as an opportunity versus a threat, firms must begin treating IT as a strategic asset, not as a financial liability. Do not measure IT against the typical budgetary constraints that evolved from the Industrial Age of corporate oversight. Rather, unleash information management from the Industrial Age financial control tethers it has operated under for the last 40 years, and allow the function to add new value to a corporation—dramatic new value based in building information into all company processes and activities.

Meeting the IT future head on as an opportunity requires defining new information metrics that are based not only on business fitness levers of market share, revenue, profit, and cash flow, but are also based on things like information conversion rates, return on net IT assets employed, or other metrics that more accurately reflect the contribution of information to the business.

Preparing for the IT future will require creating a new IT structure and capability—an IT architecture—that can flex with the business architecture according to our Business Evolution Model. This is a key agility requirement of the Next Wave that will be driven by new thinking about information by the next generation of corporate leaders.

For example, a firm should always place the CIO as a direct partner with the CEO and ensure a clear dialogue and partnership of the business and IT practitioners. We have described how today's IT dialogue is different from that of the past. The Home CIO and Distributed CIO aspects of today's IT model allow a completely new corporate conversation about how information can be used to drive superior business performance. This will allow a firm to meet the impending IT future armed and ready with a structure and processes that are designed to deliver on the value potential of information-based business models.

INVEST IN IT TO ENHANCE EVOLUTIONARY FITNESS

Information technology will be a key adaptive mechanism in *every foreseeable future scenario.* Global firms must increase IT spending, in appropriate ways, by at least 50 to 100 percent in order to be positioned for survival. There can be no more Rip Van Winkle IT management philosophies, based on total underinvestment in IT for 20 years followed by the sudden realization that a tremendous investment is necessary to bring the firm's infrastructure and application portfolio up to par with the industry and its competitors. Investing in IT must be done with an eye toward evolutionary fitness. That means investing in the agility and flexibility of the business and IT architectures. These can be greatly facilitated by enhancing the infrastructure of the firm, which leads to an ability to launch strategic and informational applications quicker across the business enterprise. Given the Business Evolution Model, this means a firm will be able to flex both the IT and business architectures to support business and technology initiatives. Whether the initiatives are core business franchise initiatives such as survive and compete initiatives or they are longer-term replication and adaptive initiatives, flexing the business and IT architectures is essential to implementing the appropriate changes required for better fitness of the business model to the business environment.

Infrastructure significantly increases a firm's ability to launch cross-company technology initiatives quickly, which means that a company can use business and technology initiatives to attack its competitors, as well as differentiate itself in the marketplace. Compete initiatives, for example, can lead to dramatic leapfrog effects by enhancing a specific element of customer-perceived value. These focused types of initiatives can be more easily implemented with a more robust infrastructure, combined with the ability to flex the business and technology architectures.

Information technology investments must be increased in support of creating and implementing an information-based business model, one that embeds information processes and capabilities in all facets of its execution. But this is a different type of business model, and it requires a different kind of leadership—at the CIO level and at the CEO level. The business leadership required of today's business environment demands an understanding and appreciation of the value that information brings to business execution, to market and customer knowledge, to the research, development, and delivery of cutting-edge products and services to world markets. The increasingly information-based business models of the future will require training in all elements of IT management and a keen foresight about how information innovation can be pursued as an internal core competency. Information Mastery will be leveraged not only internally but across a firm's entire value chain, uniting customers and suppliers in a value network of information exchange and trust, all bolstered by the tools and technologies of information-based business execution.

Increasing IT spending must also include developing new skills and capabilities in support of information-based business models. This means corporations must be willing to experiment with IT, to conduct research in IT, and to establish an R&D function for information-based research. Companies must establish pools of funding for research and experimentation. This information-based research should be established with a view toward developing new technologies that may someday create internal competitive advantage in the execution of fundamental company processes, such as manufacturing systems, business systems, and implementations of technology that solve unique problems for the firm, but that may also solve industrywide problems. These types of intellectual property will be increasingly valuable to firms as they are in position to license them to others within and across industries. In addition, these types of inventions or innovations in their highest form could actually be spun off as new software companies depending on the robustness of the application technology and the ability of the firm to package the technology as a commercial application.

This supports a potential movement away from imitator initiatives based on commercial software technology. We discussed enterprise resource planning (ERP) implementations earlier in the book. If a firm's direct competitors have all implemented an ERP solution to standardize company operations, or, for that matter, any major commercial application software package, how could that firm possibly achieve competitive advantage by implementing that same application? This "keep up with the Jones" mentality of commercial software is not necessarily the wisest course of action for a firm. A wiser course of action might be to choose a different type of initiative to invest in, being sure that proper analysis shows the firm is not losing ground to its competitors by not implementing a particular technology solution.

I believe that with the new development tools and component technologies available today, corporations can quickly develop applications to achieve specific corporate objectives without necessarily resorting to large monolithic commercial software applications. Web services is an emerging arena that appears to be the next major battlefield between Microsoft versus everyone else. J2EE (Java™ 2 Platform Enterprise Edition) is a standard for web services supported by an alliance comprised of IBM, Sun Microsystems, Hewlett-Packard, BEA Systems, and others, which transforms the Internet into a massively distributed operating system that melds corporate hardware and software based on eXtensible markup language (XML) standards and web technologies and services. The opposing technology camp for web services is Microsoft's .Net (dot-net) platform, which is a few years behind J2EE in the number of products available as well as the openness in which it is intended to operate. This is an emerging battle that will be interesting to watch. Why are web services important?

Web services represent a more modular and flexible way to design and build applications based on the technologies of the Internet. Rather than creating large, monolithic applications or desktop-oriented client-server applications using traditional software development methodologies, businesses are beginning to build applications that are based on web services. Software is instead being broken down into its constituent parts, into services or application components, which use infrastructure services, which are also being modularized. What does all this mean? It means that the modular web services approach gives companies great flexibility in system design, and that by assembling a few web services into new configurations, a business can create new application services for its users or customers. This is similar to what GE is doing with its internal web initiatives. GE is essentially building simple web-based applications that are bundled with e-mail services, which gives the company a simple way to connect all users using existing web and messaging infrastructure services.

Web services appears to be a new application development paradigm, driven by the massive adoption of the Internet by corporations and individual users, that will increase the total amount of software development work being performed in house by leading-edge corporations. This will help drive information-based strategies that help companies maintain secrecy and strategic opacity.

One major reason for taking a "build" versus "buy" approach includes maintaining strategic opacity, as well as company control, of the corporate initiative being implemented. Maintaining strategic opacity allows a firm to begin implementing an information-based business model without providing competitors with clear indications of how new competitive advantage is being accomplished.

Dell Computer is a classic instance of this approach. Dell's make-to-order business model is imitated by other PC manufacturers, from its web site to its supply chain management philosophies; however, these imitators are not achieving the same success. There are a few reasons for this. First, many of Dell's business processes and computer systems have been built over the years as it refined its make-to-order and supply chain execution processes. Being a first-mover into the world of selling PCs directly to consumers and corporations, Dell has been able to achieve significant competitive advantage in reduced inventory, reduced cost structure, and direct communication with customers and suppliers on what products and features are desired by the marketplace. This first-mover advantage has resulted in tremendous accumulated corporate experience in how to operate Dell's business model as well as its information processes in support of its business model. Dell's corporate culture is tuned to the fast pace of a direct marketing model, and its product development and launch processes are equally tuned to the speed and agility necessary to operate profitably in the fast-clockspeed computer industry. So while other firms can easily imitate Dell's web site look and feel, its navigation, and its product configurator technology, they cannot easily duplicate the underlying business process and information systems that really execute the make-to-order business model of Dell Computer. These features of Dell's business model are opaque. They are not visible to competitors because they are based on a significant investment in home-grown solutions to drive their business.

Second, even assuming that competitors knew *how* Dell Computer is able to operate its business model, they would be hard pressed to design and implement the business architecture and the IT architecture required by Dell Computer. This time compression diseconomy, where a firm cannot catch up with another firm by developing the processes, knowledge and skills, and information technologies required to execute a particular business model or business initiative, results in the maintenance of competitive advantage until the business landscape shifts to favor some other combination of competitive strategies and tactics. Strategic opacity is a competitive advantage in and of itself and can be used to mask competitive thrusts by a corporation in executing various business and technology initiatives to assume or maintain a leadership position in its chosen markets.

This potential shift back to in-house software development augmented by strategic suppliers, assemblers, component providers, and platform vendors will be driven by a desire for corporations to prevent strategic initiatives from being easily copied by implementing commercial applications. This will lead to revenue streams based on licensing and royalties from homegrown software that may be spun off or licensed to others.

If commercial software applications are selected, winners will be the early adopters, who will gain initial competitive advantage by being first-movers to implement a new strategic software application. In the Business Evolution Model, these would be considered compete initiatives. If a firm is a late adopter of a commercial software application, the advantage is gone, and playing catch-up may not be worth the investment. That particular corporation should look at its operations and seek other initiatives that provide competitive advantage. Corporations should not be swayed by persuasive vendor sales pitches that exhort a firm to buy software because one of its direct competitors has just purchased it. That does not constitute a good business case for implementing a software system. Savvy corporations will have competitive intelligence capabilities that help ascertain what competitors are doing with product and pricing strategies, sales and marketing tactics, information systems, and other strategic initiatives.

Corporations are still underinvesting in IT capabilities and assets. They must truly break from the past spending patterns and realize that information contributes vastly more value for the investment dollar than many other budgetary items and that additional spending to enhance the IT architecture will be rewarded with business agility, strategic competitive advantage, and better corporate fitness. In addition, giving IT a role in generating top-line gains as well as driving bottom-line savings will provide more incentives to drive innovation of information-based business solutions.

DEVELOP BOARDROOM IT AWARENESS AND PROMOTE IT PROFESSIONALS TO OPERATIONS ROLES

As a result of Y2K efforts, IT leaders have *proven* that they *do* indeed understand the business and how information systems impact its success. Information technology leaders were cast into the limelight with the Year 2000 phenomenon. They had a chance to interact with senior leaders of their corporations and demonstrate their ability to meet a major challenge. Even though the Year 2000 was overrated and essentially became a nonevent, consider the positive developments that emerged from the planning and execution of Year 2000 preparations.

First, companies developed comprehensive inventories of all the computing equipment in their business enterprise, which demonstrated how deeply IT impacts the day-to-day performance of even the most mundane business functions. This was an eye-opening experience for many professionals because it clearly showed how deeply dependent on computer technology corporations really are, from in-plant embedded controllers to the supply chain relationships with trading partners.

Second, Y2K preparations enhanced the IT–business dialogue by engaging business leaders in Year 2000 preparations side by side with IT practitioners. This interaction informed business leaders that the IT professionals working for the company do have a solid understanding of the business and the fundamental issues driving business success. The teamwork of the IT organization with business operations was a sneak preview of how information-based business processes can be implemented faster and better than before because the two organizations know how to work together better than before. They are now able to speak the same language about software, hardware, the Internet, and e-business issues. So there is not merely a dialogue between IT and the business, there is a shared terminology between them that allows them to understand their respective roles in the company's success. There is a shared appreciation of the power of their union, of their teamwork, and of their shared vision for the firm's success.

These two broad factors will support the transition of visionary firms toward the information-based business model and the value discipline of Information Mastery. But it must still begin at the top of the organization, with the executives of the corporation making the appropriate decisions for the future of the firm. The leaders of the Next Wave will understand that they are at an inflection point in the history of information technology, which means that corporations must be ready to begin competing on an information basis as much as on their physical assets. Leaders of the Next Wave must begin evaluating the next generation of leadership required to run their corporations. They must begin training key executives on the value of information. They must educate themselves on how IT can be better embedded in the foundation of core company processes and operations. Leaders of the Next Wave must develop a clear agenda for driving their business models based on information-intensive capabilities.

The next 5 to 10 years will be marked by IT management getting promoted to *key leadership roles* because their skills are *absolutely necessary* for the survival of firms in the modern age. Do not be surprised if the next generation of CEOs comes from a technology background. This transition must happen soon, because today the information function contributes as much value to the sustaining functions of a corporation as the physical assets do. CEOs minimally must have a direct partnership with the IT leaders of the firm and begin promoting IT-savvy executives to senior roles within the organization. All corporate leaders must be trained in the following concepts in order to prepare for the Next Wave:

- Business evolution and the role of IT in facilitating adaptive fit of the business model
- Information-based business modeling and how to compete based on information
- Information Mastery as a value discipline
- The need to flex the business architecture and the IT architecture in order to implement business and technology initiatives successfully in support of evolutionary objectives

Business leaders of the Next Wave must remember that information technologies permeate every facet of the business organization, so they must be sure to represent all functional disciplines in crafting their Information Mastery agenda, which is their IT adaptive framework for the future. This means that all information disciplines and all business disciplines—factory automation and controls engineers, manufacturing systems personnel, as well as the traditional IT disciplines—all have key roles to play in your future. This is a must for Information Mastery.

ENSURE CORPORATE AGILITY AND EVOLUTIONARY CAPABILITIES

The business evolutionary framework we have introduced brings to the fore the essence of Business Darwinism: the ability of a corporation to change and adapt to its immediate environmental challenges as well as to prepare for future environmental challenges based on its ability to compete using an information-based business model. Corporations differ from living organisms in that they can choose the trajectory of their evolution to a large extent. That does not mean that a corporation can turn on a dime and become a completely different entity overnight. Nokia serves as an example of a corporation that began in one industry, diversified into multiple businesses, then ultimately transitioned itself into a high-technology cell phone pure-play.

But the path to cell phones derived from existing and acquired corporate DNA and core competencies, as well as learned corporate culture, behaviors, and skills. Nokia, through a series of conscious corporate decisions and perhaps some serendipity, acquired the business unit diversity and R&D capabilities to be successful in cell phone manufacturing well before the decision to enter the cell phone market. Nokia had already begun acquiring and developing the corporate DNA for its cell phone success long before it formally entered the cell phone market. Ericsson's decision to enlist Nokia as the provider of cell phones for its early analog cellular network launched Nokia on its current trajectory, but this still would not have been possible without Nokia's earlier forays into electronics—computers and televisions—as well as its experience with radio telephones.

A corporation can consciously diversify itself in anticipation of environmental changes that may render certain businesses more advantageous than others. Our Business Evolution Model suggests that a firm will be in a better position to successfully make these evolutionary transitions with the agility provided by two significant capabilities: investing in an IT architecture that allows the firm to flex to support needed business and technology initiatives, and developing a business architecture that can flex simultaneously. If a company is implementing Survive initiatives that deliver operational excellence to the existing business model or Compete initiatives that provide focused competitive advantage in execution of the same business model, flexing the business and IT architectures is critical for initiating and completing business and technology change in support of the defined business model. Corporate agility facilitates the tuning and refinement of the business model of the core business franchise.

Corporate agility and evolutionary capabilities are truly put to the test during transitions from one business model to the next, through corporate replication processes. The repositioning of a company's business model across a generation of technology change, business change, or leadership change requires the best agility skills of a firm. Corporate replication demands a reexamination of the corporate strategy and the business model in order to make the required changes to ensure a viable corporate future. As discussed previously, an assessment of the firm's total capacity for change must be performed to determine how much change can be tolerated in the replication process of the firm. The Hewlett-Packard case study showed a company that is pushing the limits of change in its quest to remake itself as an Internet products and services company modeled after the best attributes of IBM, Sun Microsystems, and other leaders in their respective categories. Can HP attain the necessary corporate DNA to support this transition? Will the vast changes being driven by CEO Carly Fiorina ultimately break HP, or can the business and IT architectures be flexed successfully to lead to the new HP Way? These transitions across generations of change are difficult times for the best corporations in the world, and they require strong leadership and agility skills that may not exist. HP is in the process of changing fundamental behaviors that have been practiced for decades. HP has not necessarily built the capabilities to successfully introduce organizational change to this magnitude (nor have many corporations for that matter) and to flex the IT and business architectures in support of business and technology initiatives that derive from a new business model concept.

Finally, the skills required to adapt a firm to multiple, potentially unknown futures are equally critical for long-term business evolutionary fitness. The adaptive capabilities of a firm involve business diversification and core competency creation and acquisition. Adaptive capabilities include strategic mergers and acquisitions as well as the internal, organic R&D expertise of a firm. All of these activities are required to develop the corporate DNA to support the next business replication, a firm's transition to its next chosen future based on the body of acquired skills, core capabilities, corporate knowledge, and organizational learning.

Recall that while replication efforts reposition a company for its next future, adaptive efforts preposition a company for multiple futures. Both are critical for ensuring the long-term fitness of a firm and the viability of its future. Corporate agility is essential for a firm to be able to successfully complete its transition to its next future, and that is where the business and IT architectures are flexed to drive the required changes. But they are flexed only after the corporate strategy has been reexamined and refined, and an information-based business model has been created that provides maximal business fitness. Instituting corporate agility is no mean feat for any firm, because it implies that the processes and structures supporting business change are transient by nature. The only constant is change, and therefore institutionalizing change takes practice. Companies, organizations, strategies, and business models to date have resisted change, and the IT architectures that resulted from these habits were built to resist change. But in order to flex a business architecture, and in order to flex an IT architecture, the corporate muscle must be built up, a company must "work out" and exercise, to be ready for change when it is required for a replication initiative. Flexing corporate muscle takes practice and conditioning.

This may create a new title in corporations of the future: *Chief Agility Officer.* A Chief Agility Officer (CAO) will oversee adaptive planning and execution, as well as govern the business replication processes of a firm. The CAO will ensure that the firm has the necessary skills to adapt to known competitors and unknown changes, to the long-term business environment that will continually confront all corporations. The CAO may have dotted-line oversight over aspects of IT that relate to corporate agility, since as we have discussed earlier, IT investments play a significant role in a firm's ability to add new information systems, to launch new business and technology initiatives quickly to gain competitive advantage quickly and ensure business fitness.

The CAO will be responsible for a corporation's total business diversification strategies, for maintaining strategic degrees of freedom with the business model as well as with the IT architecture. Possible responsibilities could include planning for business replication as well as conducting adaptive activities, M&A initiatives, and overseeing long-term R&D projects. The most important role, however, will be melding all of these diversification and core competence acquisition processes into the company's total ability to shift its business model, business processes, and business and IT architectures in a completely new direction based on what the firm's corporate DNA and core capabilities are.

Consider Intel's diversification efforts of the last few years. Intel designs and manufactures world-class microprocessors. Intel's innovation capabilities—for both its products and its manufacturing processes—are widely acknowledged by its peers and admirers worldwide; however, under CEO Craig Barret, Intel is undergoing a major change—diversifying itself into multiple businesses that one would not have expected from Intel. These include Internet services such as web site and application hosting, as well as selling branded Internet appliances. Intel could not have contemplated these changes without instituting the business agility to execute them. This is adaptation at its finest—adding diversity in the face of uncertainty, which is the ultimate evolutionary advantage. Diversity and variation wins the adaptation and natural selection game.

Business agility can be manifested in many ways, from strategy shifts resulting in business replication to adaptive activities resulting in acquisitions of new business units that may become core competencies over time. Business agility, though, also comes through launching Survive and Compete initiatives with the current business model. Competing on time has long been known to be a critical capability for any corporation, providing demonstrated results for the firms that can design and implement time-based initiatives. Stalk and Hout summarize the advantages of time-based competition: "When a time-based competitor can open up a response advantage with turn-around times three to four times faster than its competitors, it will almost always grow three times faster than the average for the industry and will be twice as profitable as the average for all competitors."[2] Time-based competitors are a new breed of company, according to Stalk and Hout, in that they compete and manage themselves in new ways, using agility, flexibility, and speed. They obtain their astonishing results by focusing their organizations on flexibility and responsiveness.

Agility, flexibility, and speed are the watchwords of the digitally evolved corporation that can flex both its business and IT architectures in response to changing environmental and business conditions. In a sense, corporate agility and flexibility are time-based strategies. They are capabilities that facilitate a firm's preemptive strategies against competitors, as well as facilitating a firm's response to changing conditions in its business landscape—market and customer preferences, competitive moves, and environmental changes such as regulatory changes, raw material price fluctuations, currency fluctuations, and other macroeconomic changes. Corporations that have the internal capabilities to quickly adapt to change, as well as initiate change to launch needed business and technology initiatives, will be best positioned to compete in the Information Age. These business evolutionary skills are mandatory for companies to compete. The speed of business evolution within generations of change, such as survive and compete initiatives, as well as across generations of change, like replication and adaptive initiatives, will determine the winners and losers.

DIGITAL HUNTER-GATHERERS AND CORPORATE VELOCIRAPTORS

The technology of today has created a modern version of hunter-gatherers—digital hunter-gatherers. The early hunter-gatherers were mobile people, who lived off the land and carried all of their worldly possessions with them. The transition from hunter-gatherers with small, mobile technology compares nicely to today's digital hunter-gatherers, with smaller and more powerful mobile technologies to support increasingly mobile techniques for making a living in the digital economy. We have come full circle in our adoption and packaging of technology in support of our need to make a living. The original hunter-gatherers were only able to use technology that was small and portable, easy to pack with them in support of their lifestyle based on constant movement in search of food and sustenance. Their mobility placed limitations on the tools and technologies used for survival.

Today's digital hunter-gatherers are also limited in how they can use their tools and technologies. The limitations in this case are imparted both by increasingly mobile lifestyles, as well as the need to be connected to the home office for access to mission-critical information that helps them perform their business missions. There are many examples of digital hunter-gatherers in business today. Sales teams are digital hunter-gatherers. Management consultants are digital hunter-gatherers. Work teams are digital hunter-gatherers. The digitally evolved corporation will use information as its weapon, much as the spear and knife were early weapons for hunter-gatherers. The ability to distribute critical information to these digital hunter-gatherers will be ever more important as workforces are more distributed, as offices are increasingly global, and as business execution becomes more remote from corporate headquarters.

For example, sales teams will be organized like bands of hunter-gatherers with a single purpose—bagging game. In this case, the "game" is customers, and the competition is other competing firms. This band of digital hunter-gatherers will be digitally organized into connected workgroups and armed with weapons—information-based weapons—to help win customers and market share. These digital hunter-gatherers will be provided with information about their competitors, their sales tactics, and their products and services to be better able to compete against them. Digital hunter-gatherers will be armed with the latest product data, as well as the latest market and customer preferences, and will be able to deliver customized value propositions for a particular client on the spot, and close the deal in a much shorter time than without the information-based tools and weapons. These digital hunter-gatherers will be hyperefficient as a result of real-time access to necessary information in support of their particular job functions, whether it be sales, consulting, or other field operations. Digital hunter-gatherers are implementations of time-based competition, but they are also evolutionary behaviors based on competing information. Information-based competition and time-based competition are closely linked in delivering superior corporate fitness, performance, agility, and adaptability. But information-based capabilities are required to be a time-based competitor. Information facilitates speed, agility, and flexibility.

When the movie *Jurassic Park* was released to the world in 1993, it captured the hearts and minds of a generation of children and adults who had often wondered what life was really like during the Jurassic Period. The Jurassic Period was the Golden Age of dinosaurs, the time when the Earth was ruled by beasts such as Tyrannosaurus rex and the infamous velociraptors that terrorized the principal characters in the movie. Velociraptors displayed the cunning and ruthless aggression we attribute to these fierce prehistoric meat eaters based on scientific evidence and their curved middle claw, which scientists infer was used to slash their prey. Velociraptors are believed to have hunted in packs and were very fast runners capable of speeds approaching 40 miles per hour. Their scientific name is *Dromaeosaurid deinonychosauria,* but velociraptors are known by nicknames such as "swift seizer" and "quick plunderer."

The increasingly mobile and digitally enabled members of today's workforce allow companies to deploy resources more quickly in pursuit of strategic and tactical objectives. The ability to quickly commission work teams connected by mobile technology and armed with customer and competitor information is similar to launching a pack of corporate velociraptors. These corporate velociraptors will work as teams with speed and intelligence to capture new customers and seize market share ahead of the competition, and they will do so with the precision afforded them by the information-based competitive weapons of the Next Wave. They will be ultra-informed with all the information at their fingertips to make deals happen. This is more than today's version of customer relationship management (CRM) and sales force automation. This is an organizational model based on delivering mission-critical information to the connected, digital hunter-gatherers and corporate velociraptors. This is an action-based employee deployment model similar to the logistics systems of the armed forces, except the material is the necessary information to conquer a targeted set of customers, to win a region or a state from a competitor, or to own a market or an industry.

The power of information-based competition can be exploited in many ways. The concepts of digital hunter-gatherers and corporate velociraptors are simply potential implementations of information-based competition and digital weapons using mobile yet connected workforce deployment models. Sales teams and product development teams can all work together in coordinated ways to perform their specific duties, armed with digital weaponry and coordinated by information systems, all in execution of an information-based business model.

REAL-TIME EVOLUTION

In today's volatile business environment, building variation into a business model or organizational framework is critical for enhancing its ability to survive high-change environments. This can take the form of processes, technologies, and behaviors all designed to enhance survivability of a firm. The speed at which business change occurs is alarming to some, but to others it is business as usual. High-clockspeed industries like semiconductors and electronics are accustomed to rapid product cycles and accelerating product obsolescence, whereas other industries are not comfortable with that pace of change. Companies that are prepared for change, however, and that can take advantage of change by using it against their competition, will be positioned to win. These firms have the overall business vision and capabilities to anticipate and respond to change and to build the appropriate evolutionary skills into their corporate strategies and their business models to ensure a vibrant future. Not all companies will. Many corporations do not have the basic evolutionary capabilities to survive a single generation of change, much less multiple generations of change across decades of competition. The firms that have managed so far are advantaged only in that they have been through cycles of change before. But we are entering a new era of competitive intensity based on global markets, increasing information content in products and services, and an increased need to use information-based capabilities to survive.

Microsoft, for example, has already been through several episodes of a corporation evolution in its short history, including its rise as a software and operating system powerhouse, to its Internet and application software dominance. Today Microsoft is building game consoles; it is expanding into online services to compete with America Online; and it has invested in a slew of other start-ups and business ventures to provide the evolutionary basis for its future growth and expansion. Microsoft is building corporate DNA and genetic variation into its future business through these investments, through mergers and acquisitions, and through its hefty R&D expenditures.

Today's business environment, as mentioned in Chapter 3, resembles punctuated equilibrium, characterized by the sudden burst of evolutionary activity and the rapid rise of new species of corporations. As we also stated in Chapter 3, however, this is simply a time-compressed period of business evolution based on a rapid rate of environmental change, which suddenly casts favor over the then-well-adapted business models and the kinds of companies that can execute those business models. It is almost real-time evolution we are witnessing. The Internet phenomenon was a case in point. The environment changed, new companies emerged based on new business models and new technology, and then the business version of natural selection pruned the viable firms with solid fitness capabilities from those that were unfit, that could not provide sustainable business performance.

Dell Computer is considered one of the most "fit" companies in the world with its make-to-order business model and its direct sales process. Dell, in several ways, represents the model of business evolution in the fastidious way that it avoids inflexibility and architects change into the way it conducts business. It is no surprise that the business metrics preferred by Michael Dell are those that we defined early in this book: revenue profit, cash flow, and market share. A quote from Michael Dell is instructive:

> To compete successfully in any industry, you must first understand its fundamental economics, which can reveal new customer opportunities, products and services. If you are starting or running a business, and you choose to leave the economics until last, you won't actually be capable of developing the customers and product strategies that will be necessary to achieve balanced success, which I define as growth of *market share* (or *revenue*), *profitability,* and liquidity (or *cash flow*).[3]

Dell is able to respond in real time to market conditions because it is constantly in direct contact with customers and suppliers. Dell knows what the market preferences will be for products and services, and what prices customers will be willing to pay for new products and services. Dell can evolve its business model in real time because it is continually monitoring and sensing the changes in market and customer preferences, as well as changes in the business environment and competitors' strategies and tactics.

Real-time evolution is based on a firm's ability to monitor, sense, and adjust its business model on the fly, dynamically, based on feedback from the business fitness levers. This is particularly critical in the case of survive and compete initiatives, which occur with generations of change, not necessarily across generations of change. But preparing for the business future is also a real-time activity, which is why adaptive initiatives are ongoing processes for corporations. The set of processes and activities that preposition the firm for multiple futures are critical for ensuring the genetic variability and corporate DNA to allow the firm to have multiple evolutionary options when it is time to cross a generation of change. These activities and processes facilitate business change given the acceleration of environmental change in the business landscape.

Real-time evolution attempts to remove as much of the organizational inertia and technological lag from the process of adapting to business change, which is why flexing the business and IT architectures is so important. Building information-based business models to facilitate agility and flexibility of response synchronizes the organizational structure and processes with the information needs of the corporation. This is why the old concept of poor alignment of IT with the business is merely an excuse from Industrial Age methods of managing increasingly information-based businesses. Poor alignment was not IT's fault, and it was not the business's fault. It was simply an outcome from a system of corporate management that arose to impose control over a discipline that was in its infancy and that is still rapidly evolving and changing. Today's information-based business models defy Industrial Age paradigms of management. The new role of IT in digitally evolved companies is one where software must drive the hardware—which in this case is the corporation, the company's physical infrastructure. If the application needs of the corporation are defined concurrently with the strategy of the firm (information-based business modeling), the lag between the business and IT will disappear. This is the corporate version of adaptation. If the infrastructure is built to allow rapid application deployment in support of rapid cycles of learning, then IT will be able to implement software more easily than otherwise. That is how real-time evolution can occur in companies of the Next Wave.

THE DARWINIAN ROAD AHEAD

What a time we live in! This is an unprecedented period in history, and we are just beginning to see how things will change given the reach and impact of information technologies in all aspects of human existence. According to some analysts, we are only one-fifth of the way through the technological opportunities inherent in computers and communications. That means we have four times as much change coming as we have experienced in the past 40 years. That is incredible to think about. As a species, human beings have witnessed an onslaught of technology-driven change, beginning from our early use of stone tools and harnessing fire, to our increasing use of information technologies in our everyday lives.

As humans, we are a unique species on earth. We are unique in that we actively shape our environment and the landscape we live in. We shape it in both good and bad ways, depending on what perspective one chooses, but nonetheless we change it. We are a digital species. We evolved language and culture, created technology, and domesticated our food production, writing, and associated communication technologies. We invented machines to help us count and devices to help us communicate. We carry our digital devices with us everywhere we go it seems: cellular phones, two-way pagers, Palm Pilots and related personal organizers all are creeping into our lives deeper and deeper. But what does this all signal? It means simply that we are so used to being connected digitally with one another, with our work environments, with our personal environments, that we will go to great lengths to ensure that we can reach and be reached to communicate and exchange information.

That is the human experience, communication and information exchange. That is what human culture was founded upon. Our culture is becoming increasingly digital as opposed to strictly oral and written. Being human is about being digital today. We have always been digital to some extent; however, we just did not realize it until our DNA structure was decoded. The language of human reproduction is digital and bears the uncanny resemblance to the computer concepts that are dramatically shaping and driving business organisms today—namely corporations. The digital analogy of humans to corporations, as well as the cultural analogy of humans to corporations, fits nicely as a way to view the behavior and evolution of these "species."

Make sure you have the adaptive capabilities to survive in this wave of rapid change using the punctuated equilibrium analogy. Do not let your firms, or yourselves, become victims of business and information Darwinism. We are in the Age of Information. Information is a key adaptive capability for survival for the foreseeable future. Do not be deselected by ignoring the growing information imperative of the Next Wave. Remember, the rules of survival have been known for a long, long time: Adapt or die. That is the law of the jungle today.

NOTES

1. Gary Hamel, *Leading the Revolution* (Boston, MA: Harvard Business School Press, 2000); see also Gary Hamel and C.K. Prahalad, *Competing for the Future* (Boston, MA: Harvard Business School Press, 1994).
2. See George Stalk, Jr. and Thomas M. Hout's groundbreaking book *Competing Against Time* (New York: The Free Press, 2000) for a compelling analysis of time compression strategies.
3. Michael Dell with Catherine Fredman, *Direct from Dell* (New York: HarperBusiness, 1999), p. 201.

INDEX

A

Adaptation, 53, 160. *See also* Change; Corporate culture
  adaptive mechanisms, 3, 4
  proactive, 77, 78
  short and long time frames for, 76, 77
Adaptive activities, 160, 162, 192–95, 223–30, 234, 253, 261
  and Business Evolution Model, 213
  replication activities compared, 223
Adaptive initiatives, 154, 155
Agility, 23, 58, 107, 114, 242
  digital, 47
  ensuring corporate agility and evolutionary capabilities, 252–55
  operating agility, 141, 143
Architecture
  business. *See* Business architecture
  information technology. *See* Information management processes

B

Breakeven points, lower breakevens and strategic flexibility, 141, 144
Business architecture
  flexing, 168–71
  and IT architecture interplay, 174, 175
Business capability, 72
Business drivers, information as, 6, 241, 242
Business environment, 56–59, 165, 216
Business Evolution Strategy model, 156–92
Business execution, and information-based business processes, 16
Business fitness. *See* Fitness
Business initiatives, prioritizing, 178
Business mission, 128
Business models, 2
  blended business model, 41, 42
  breakeven points, 141, 144
  Business Evolution Model, 159, 160, 172, 177, 181, 191, 192, 209, 230
    and adaptive activities, 228, 229
    Hewlett-Packard example, 181–90
    Nokia example, 219–23
    sample questionnaire, 179–81
  business first, 23
  company boundaries, 126, 138, 139
  and competition, 123, 124
  components of, 125, 126
  configuration, 126, 130–32
  core strategy, 126, 128, 129
  corporate strategies and, 123–28
  corporate structure and core capabilities, changes, 158
  customer benefits, 126, 135, 136
  customer interfaces, 126, 132–36
  e-business and IT as execution mechanisms for business strategy, 23
  First Wave, 24, 44
  Information Age, 10, 11
  information-based, 7, 123–55, 234, 241, 242, 252
  information-based force multipliers, 125, 126, 144, 145
  Information Mastery, creating agenda for, 145–55, 240–43
  information technology and, 46, 123–25, 130–32

Business models *(continued)*
  Microsoft, 69–71
  operating agility, 141, 143
  portfolio breadth, 141–43
  profit potential, 126, 139–41
  repositioning, 252, 253
  strategic flexibility, 141–44
  strategic resources, 126, 127, 129, 130
  value drivers, 125, 126
  value network, 126, 136–38
  variation, need for, 257–60
Business processes, 74
  core processes, 129, 170, 195–97, 199–207
  information-based, 13–16
Business to business (B2B), 42, 137
  and enterprise software applications, 110
Business-to-consumer (B2C) commerce, 22, 42

C

Cash flow, as fitness metric, 175, 176
Change, 34, 75, 76, 115, 149, 162, 234. *See also* Adaptation
  business environment, changes in, 216
  and business evolutionary strategies, 157
  business model, repositioning of, 252, 253
  capacity for, 163–68
  and competition, 76
  corporate change vectors, 166–68
  high-change environments, 257–60
  and information technology structure, 95
  leadership, change in, 215, 216
  and macro-model of business evolution, 158–62
  ownership, change in, 216
  pace of change, 56–58
  preparing for the Next Wave, 47
  technology-driven, 3, 34, 35, 232
  tolerance, 224
Chief Agility Officer (CAO), 254
Chief Information Officers (CIOs), 9, 17, 89, 241, 242, 245
  Distributed CIO Function, 237
  Home CIO, 236
  managing IT architecture, 101
Client-server architectures, 83, 94
  and departmental software applications, 85, 86
  enterprise software applications, 87, 88
Coalitions, and value network, 137
Communication, 260
  use of PCs, 88
Company boundaries, 126
  role of information in defining, 138, 139
  strategic resources and value network, 138
Competition, 60–62, 194–95
  and business model, 123, 124
  and change, 76
  competitive initiatives, 152, 153, 192, 193, 207–9
  competitive technologies, 46, 47
  and evolution, 54–56
  how corporations compete, 67–69
  information, importance of, 6, 7
  and information-based business, example, 11, 12
  strategies, 207–12, 229
    survival initiatives compared, 207
Computer Age, 39, 43, 44, 69
Computers. *See also* Software applications
  computer literacy and workforce, 235–37
  development of, 39
  mainframes, 82, 94
  minicomputers, 82
  PCs, 82, 85, 94, 99
Configuration, 126, 159
  core strategy and strategic resources, 130
  role of information, 130–32
Consortium participation, adaptive activities, 225

Core capabilities, 59, 60, 72, 73, 107, 158
Core competencies, 72, 73, 129
Core information strategy, 128, 129
Core processes, 129
core defined, 196, 197
efficiency, 197, 198
insurance industry example, 199–207
protecting, 195
Core strategy, 59, 60, 90–92, 123–30, 158, 159
Corporate culture, 3, 4, 21, 32, 72–75, 165, 166
Corporate DNA, 4, 5, 32, 72–75, 162
Corporate genetics, 72
Corporate muscle
business architecture and IT architecture, 168, 169–75
fitness levers, 175–81
Corporations
as anti-entropy machines, 65, 66
core capabilities, 59, 60, 72, 73, 107, 158
core competencies, 72, 73, 129
core processes. *See* Core processes
evolutionary metaphor. *See* Evolutionary metaphor for business
history of and evolutionary concepts, 62–66
information technology and business operations, 250, 251
long-term activities of, 156, 157, 160, 168, 173, 178
macro structure, 90, 91
nature of, 64
restructuring, 90, 91
short-term activities of, 156, 157, 160, 168, 173, 178
strategies, 59, 60, 90–92, 123–30, 158, 159
structure of, 59, 60, 89–91, 158, 169
Cultural adaptation. *See* Corporate culture
Customer benefits, 126
core strategy and customer interface, 135
role of information in benefit creation and delivery, 135, 136
Customer interface, 126
and core strategy, 135
customer-facing information management, 133
customer self-service, 133, 134
fulfillment, 132, 133
information and insight, 132, 134
pricing structure, 133
relationship dynamics, 132–35
support, 132, 133, 135, 136
Customer relationship management (CRM), 14, 208
and informational technology, 112, 113
Customers
intimacy, 13–15, 24, 27
proximity to, 24
securing market share and protecting customers, 198, 199
service, 198

D

Dell Computer, 32, 248, 249, 258, 259
information-intensive mode of competition, example of, 11–13
Differentiation, basis for, 128
Digital Business Design, 9, 10

E

E-commerce, 21–23, 33, 109, 110
companies that understand Internet opportunity, 23–27
failed business statistics, 44
Efficiency, 126, 139–40
Electronic data interchange (EDI), 137
Enterprise resources planning (ERP) software, 87–89, 108, 247
dangers of, 108–10
transactional systems and, 111
Environment
business environment, 165, 216
and evolution, 56–59
effect of on evolution, 52

Evernet, 45
Evolutionary activities
adaptation. *See* Adaptive activities
competition. *See* Competition
reproduction (replication). *See* Replication activities
survival. *See* Survival
Evolutionary metaphor for business, 3, 32–34, 51, 52, 149–55, 163, 164, 192–95
adaptation, 53
competition, 54–56
corporations
adaptation, 75–78
competition, 67–69
corporate culture, 74, 75
corporate DNA, 72–75
evolution of, 62–66
reproduction, 65, 66, 69–71, 75
survival, 66, 67
corporations and evolutionary activities, 61, 62
corporations as living organisms, 59, 60
environment, 52, 53
environment of business, 56–60
essence of business Darwinism, 252
evolution as guide to future, 52
natural selection, 52–54
punctuated equilibrium
and the business environment, 57–59
and change, 56, 57
real-time evolution, 257–60
survival of the fittest, 52, 53
Executives
leadership
changes in, 215, 216
roles, 20, 251
Next Wave executives, traits of, 18
Expense, IT viewed as, 10

F

Feedback, fitness levers, 175–81
Fit
business model elements, 141
and profit potential, 126
Fitness, 214, 232
metrics, 175–81, 211, 214, 233
and adaptive activities, 227
Front-end/back-end structure, 93
Functional structure, 92
Future trends
analysis of, 234, 235
information technology as opportunity, 244, 245

G

General Electric, early use of computers, 84
Genetic evolution, 4
Geographical structure, 93

H

Hewlett-Packard, 253
business evolution example, 181–90
change in leadership, 217, 218
corporate restructuring example, 165, 166, 171

I

Industrial Age, transition from, 8, 28, 38
Industrial automation, 26
Industrial Revolution, 37–39, 51
Information
access to, 7
as adaptive mechanism, 5–8
as an asset, 8
assets, 16
as business driver, 6
company boundaries, role in defining, 138, 139
competencies, assets, and processes, 129, 130
economics of, 7
information-based business models, 7
metrics, 16
as replacement for inventory, 12
value of, 5, 7, 16, 17, 23, 29, 30, 131

Information Age, 5
business model, 10, 11
transition from Industrial Age, 8
Information-based business models, 7, 123–55, 234, 241, 242, 252
Information-based business processes, 13–16
Information-based force multipliers, 125, 126, 144, 145
Information Darwinism, Principle of. *See* Principle of information Darwinism
Information management, 15, 16, 96–98, 100, 127, 250, 251
architecture
business architecture and IT architecture interplay, 174, 175
defined, 102–4
flexing, 168, 169, 171–75, 233, 234
information technology, 101–5
management patterns, 116–20
mapping IT architecture to business fitness, 105
customer-facing information management, 133
developing IT portfolio, 114, 115
and Information Mastery, 120–22
informational technology, 104, 105, 111–13, 115
infrastructure, 105–10, 114, 115
origins of and organizational strategies, 96–98
role of IT, 100, 101
strategic technology, 105, 113–14
supplier-facing information management, 137
transactional systems, 105, 106, 110–12, 115
Information Mastery, 15–17, 47, 233, 251
attributes of, 16
and business model, 125
creating agenda for and business model, 145–55, 240–43
executives, attributes of Next Wave, 19–21
information technology architecture and, 120–22
methods of achieving and configuring the corporation, 130–32
preparing for Next Wave, 238–40
steps to, 244
as value discipline, 239
value metrics, 239
Information technology, 5, 81
business implications, 45, 46
and business model, 46, 123–25, 130–32
and business value, 23
core processes, 173
corporate leadership, 20, 251
corporate strategy, as driver of, 92
culture of, 21
developing new skills and capabilities, 247
expectations of, 21
and foretelling future trends, 235
future of, 237, 238, 247, 248
as opportunity, 244, 245
historical background, 82–89
information value metrics, 173
investment in and Principle of Information Darwinism, 8–12, 17–19, 47, 246–50
investment patterns, 115–20
management. *See* Information management
organization and structure of, 20, 89–98, 100, 131, 172
organizational principles, 97, 98
organizational and technology learning processes, 173
and Principle of Information Darwinism, 8–10
ratio of spending and gross revenues, 28, 29
role of and core strategy, 131
role of as a value discipline, 19, 20, 96

Information technology *(continued)*
spending
categories of, 105
rates, 111–13
strategic approaches, 148, 149
strategic functions, 89, 100
strategic information assets, 173
strategies, 97
structure of, 20, 21, 89–91, 245
success, new metrics of, 131, 132
value metrics, 239
Informational technology, 105, 106, 111, 113
Infrastructure, 105–10
Innovation, 35, 146, 147, 165
adaptive activities, 225
rate of and capacity for change, 163, 164
Insurance industry, core business survival and competition example, 199–207
Intel, 254
transitioning technology, 218, 219
Internet, 233
attributes of, 43
changes in IT architectures, 88, 89
companies, 22
corporate adoption of, 88, 89
importance of, 40, 46
increasing usage of, 45
Internet Age, 43
Internet business models, hybridization of, 41, 42
as marketing tool, 88
n-tier Internet architectures, 83
networking, trend toward, 43
rapid acceptance of, 40, 42, 43, 46, 99, 236
Web services, 247, 248
Internet Age, 69
Inventory, information as replacement for, 12

J
Joint ventures, adaptive activities, 225

K
Knowledge management processes, adaptive activities, 225

L
Leadership
change in. *See also* Hewlett-Packard
and IT, 210, 251
and replication initiatives, 215, 216

M
Make-to-order manufacturing, 11, 12
Management of IT. *See* Information management
Manufacturing operations, outsourcing, 208
Market proximity, 24
Market share, 68, 69, 198, 199
as fitness metric, 175, 177
Marketing and Internet, 88
Matrix structure, 93
Mergers and acquisitions, adaptive activities, 225, 227, 228
Metrics, business fitness, 170, 175–81, 211, 214, 227, 233
Microsoft, 85, 258
business model, 69–71
Motorola, Business Evolution Model example, 210–11
Mutation rates, 163–68

N
N-tier Internet architectures, 83
Natural selection, 52–54
New Economy business model, 2
First Wave, 2
Next Wave. *See* Next Wave business model
Next Wave business model, 69
beginning of, 9–11, 45
executives, traits of, 18, 19
future developments, 235–37
and Information Mastery, 15, 238–44
information technology and, 237, 238
Internet and, 44

leaders of, 251
preparing for, 47, 48, 238–40
strategic information management, 19
traits of Next Wave winners, 11
Nokia, 252
information management example, 24–27
replication initiatives, example of, 219–23

O

Old Economy business model, 2
Operational excellence, 13–15, 27
Organizational learning processes, 170
Organizational structure models, 90
Organizational supply chains, 72
Outsourcing
manufacturing operations, 208
suppliers, 138
Ownership and replication initiatives, 216

P

Partners and value network, 136, 137
Portfolio breadth, 141–43
Pricing structure, 133
Principle of Information Darwinism, 8–10
information-based processes, 13–15
information technology as strategy, 8, 10–12, 17–19, 47, 246–50
Printing press, 233
and development of technology, 35–37
Process structure, 93
Product development process, 208, 210, 211
Product leadership, 13, 14, 27
Product structure, 93
Profit, as fitness metric, 175
Profit boosters, 126, 141
Profit potential of business model, 126, 139–41
Punctuated equilibrium, 258, 261
and evolutionary change, 56–59

R

Replication activities, 117, 153, 160–62, 193, 195, 229, 230, 234, 253
adaptive activities compared, 223
and Business Evolution Model, 213–18
transitioning technology
Intel example, 218, 219
Nokia example, 219–23
Research and development, 226, 227
adaptive activities, 225
and IT, 21
Revenue as fitness metric, 175

S

Scientific management, 38
Scope of product/market, 128
Software applications, 81, 248, 249. *See also* Computers
and client-server architecture, 85
enterprise software. *See* Enterprise resources planning (ERP) software
financial, origins of, 83–86, 89
and manufacturing industry, 86, 87
and Web services, 247
Speed, 23, 58
Strategic assets, 129, 159, 170
information technology as, 245
Strategic flexibility, 141–44
Strategic resources, 126, 127, 129–30
value network, linking to, 136–38
Strategic technology, 105, 106, 113–14
Strategic weapon, IT as, 10–12
and corporate strategy, 91–95
executive training in strategic information management, 19
Success, factors in, 68
Suppliers
company boundaries and outsourcing, 138
supplier-facing information management, 137
and value network, 136
Supply chain management, 208, 209

Survival
of the fittest, 52, 53, 66, 67, 69
goals, 117, 192, 193, 195
initiatives, 152, 194, 207, 212, 229

T

Technology
acceleration of, 44
digital technology, 260, 261
and hunter-gatherer metaphor, 255–57
as driver of change, 3, 34, 35, 232
historical background, 35–40
communications and transportation, 38, 39
computers, 39, 40
Industrial Revolution, 37–39
integrated circuits (microchip), 39
Internet and, 36, 40
printing press, 35–37
transistor, invention of, 39
initiatives, prioritizing, 178
recent technotrends, 44
and replication initiatives, 215
supply chains, 72
transitioning
Intel example, 218, 219
Nokia example, 219–23
types of technology choices, 102, 103
Transaction costs, 64, 65
Transactional systems, 105, 106, 110–11

U

Uniqueness, 126, 140, 141

V

Value chain, 169, 172
Value-creating activities, 24
Value delivery, 13, 24, 33
Value disciplines, 13, 19, 239
information mastery as, 15–17
Value metrics, 239
information, 173
Value network, 126, 136–38
strategic resources, linking to, 138
Venture capital, 2, 3

W

Web services, 247, 248

Z

Zachman Framework, information systems architecture, 101, 102